The Bounds of Interpretation

Linguistic Theory and Literary Text

ELLEN SCHAUBER AND
ELLEN SPOLSKY

THE BOUNDS
OF
INTERPRETATION,

LINGUISTIC THEORY AND
LITERARY TEXT

STANFORD UNIVERSITY PRESS 1986
STANFORD, CALIFORNIA

Stanford University Press
Stanford, California
© 1986 by the Board of Trustees of the
Leland Stanford Junior University
Printed in the United States of America

CIP data appear at the end of the book

Published with the assistance of
the Andrew W. Mellon Foundation

רבי טרפון היה אומר. . . . לא עליך
המלאכה לגמור ולא אתה בן חורין
להיבטל ממנה.

פרקי אבות 2.16

Rabbi Tarfon used to say. . . . It is not
incumbent on you to complete the work, but
neither are you free to abstain from it.

Avot, 2.16

For our parents
Shirley Schauber, Harry Schaps, and Zelda Schaps,
and in special memory of Bernard H. Schauber

Acknowledgments

As co-authors of this book, we come to its issues from different academic perspectives: Ellen Schauber is a theoretical linguist, and Ellen Spolsky is a literary critic. The book is accordingly the product of much discussion (often heated and protracted) and also, inevitably, of much compromise. We can only hope that we have achieved from these dialogues, to borrow the elegant phrasing of René Wellek and Austin Warren, "a real instance of collaboration in which the author is the shared agreement between two writers."

The discussions that resulted in this book of course extended beyond the two of us. We have been fortunate that so many competent and experienced listeners, willing at all stages to read, debate, and explain, have helped in our progress toward understanding. We are grateful for the generosity and patience of friends, colleagues, and students at the University of New Mexico, Northwestern University, and the 1980 Summer Linguistic Society of America and TESOL Institutes, in particular: Ellen Barton, Linda Brodkey, Robert Cooper, Michael Fisher, Joshua Fishman, Gerald Graff, Vera John-Steiner, Judith Levy, Bonnie Litowitz, Phyllis Lyons, Charlene McDermott, Rae Moses, Linda Schinke-Llano, James Shay, James Wertsch, Claudia Williams, Ellen Wright, and all the students in the seminar in linguistics and literary theory at the LSA Institute and in the seminar on the genre of romance at Bar-Ilan University (1980–81). Special thanks go to Ray Jackendoff and Mary Louise Pratt. Our greatest debt is to Bernard Spolsky, whose help and encouragement from beginning to end cannot be overestimated. Any shortcomings that may remain, despite all this help and good advice, are of course our own responsibility.

The writing of this book was further supported by sabbatical leaves from the University of New Mexico and from Northwestern University, and by research support from both these institutions and from Bar-Ilan University. Helen Tartar and Stanford University Press have been a wonderful support through the final manuscript revisions. Thanks are owed as well to Garland Bills, Chair of the Linguistics Department at the University of New Mexico, and to Barbara Gates, Sue Katz, Mary Kollander, and Mary O'Rourke for all their organizational and typing assistance.

Through it all, three budding linguists and literary critics valiantly sustained us. Our deepest thanks go to Marc Schauber and Ruth Spolsky, and to Joel Spolsky for his help in the preparation of the References.

E.S.
E.S.

Contents

Contents

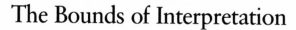

The Bounds of Interpretation

Linguistic Theory and Literary Text

An Introduction

Linguistics as Literary Theory

There is leakage. Ideas thought to be safely stored overflow their containers, slip out of closed cupboards, travel through halls and down stairwells, seep under doors we had thought shut. We were dealing, we had assumed, with inert matter, bottled and labeled— but we find stains on our books and papers. As children we mimicked the television detective who called for "just the facts ma'am, just the facts," as graduate students in literature we read "just the text," or in linguistics, studied "just the sentence." Boundaries were clear, doors were marked OFF LIMITS. Inside each separate room was the object of analysis: the poem or the sentence, corpselike.

We find, recently, that some of the doors can be unlocked, some of the boundaries bounded. It is becoming increasingly clear not only that linguistics, philosophy, cognitive psychology, and literary theory share some basic concerns about the nature of interpretation (this has always been so), but that some writers in these fields are beginning, at last, to address the need for a common language. This has not always been so. Linguistic theories brought to literary service have more than once disappointed literary critics, being criticized for contributing little more than a scientific-sounding jargon. Linguistic theorists, for their part, have mostly ignored the evidence of literary texts. They have assumed that the language of those texts was formally different from the language of "ordinary speech" and therefore not useful as data in the development of the theory. However, recent literary theory has amply demonstrated the impossibility of describing a separate literary language.[1] Thus, even apart from the general problem of textual interpretation, there can be no independent literary theory that is not a general theory of interpretation. Likewise, it is now a general perception among linguists that any comprehensive linguistic theory must be a general theory of interpretation. Linguistic theory, therefore, is not, as it is sometimes considered, a help to literary theory; it is identical with it.

Aside from the not inconsiderable problems of understanding an unfamiliar technical language, literary critics were unimpressed by linguistics, in part because it did not offer a procedure for the discovery of new interpretations, the production of which had traditionally been the business of literary critics. Even when the focus of literary scholarship shifted to theoretical concerns, a linguistics that focused on the sentence while ignoring pragmatic aspects of language was bound to be disappointing. As Mary Louise Pratt (1977) explains, it simply did not have the descriptive power to match the goals and concerns of literary theory. In the meantime, both literary theory and linguistics have changed: the former has been pushed by challenges from without to new levels of methodological rigor, and the latter has expanded in response to challenges from within. The tenor of the current metatheoretical debate in linguistic circles argues the ultimate need for a comprehensive theory of text interpretation that extends beyond the boundaries of a formal syntax, and semantic investigation has progressed to issues much more sophisticated than were recognized by the structural linguists whose work was first borrowed for literary stylistics.

In the belief that the isolation of the two fields is inimical to both and that further rapprochement is both possible and desirable, we offer the preference model as a claim for the power of generative linguistic theory as a theory of literary interpretation. In this book we begin that process of rapprochement by showing how rules that concern linguists (specifically, a combination of well-formedness

[1] Among the literary theorists who have argued that the notion of two separate languages, one literary and one nonliterary, cannot be maintained are Pratt (1977), Reichert (1977), Culler (1975), and Fish (1973).

and preference rules) can help solve one of the most pressing current problems facing literary critics: how to allow a variety of conflicting interpretations for a given text without abandoning all possibility of controlling the range of those interpretations, or judging among them. We hope to provide a model that will describe how, flooded with information but deprived of crucial bits, readers produce interpretations. Competent interpretations differ from one another and change over time, but even so, readers make do. A note of caution is perhaps appropriate: this study stands near the beginning of the project of finding a language in which linguists and literary theorists can communicate. Readers in both disciplines will inevitably find terminological and conceptual difficulties in our description of the model, such as its authors found as they worked together. It is not always easy to distinguish between a legitimate mutual approach to a mutual problem, which holds out the promise of a shared understanding, and a tactical compromise or fudge in which disagreement may be buried rather than explored or resolved. Much work remains to be done, and much patience is required.

Part I

The Preference Model

Chapter One

The Preference Model of Interpretation

The preference model is a competence model that, we claim, moves beyond some of the impasses encountered when earlier versions of generative linguistics were put at the service of literary interpretation. Because of its major innovation, the addition of preference rules to well-formedness rules, the model also moves beyond the critique of method recently mounted in literary theory. Linguists have long recognized that in principle it is impossible for any theory to be totally objective, to evaluate itself from far enough outside its own operations to comprehend itself fully. Edward Sapir told us in 1921 that "all grammars leak." We understand this assertion as not merely an admonition or comfort to formalist systematizers searching for a watertight grammar but as an acknowledgment of the capacity of the grammars by which human beings talk, think, and live to cope with both insufficiency and supplementarity—and still be grammars. The preference model, we claim, is such a grammar. The ability to accommodate new, variable, contradictory, and endemically insufficient data is the basis of the interpretive competence that people exhibit every day. That necessary and sufficient conditions for the creation of meaning are not usually available does not prevent all understanding; thus, a model of interpretation must account for the emergence of meaning without satisfying such absolute conditions.

The linguist Ray Jackendoff, first with Fred Lerdahl in their joint work on a generative grammar of music (1980), introduced the preference rule into generative theories; Jackendoff later developed the concept into a general cognitive semantics (Jackendoff, 1983a). Preference rules supplement the well-formedness rules of which generative grammars were entirely composed. Jackendoff, for example, bases his work on the Extended Standard Theory (e.g., Chomsky, 1972a, and Jackendoff, 1972). Instead of specifying, as do well-formedness rules, an exclusive, yes-or-no categorization, preference rules describe the interaction of a number of fixed and variable factors that enter into a categorization decision. A preference rule describes the categorization of fuzzy data, accounting for categorization judgments based on the satisfaction of some subset of conditions of a definition and recognizing that certain of those conditions can be satisfied in varying degrees. Thus things can fit more and less, depending on how many conditions they match and how closely.

Jackendoff makes the following claim:

I see a preference rule system as a way to accomplish what psychological systems do well but computers do very badly: deriving a quasi-determinate result from unreliable data. In a preference rule system there are multiple converging sources of evidence for a judgment. In the ideal (stereotypical) case these sources are redundant; but no single one of the sources is essential, and in the worst case the system can make do with any one alone. Used as default values, the rules are invaluable in setting a course of action in the face of insufficient evidence. At higher levels of organization, they are a source of great flexibility and adaptivity in the overall conceptual system. [1983a:157]

A preference grammar or model—that is, a grammar composed of both preference and well-formedness rules—is thus particularly well suited to the formal description of texts in which decisions about meaning are not automatic or clear-cut but are more likely to require judgments that cannot be labeled right or wrong, only assessed as relatively stronger or weaker. A preference model provides, moreover, a framework for talking about creativity and change in an interpretive system and about the weighting of communal and personal conditions of significance that variously influence the system.

The preference model that we outline in this book depends on three assumptions, all of them contentious. The first is the Chomskyan idea of a grammar as a competence model (1975a:7)—a set of internalized (although not necessarily unconscious) rules that enables one to be a competent speaker or reader. Competence models are based on a distinction between competence and performance—between linguistic rules as a description of ability and specific instances of linguistic usages, instances that may or may not mirror this capability. The preference model depends on an analogy between the native speaker of a language and the experienced reader of a literary work, arguing that the behavior of both is at once rule-governed and creative; that it is creative in part because it is rule-governed (see Chomsky in Parret, 1974:29). Our literary competence model takes into account, however, a fact that is irrelevant to a linguistic competence model but crucial to any model of pragmatic competence—that, given the same linguistic competence, some people are more capable readers of literary texts than others. Accounting for the effects of varying literary experience within an idealized competence model presents problems that Chomskyan competence grammars have avoided by exclusion.

Chomskyan competence grammars have assumed that normal variation in experience will not affect the ability to create a grammar, and thus whatever relevance such variations could have would be in the realm of performance (see Chomsky, 1975a:46, n. 10 for a discussion of these points). However valid such an approach may be for the study of syntax, it is impossible to make the same argument for variations in literary experience. In fact, a description of the ability to deal with variation is crucial to any account of literary competence.[1]

Our second assumption, necessary to describe rule-governed competence, is that literary interpretation is based on categorization. The preference model is a genre theory, a theory of kinds; it presents meaning as ascribed to literary works on the basis of complex categorization judgments and recognizes that such judgments are based on a range of conditions. Kantian universal categories

---

[1] The sociolinguists Dell Hymes (1974:93n.) and William Labov (1972b) have argued similar positions. Other linguists, e.g., George Lakoff (1972) and James McCawley (1981), have tried to account for intuitions of variable strength with formal competence rules. See also an interview with McCawley in Parret (1974) in which he argues that Chomsky's category of performance is insufficiently delineated to make his distinction between competence and performance useful.

have a place in the model, but they are not privileged, or even absolutely distinguished from culturally provided types or from the particulars of experience, which can also act as types.[2]

Current theories of categorization gravitate toward one of two poles. One set of positions is based on the (usually unstated) assumption that clear categorization is possible and therefore that some sort of objective data (e.g., "literal meaning") can be conventionally recognized and used in understanding texts. The positions clustered around this assumption account for what agreement may exist among interpreters about the meaning of a text. Other positions deny either the existence or the relevance to interpretive acts of any literal ("neutral") data, and thus seek to explain phenomena unaccounted for in the first set, such as disagreement among interpreters. In spite of the fact that much of the work designed to support either of these positions in fact argues their interdependence, many if not all of the theorists who have discussed the issue argue that the logic of the two positions is mutually exclusive.[3]

Both sides assume that indeterminacy bleeds, that even a little will hopelessly contaminate the system. In contrast, we claim that a comprehensive model must account for inherent indeterminacy without abandoning the project of charting such determinacy as

[2] Jackendoff (1983a) argues that types and tokens have the same internal structure. This is what allows the comparison of the two, and, furthermore, allows the formation of a type from the experience of a token. A type is a token with the additional feature "-hood", an abstraction away from the particular instance to its categorical state. The rationalist problem (see Hirsch, 1967) of how particulars are knowable thus disappears.

[3] Wittgenstein (1953:I. 43) argued that no stable core of meaning could be found for a word outside the context in which it was used, yet he had to exempt a category of technical definitions from his generalization. E. D. Hirsch, Jr. (1967:146), placing himself squarely on the side of the objectivists, argued that the meaning of a text is identical with the text's "intrinsic genre," that is, the genre and therefore the meaning that the author intended. He was forced to make a new category, which he called "significance," for meaning that could not have been intended but arises in the context of the reader; in other words, he let in by the back door what he was not prepared to welcome at the front. John Searle, too, had to accommodate a way of meaning with which he was uncomfortable. His system of speech acts, modeled on the Chomskyan notion of a grammar, was a set of shared conventions, but he also had to recognize (1969:36ff. and 68) that even a conventional system permits "preconventional communication" (Strawson's term, 1971:174). Although Searle acknowledges (1971:9) that the question of the extent to which speech acts are conventional is "one of the most important unresolved controversies in contemporary philosophy of language," the issue in fact impinges on the plausibility of theories in all language-based disciplines.

exists in hermeneutic systems. The theory must account as much for agreement as for disagreement, for the act of categorizing as well as for the fact that categorization is often unclear and that categories can change. Furthermore, by distinguishing inferred functional categories (the role of any unit in a given context) from structural categories, the model seeks to recognize multiple valid interpretations, while it retains the power to exclude some interpretations as invalid or ill-formed.

One of the most famous demonstrations of the weaknesses of an interpretive system based on categorization but unable to account for gradient judgments is Wittgenstein's argument (1953: I. 66) against the possibility of defining the word "game" independent of its use. Derrida's article on the inevitable impurity of genre (1980) is in a similar vein. Jackendoff (1983a: 112ff.) sums up linguists' arguments about the issue. Theorists who have adopted any absolutist version of categorization have found defining the category of literary texts impossible, although it might seem that such a definition is a primary task of a literary theory. Those, like Aristotle, who have assumed that definition is objectively possible have produced definitions that are unsatisfyingly partial or inflexible. Those who have assumed the impossibility of absolute categorization have given up the task of defining a category of literature, arguing either that in principle it cannot be done or that it is not an interesting issue. New category names, such as "narrative," seek to avoid such oppositions as literary to nonliterary and fiction to nonfiction. But, of course, whatever the categories are called, the problem of categorization remains.

The problem theorists have had in defining a category of literary texts is perhaps only the most striking of a group of related problems. The example of categorization suggests why it has also been difficult, if not impossible, for literary theorists to describe the activities of literary critics in a way that matches their intuitive understanding of the complexities those activities involve. All readers of texts, academic or not, in fact depend on a category labeled "literary," regardless of whether they can provide a principled definition of it, just as they use other concepts, like "game" or "genre." As has often been noticed (see, e.g., Culler, 1975), academic critics, in particular, can accept more than one interpretation of a particular text and even welcome multiple interpretations, while at the same time rejecting others, that is, categorizing some interpretations as well-formed and others as ill-formed—and ranking some of the acceptable interpretations as better than others. Obviously, a system that works only with absolutes cannot account for such gradient judgments: if it cannot recognize a category (no matter how fuzzy) of literary texts, then on the same grounds it cannot separate a well-formed from an ill-formed interpretation, or a good from a better interpretation. Since readers can and do make these judgments, it follows that theories based on absolutes are necessarily inadequate.

Because the preference model assumes that most categorization is fuzzy, it refocuses attention on the conditions that allow fuzzy categorization. It uses preference rules to account for the interactions of the fixed and variable factors that are involved in categorization decisions, hence for the decisions that form the basis of interpretation. Specifically, by allowing an extension of the notion of rule beyond the logical constraints of well-formedness rules, preference rules enable us to describe systems in terms of rules that vary from the mathematically precise to the impressionistic.

This book seeks in part to chart the aspects of a theory of interpretation for which indeterminacy precludes formal description and to separate those aspects from the comparatively determinate. The differences between the determinate and the indeterminate are roughly reflected in the kinds of rules by which they are described. In places, the preference model depends on the formal rules that others have proposed.[4] In other places, where formal rules seem inappropriate, we have begun the task of writing preference rules that properly reflect a combination of determinacy and indeterminacy. These fairly informal rules may be susceptible to greater formalization. Preference rules are transparent in an important way: they are compounds whose parts retain their labels. The preference rule describing any given categorization judgment labels separately the contributing factors about which an interpreter can and cannot be certain. Furthermore, it separates several sources of indeterminacy. For example, it recognizes and separates out the aspects of language

---

[4]It is impossible to provide a summary of such rules, but for examples see Akmajian and Heny (1975) and Chomsky (1957, 1965, 1973, 1977a, 1980, 1981) for syntax; Schane (1973), Hyman (1975), Chomsky and Halle (1968) for phonology; Evans et al. (1980) and Jackendoff (1983a) for semantics; Cole and Morgan (1975), Cole (1978, 1981), Gazdar (1979), Searle, Kiefer, and Bierwisch (1980) for pragmatics.

that can be characterized absolutely (e.g., many aspects of the autonomous linguistic system) from those requiring a notion of gradience. A preference rule does not make a decision or resolve difficulties but rather describes the various sources and weights of an interpreter's certainties and uncertainties. This weighting provides one method of explaining variation: because of nonlinguistic factors, readers and communities of readers weight different factors differently.

We make a third assumption, derived from the second: that a new model of interpretation should aim not just to be a better methodology or metaphor but to be responsible to the biological possibilities of the human brain in whatever ways the current state of the cognitive sciences allows.[5] Indeed, such a position is inherent not only in Chomsky's assertion that linguistics is ultimately a subdivision of psychology but also in Derrida's great debt to Freud. Although Chomsky's model is not a psychological one in the sense that it claims its rules represent actual psychophysical structures, it nevertheless assumes that all the information in the grammar will have an indirect but real relation to neural processing.[6] Some recent linguistic work has indicated that the validity of a grammar may ultimately be judged by how closely the form of its rules approaches psychological reality (see, e.g., Bresnan, 1978). We are, of course, much farther away from knowing how our brains work than we would like to be.

We recognize that questions have been raised, often reasonably, about the value of competence models on the grounds that no useful

[5] Although we part company here with Culler's 1975 suggestion that linguistic competence offers only a metaphor for literary theory, his suggestion that literary competence could be described as a grammar encouraged us to begin our work. Fish (1970) and Van Dijk (1972) had previously suggested the analogy between literary and linguistic competence, but Culler was the first to work some of it out. Bové (1976) objects that Culler's analogy does not allow sufficient scope for the effects of historical change on the notion of a "competent" interpretation or in fact for any relativism, historical and/or personal. (Sampson [1979:129] made a similar complaint against Chomsky's notion of competence.) Prince (1976) and Smith (1978) have also pointed out the incompleteness of Culler's exploration of the analogy he proposed. For some discussion of the current state of research in the cognitive sciences as relevant to linguistic theory, see Fodor (1983) and Jackendoff (1983b).

[6] The theory Chomsky envisioned was a theory of mind, not just of sentences. For his conception of the relationships between his work and psychology see Parret (1974:29–30; Chomsky, 1975b and n.d.). A competence grammar, however, does not aim to define actual psychological or neurological processes; see Langacker (1972:135).

distinctions between competence and performance can be made when accounting for actual rather than idealized data. Whereas Chomsky's domain of "language out of context" may be described in technical terms alone, the pragmatic and literary domains cannot, for they necessarily involve context and thus must include situation-specific categories. Despite some inadequacies in the autonomous linguistic model for other domains, it would be a loss not to take seriously the implications for literary interpretation of the methodological claims embodied in the Chomskyan revolution. The most important of these claims are, first, that linguistic creativity is a function of an underlying system of rules, and, second, that understanding such creativity requires defining what are possible rules and stating how rules can interact.

Therefore, we offer both our method and our conclusions as a contribution to the self-examination currently taking place in literary studies and among all those interested in understanding discourse. Until now, attempts to establish distinctions between literal and nonliteral meaning or to identify units in an interpretive system have been hamstrung by the absence of a comprehensive model of interpretation. An interpretive system, however, is a system of moving parts, not predefined entities, and so its units must be defined in interaction. Only a comprehensive model allows this. We attempt to present such a model, with the greatest methodological rigor presently available. If we could, in advance, define our terms or argue definitively for our basic assumptions, there would be less need for the preference model, for one of its tasks is to define the primitives of an interpretive system by charting how they interrelate in a description of competence. The model's descriptive ability will be its own best argument, and its success in approaching an inherently indeterminate topic will help to demonstrate the reasonableness of positions that, independent of it, are problematic.

Another way of making this argument is to point to its functional relativism. Primitives and axioms, whether or not they have any reality, are not very useful outside a theoretical construct. The validity of a model does not depend wholly on the validity of its premises. Rather, the soundness of the premises is determined by how well they function within the system. In a model, the various parts make demands on each other, enable predictions about each other, and ultimately reinforce each other as a system, even when the system itself questions the notion of a totally closed system. If it is success-ful, the preference model should both make clearer the problems inherent in formal explanations of language in context and allow description and explanation of such language. Any successes of the model in these areas should argue that a primarily formal approach can make significant contributions, regardless of its inherent validity.

This last point is worth emphasizing. The underlying assumption of all model-making, all grammars, is that human activity is rule-governed. Generalizations can be made, and to some extent rules can be specified. Even where theorists cannot specify what the rules are (we are, after all, standing in our own shadow), their existence is assumed. In committing ourselves to making a model of reading rather than restricting ourselves to a critique of others' models, we have inevitably committed ourselves to a position that is, not inci-dentally, hostile to various forms of the recurrent romantic fallacy, which in one version or another claims to have discovered areas be-yond systematizing, beyond rules, areas that, when the claims are taken to their logical end as they are in some versions of poststruc-turalism, undermine the possibilities of any systematic generaliza-tion whatever.[7]

It may be that the critique of method mounted by deconstruc-tionist philosophy has been welcomed so warmly in some literature departments because deconstruction is ultimately so congenial to the aesthetic fallacy that holds the production and understanding of literary texts to be defined by the breaking of rules, by such texts' being somehow beyond precise description. But the confusion caused here by the notion that rules must be normative is no longer seriously at issue. The real issue is the possibility of arriving at a systematic description of how grammars (specifically systems of in-terpretation) work and do not, and change and do not. The chal-lenge is to describe a grammar within which norms not only are preserved and learned but also can be systematically questioned and broken.

In the chapters that follow we will outline the preference model in greater detail, describing the subsystems of which it is composed and the kinds of rules that describe those subsystems. Part II deals

[7]Lentricchia (1980) argues the homology between romantic concepts of poetry and recent literary theory, both new critical and deconstructionist.

with genre categorization as the prototype of interpretive judgment. We examine some exemplary preference judgments and then discuss the significance of preference rules for the description of generic change. Part III proposes a further specification of the basic interpretive operations of the model (reference, transformation, and inference) and then analyzes some critical readings of unconventional metaphors and of literary characterization in terms of the preference model. Part IV attempts to test the model's ability to specify distinctions between interpretive communities, and then, finally, to describe a category of literary texts.

Chapter Two

The Systems of
the Preference Model

The preference model accounts for the literary competence of an experienced reader as three separate systems: (1) *linguistic competence* (in the narrow sense), which is described by an autonomous linguistic system, (2) *pragmatic competence*, described as a variety of context-based subsystems, and (3) *literary competence*, described as various subsystems of literary conventions. Each of the systems is described by rules that define its operations.

THE THREE SYSTEMS

The first system is the formal autonomous linguistic system of phonology, syntax, and semantics. An autonomous linguistic system limits its domain to structural descriptions of strings of words out of context.[1] Debate still continues on how many subsystems there are in the autonomous system and on the whole question of the scope of the system. Theoretical linguists differ on such points as the role of the lexicon, whether semantics constitutes a separate

---

[1]The possibility of an entirely decontextualized (autonomous) and yet comprehensive grammar is probably remote, but see Lyons (1977:590) for an argument for the usefulness of an at least "maximally decontextualized grammar" (which, incidentally, demonstrates the need for a way of handling gradience).

subsystem independent of syntax, or how much of meaning can be accounted for within a formal semantic system, how much can be accounted for within the lexicon, and how much is better dealt with in a context-related pragmatics.[2] But no matter where the outer limit of the autonomous system is located, it is clear that much of what people need in order to understand meaning is contextual and is, by definition, not described therein.

The second system, the pragmatic, describes readers' competence to understand language in relation to its contexts. For some linguists and philosophers the phenomena described by pragmatics may be limited either by defining it as a realm of communicative competence (Hymes, 1974; Rommetveit, 1979) or by excluding unintentional communication (Bach and Harnish, 1979; Levinson, 1983).[3] This limitation might seem to make sense where the goal is a relatively synchronic description of how people manage communication, but it would not be able to describe much of what is considered to be literary interpretation. Few literary interpreters have ever felt bound to measure success by any standard of communicative clarity, or to limit their understanding to the text's intended communication.

Although we refer to the pragmatic system in the singular, in fact it consists of many areas or subsystems. Some linguists have attempted to extend earlier formal theories to describe some of these new areas,[4] and others, like Joan Bresnan (1982), Gerald Gazdar (1979, 1981), Barbara Partee (1975), and David Perlmutter (1980),

[2] On the relationship between speech acts and formal theory, for example, Searle (1975*b*) criticizes Ross (1970) and Gordon and Lakoff (1971) for attempting to include speech acts within the domain of formal theory rather than within pragmatics. The relationship between semantics and pragmatics is continually redefined. See, for example, Cole (1981), Kempson (1984*a*), and Sperber and Wilson (forthcoming). Jackendoff (1983*a*: 105–6, 208) concludes that the distinction between semantics and pragmatics may not be theoretically significant.

[3] And for some, like Kempson (1984*a*, 1984*b*) and Sperber and Wilson (forthcoming), pragmatics is a theory of utterance rather than sentence interpretation. To quote Kempson (1984*a*: 17): "And here, finally, we have the basis for characterising discourse-related phenomena without having to abandon the assumption that a grammar is a sentence-generating mechanism. . . . Not a set of rules which predicts actual interpretation but rather . . . a set of instructions on utterance interpretation, a set which may include . . . more specific indications of context-construction, or even indications as to the speaker's attitude to what he says."

[4] Ross (1970) and Sadock (1974), for example, are attempts within generative semantics to include speech acts within autonomous linguistics. Katz (1980) addresses the same issue from an interpretivist point of view rather than from that of the gener-

are looking for new formal theories to redefine autonomous (non-pragmatic) meaning, and, therefore, pragmatics by exclusion.[5] But some, Paul Grice for example, have taken the position that the language behavior to be described in this area is sufficiently different from the language behavior described by the formal linguistic system to make the same descriptive mechanisms useless.[6] Stephen Levinson (1983 : 12ff.), in agreement with Grice, points out that although one's definition of the phenomena to be studied under the rubric pragmatics depends partly on where one fixes the limits of syntax, the difficulty of placing the boundary does not imply that semantics and pragmatics may be described by one system. His summary of the arguments against the possibility of a unified formal model concludes (p. 15) that "from what we now know about the nature of meaning, a hybrid or modular account seems inescapable." In fact, pragmatics may not be entirely a specifically language system, but may also include a set of subsystems describing general cognitive capacities, like reasoning, and general social phenomena, like turn taking.[7] In any case, for language competence, pragmatics depends on the formal language system. Although it is similarly systematic and rule-governed, it is, as Levinson notes (p. 21), "essentially concerned with inference" and therefore does not seem to be amenable to the same kind of formalization as syntax.

An important subset of rules within the pragmatic system is what we call the *conditions of significance*. These conditions embody the

---

ative semanticists. The linguist Frederick Newmeyer explains (1980) that the failure of the generative semanticists to limit the domain of factors relevant to performance forced them into an unsatisfactory reductionist position. Culler (1981) makes the same point in explaining Derrida's criticism of Austin as recognizing the impossibility of ever delimiting "relevant" context.

[5] Chomsky's Government and Binding Theory (1981), for example, once again narrows the scope of semantics, recognizing that, although syntactic relations may govern meaning (scope of negatives or quantifiers, disjoint reference, possible thematic relations), most of meaning is outside the purview of his formal system. See Cole (1981) for a variety of recent positions on the relationship between semantics and pragmatics.

[6] Grice, believing discourse rules to be rational rather than conventional, has suggested (personal communication) that a theory of speech acts is a part of a theory of action.

[7] See Newmeyer (1983) for a general discussion of the concept of the modular structure of the grammar, and see Jackendoff (1983b) for problems with delineating individual modules and for evidence of interaction among them.

hierarchy of interpretive values, or weightings, of a community or of an individual. They are not, as some critics have thought, identical with the whole of the interpretive system itself. Rather, they are the conditions that, for each genre of a text, define the relationships of texts to the values of the reader or of the community as a whole. Specific interpretive rules can, depending on the conditions of significance, be favored or considered insignificant, but if they are collapsed with conditions of significance, one cannot understand gradient relationships between interpretive possibilities as these possibilities vary from genre to genre. We find it useful to retain the distinction between, for example, failure to understand an author's intention (being unable to recover it) and noticing it but being unwilling to accord it value.

The third system, the literary system, describes an additional or supplementary competence gained by experience and training. A reader may be able to understand the language of a literary text, but an experienced reader will not accept as well formed an interpretation of a literary text that does not take into account the literary system. Culler puts it this way:

> A knowledge of language will take one a certain distance in one's encounter with literary texts, and it may be difficult to specify precisely where understanding comes to depend on one's supplementary knowledge of literature. But the difficulty of drawing a line does not obscure the palpable difference between understanding the language of a poem, in the sense that one could provide a rough translation into another language, and understanding the poem. [1975:114]

Culler uses the term "language" ambiguously to refer both to the knowledge Chomsky called linguistic competence and to all nonliterary language knowledge, including relevant pragmatic or "encyclopedic" knowledge. Our terminology makes a distinction between the two. We use the term "linguistic competence," or "autonomous linguistics," in the narrow Chomskyan sense of language that can be described separately from context (Chomsky, 1975a: 46, n. 10). We use the term "pragmatics" to mean the systems necessary to language understanding that are context bound and thereby separable from the autonomous linguistic system. Finally, we use the term "literary competence" to mean both competence in the three systems necessary for literary interpretation and also the system of literary conventions itself, as distinct from the autonomous and pragmatic systems.

Although the meaning of these various terms will in most cases be clear from the context, the terminological difficulty raises the important issue of distinguishing interactive parts from the whole. Because the preference model has separate but interacting systems—a common property of formal systems—it both displays the problem and provides a forum for grappling with it: we have to observe separation and interaction simultaneously, in order to make distinctions where boundaries are necessary even if unclear. The preference model also makes distinctions between the *structural* and *functional* aspects of literary competence, also a common approach in formal systems, and one that turns out to be especially crucial to the explanation of systemic change.

In principle, isolation is the best and perhaps the only way to study the phenomena that interest us here. But isolation presents two methodological problems: having separated systems, the model must then specify how they are recombined in an interpretation; and since systems can be subdivided endlessly, the question of how much subdividing should be undertaken must be resolved not only by considering the types of rules necessary for describing each potential subsystem, but by considering the relative costs and benefits of such isolation. The recent history of literary theory reveals how easy it is to obscure important differences between interdependent systems by failing to understand the nature of the gap between syntactic form and meaning. As Stanley Fish (1973) has pointed out, this was the primary error of stylistics. Although the literary system may be in one sense merely a pragmatic subsystem, it is our interest in describing literary competence that directly argues for separating out this particular system here.

Within our terms, pragmatic competence presumes linguistic competence, and literary competence presumes both pragmatic and linguistic competence. The only way a reader can begin to understand the language of literary texts is by assuming that the literary language is dependent but not necessarily identical with the meaning that language has outside the context of literary interpretation. Literary language is not formally different from nonliterary language, and the language of any text has to be interpreted according to the context of the exchange and the governing conventions of that context. When an author or narrator is addressing an audience, various conventions of exchanges are understood to apply. Whatever systems describe ordinary language competence must be a part of competent reading. Normally, the reader assumes that the author accepts the ordinary implications of the language he or she uses (unless the author indicates otherwise). But for any literary text, interpretation will also be partly determined by literary conventions. Tension may result when these two sets conflict, but the tension will not cancel the normal operations of language.

The three systems of the preference model describe the store of conditions and rules by means of which a reader arrives at interpretations of language texts. A *rule* is a *set of conditions*; it can also be said to describe a gestalt understanding of the set of conditions that constitute it. Another way of putting it would be to say that a rule is a set of conditions, one or more of which are instructions about what to do with the other conditions. A rule is said to *apply* when a reader can match a particular text to the conditions of the rule, or, as Jackendoff (1983*a*: 23ff.) puts it, can match a mental representation of the text with the mental representation of the rule. Except in the autonomous linguistic system in which most rules are well-formedness rules, the *degree of fit* between a text and a rule will not always be perfect, but when a reader feels satisfied that a sufficient number of conditions has been matched, the reader is said to be in possession of an interpretation of the text. The search for matches between strings of text and the rules or experiences within the reader's competence is the search for a satisfying interpretation of that text. The rules postulated here are descriptive rather than prescriptive in that they are arrived at by describing what is done rather than by imagining what should be done, but insofar as they also describe what is rewarded within the world of journalistic or academic literary criticism, they are in fact normative, though not, in principle, prescriptive.

Most linguists would agree that rules are useful descriptors, but they do not agree on the nature and function of rules. Opinions differ on how formal rules should be, how they should be defined, how they should be applied, how many types there are and whether different degrees of formalism are appropriate for describing different kinds of competence. Linguists who describe the autonomous linguistic system have depended on well-formedness rules. In the preference model we use two kinds of rules that will be described separately: well-formedness and preference rules. In place of the traditional distinction between necessary and sufficient conditions of definition, we make a distinction between four different kinds of conditions of *judgment*. These will be illustrated in detail in Chapter Six. Briefly, the distinctions between kinds of conditions reflect the distinction between necessary conditions and nonnecessary conditions, and between conditions that contain a notion of gradience (i.e., can be met by any number of situations of "more or less") and conditions that are absolute, admitting of no gradience.

Let us look first at the power and scope of well-formedness and preference rules.

WELL-FORMEDNESS RULES

A *well-formedness rule* (WFR) is a set of conditions all of which are well-formedness conditions (WFCs). The syntactic and phonological rules in most varieties of generative linguistic theory have been written as well-formedness rules. These are the rules that determine clear-cut grammaticality within a system. A well-formedness rule can be a rule like the WFR specifying that a sentence in its underlying form consists of a noun phrase and a verb phrase (or a predicate and an argument, or a subject, a verb, and an object, depending on the category labels the particular theory employs). A well-formedness rule could also be a set of well-formedness conditions, such as the ones that describe when the regular past tense in English is pronounced [*t*], [*d*], or [*ed*] (e.g., crushed, begged, waited). A syntactic well-formedness rule describes the fact that (*a*) and (*b*) are both well-formed sentences of English, differing in that (*b*) is the negation of (*a*):

(*a*) I like ice cream.
(*b*) I don't like ice cream.

An example of a well-formedness rule that operates in the pragmatic as well as in the literary system is the Genre Determination Rule. Hirsch (1967: 111ff.) argues the case for such a rule. In the preference model it can be stated as:

Understanding is always governed by arbitrary and heuristic genre conventions.

Hirsch's distinction between intrinsic and extrinsic genres opened up his theory of genres to justified criticism that is not relevant here. The genre-determination rule, however, is one of the epistemological foundations of interpretation: it is so abstract as to be constitutive of the interpretive process itself. It simply states that reading (listening, talking) is always done within a framework of historical expectations or genres. Notice, for example, that this well-formedness rule does not specify what the term "genre" means, or how a reader will know what the genre of a text is, or what to do when a text does not fit familiar genre categories. Readers cannot, therefore, put this rule into operation, necessary though it is, unless they also control rules that answer these other questions. This means that although the well-formedness rule is the basis for interpretive competence and cannot be dispensed with, much if not most of what has been found interesting about genres, as well as what is needed in order to distinguish genres, cannot be described by it. Well-formedness rules, therefore, however useful they have proved in syntactic and phonological studies, and however necessary in semantics, are not sufficient to the challenge of semantics or to the ultimate task of describing meaning. The rules of the theory we want must describe two qualitatively different abilities: the ability to handle necessary rules in which no gradience is involved, and the ability to make variable judgments.

PREFERENCE RULES

We find some grounds for optimism that generative theory will ultimately be able to describe variable judgments in Jackendoff's development of the preference rule (PR). Jackendoff's claims (1983a) for a semantics that is described mainly by preference rules starts with the recognition, described above as the genre well-formedness rule, that categorization is fundamental to all the semantic operations language use requires. Without this competence, not only could a literary genre not be recognized but not a single word could be understood. Jackendoff (1983a:77ff.) proposes to account for the ability to make semantic judgments by accounting for the ability to categorize. His preference rules allow the operation of Hirsch's genre rule by allowing us to answer the questions that the genre rule does not answer and that well-formedness rules cannot answer.

Categorization, as we use the concept here, refers to the competence to organize the components of stimuli so as to recognize—that is, understand—them. Apparently, perception, interpretation, and understanding cannot be described unless they are considered as varieties of an ability to relate what is present to what is familiar from past experience, in which case gaps must be recognized where past experience cannot provide understanding. One of the most basic of all conceptual capacities is the ability to recognize something familiar, to classify it as the same in some significant respects as something else. Whatever else it is, understanding must at least involve categorization. Adam's first assignment, the naming of the creatures in the Garden of Eden, constituted his understanding, his interpretation of them.

It is perhaps necessary to state explicitly that although it may be easiest to conceptualize categorization as an operation that involves things or nouns, the system of preference rules that Jackendoff describes applies equally well to all the lexical categories (nouns, verbs, adjectives, adverbs, prepositions, etc.). Some flowers are more securely describable as red, some actions are less securely judged as lying. In Jackendoff's semantics (1983a: 57ff.), not only the noun or the argument but also the verb or the predicate is understood according to preference rules.

Psycholinguists have demonstrated that interpretation is complex for even the simplest stimuli in a way that has some bearing on questions of literary interpretation. It is crucial, for example, that although there may seem to be no a priori reason why *A* in the accompanying figure should be perceived as organized at all, experiments show that it always is; it is never seen simply as a random bunch of lines or a scribble. Furthermore, there is no logical reason why it should be analyzed as "the letter x inside a square" (*B*) rather than as the arrangement of *C*, yet it apparently is.

Stimuli seem to be perceived as already organized. People do not, it seems, perceive all the logical possibilities for the organization of any given stimuli first, and then choose between them. Two explanations (not necessarily mutually exclusive) for the regularity with which subjects perceive one possible pattern rather than, or at least before, another suggest themselves. It is presumably easier to perceive forms that already have names in the perceiver's experience, like "x" and "square." Or perhaps interpreters faced with the task of analyzing the figure do so by introducing functional concepts ("the box contains the x"). Given these two possibilities, a structural unit—that is, a unit for which a function has not been inferred—would necessarily be categorized by its structural features alone. This kind of categorization, because it is independent of relevance, would be less useful than a functional categorization and therefore is perhaps less likely to be perceived. A functional unit may be recognized by a combination of some of its functional and structural properties: it is categorized both by the structures that describe it and by the functional conditions that have been associated with its structures. The introduction of function, then, is an added complexity but one that aids understanding.

One should not assume from the distinction just drawn that there are two physically separable kinds of units, structural and functional. On the contrary, any unit can in principle be labeled as either structural or functional: the choice depends on how the unit is perceived at a given point in the interpretation. A car is both molded steel on four wheels and transportation. "Hello" is a word and a greeting. Readers may attempt to recognize function, may even prefer to look for a function. It would hardly be surprising to discover that judgments were normally made on the basis of a recognition of relevance—and relevance is always a matter of context. Functional units, therefore, are categorizable only within a context whereas structures may or may not be context dependent. There are in principle, then, two different but interdependent ways in which units may be recognized—as structural units or as functional units— and a reader's ability to distinguish the two when necessary is crucial to the interpretation of new or difficult texts. As we will see in Part II, the preference model preserves the distinction.

Structural conditions provide clues to function and vice versa, but there cannot be any a priori correspondence between a particular structure and a particular function; the latter must always be inferred. Although the search for an easy algorithm for determining the relevant structural and functional units of interpretation would be in vain, nevertheless one can certainly allow that the difficulty of understanding exactly how they are recognized does not tell against the existence of such units. Obviously, until functional (relevant) units are specified, one cannot talk about dependence on particular structures or about their interactions, but one can nonetheless postulate their existence. We agree with Hirsch (1967:77) that "the hermeneutic circle is less mysterious and paradoxical than many in the German hermeneutical tradition have made it out to be." Even if the only *relevant* units are the units that are seen within an interpretation, that is, are already understood as relevant, the units that do not fit into the hypothetical interpretation may also be noticed. Memory of what is relevant from the reader's past experience accounts for the phenomenon of noticing units that are not meaningful within the immediate context. But all units, relevant or irrelevant, can be recognized as units if they belong to already familiar categories or previously known patterns. Patterns or categories that are familiar from a reader's literary and pragmatic experience act as paradigms that suggest other potentially interpretable (patternable) units. This is true even though the reader-interpreter does not yet know whether the units or patterns familiar from past experience are wholly, partially, or not at all consistent with the current context.

A more recent version of the hermeneutic circle—that is, the attack on the theoretical possibility of unit determination—is Derrida's claim (1980) that, even though interpretation depends crucially on categorization (he recognizes that Hirsch's genre rule is indeed a well-formedness rule), nothing can ever belong to a category absolutely: categorization has to be accomplished by each individual, mysteriously and imperfectly. As a competence model, the preference model is bound to account for this categorization, impure as it may be. Preference rules, as we have said, are the mechanism for building fuzziness into the system. At the same time, the introduction of context-sensitive variable rules into the system makes it impossible in principle to argue the existence of a permanent set of pure or ideal categories (Jackendoff, 1983a:82). Hirsch (1967:ch. 3) posits that interpreters have two resources: they use an inherited or learned set of categories, but they also have rules for adjusting the boundaries of those categories as the need arises. The preference model concurs: its categories are not platonic ideals but rather an inherited set of expectations and labels with which an experienced reader meets texts. They are both the context of experience and the experience of context, and they function in the model so as to allow readers to categorize texts that do not precisely fit. Certain existing category labels are legitimized to the extent that they can be successfully incorporated into the model (success being understood as a better account of the interpretations of experienced readers). The model evaluates the meaning and function of its categories indirectly, questioning the legitimacy of each category, the ways categories are described, and the ways in which they function, and it also provides an account of how those categories are simultaneously used and questioned, used and redefined.

Jackendoff (1983*a*: 132) chose the term "preference rule" for the rules by which he proposes to label and evaluate impure semantic categories "because these rules establish not inflexible decisions about structure, but relative preferences among a number of logically possible analyses." Although they are particularly helpful as semantic descriptors, preference rules are found to some extent in all the linguistic systems. They are sets of conditions of four different kinds: well-formedness conditions plus three kinds of preference conditions, all three of which can apply variably. In addition to variability of application, the three kinds of preference conditions (but not the well-formedness conditions) allow for variation by being differentially weighted. When a text is matched to a preference rule, the rule may be said to apply even when the text does not exactly match all the conditions of the rule: a partial match will still produce a judgment or an interpretation. The more conditions of the rule that can be matched to the text, the stronger the judgment; a match of fewer conditions will produce a weaker judgment. According to Jackendoff, preference judgments follow the Gestalt Law of Prägnanz, originally formulated in Wertheimer (1923). Kurt Koffka (1935: 110) states it as follows: "Psychological organization [i.e., a judgment] will always be as 'good' as the prevailing conditions allow. In this definition the term 'good' is undefined. It embraces such properties as regularity, symmetry, [and] simplicity."

In the preference model, the rule by which categorization judgments are made is a version of the Gestalt Law of Prägnanz. The rule takes the form of a gradient necessary condition:

GNC: *Prefer the best categorization possible under the circumstances.*

Two gradient necessary conditions describe "best categorization":

GNC 1: *The best categorization is that which allows the most* coherent *interpretation to emerge.*

GNC 2: *The best categorization is that which allows the most* satisfying *interpretation to emerge.*

"Satisfying" and "coherent" are thus the specifications of "best." They are determined by the set of conditions of significance in force at the time for the categorization judgment in question. They do not demand a choice between, on the one hand, a classical aesthetic notion of art as an ordering of experience, and, on the other, some more daring formulation of pleasure, such as Morse Peckham's suggestion (1965) that we in fact seek chaos, not coherence, in art. As we will explain in Chapter Eight, these adjectives simply denote whatever is considered to be satisfying and coherent by a given community of interpreters. A satisfying and coherent judgment, or set of judgments, is a satisfying and coherent interpretation. It is maximally stable; it defines the strongest interpretation or set of interpretations possible under the circumstances.

Usually a judgment will involve the application of a number of preference rules, and the strength or weakness of the judgment will depend on the extent to which the rules reinforce each other or conflict. When conditions conflict, the role played by the weighting of preference conditions in an interpretive model becomes more apparent. One can observe the effects of weighting in Wayne C. Booth's sensitive discussion of narration in *The Rhetoric of Fiction* (1961). Here Booth is searching out an accommodation between two desirable but conflicting rules, demonstrating his awareness of relative weightings: when two rules conflict and neither prevails, the conflict remains unresolved. The result is that the reader's evaluation does not seem entirely satisfying. If one rule is weighted more heavily and overrides the other, the judgment (all things being equal) will seem more secure.

Booth's understanding of the dilemma presented by an unreliable narrator depends on his estimate of the functions a reliable narrator can perform for a reader. If narrators are both reliable and omniscient, they can provide information that the reader could not otherwise know. They can manipulate the mood (p. 200) and heighten the significance of events (p. 196), mold the beliefs of the reader, that is, "define for us the precise ordering of values on which our judgment should depend" (p. 178) and relate those values to "established norms" (p. 182). Perhaps most important, they can generalize the significance of the work as a whole: can "give form to moral complexities" that make reading a novel a rewarding experience (p. 188). Booth's implicit assumption of the value of the fulfillment of all of these narrative tasks explains why the assumption that there is a reliable narrator is, for him as for many readers, so desirable, so heavily weighted, as to be the null hypothesis. Until presented with evidence to the contrary, Booth will assume a reliable narrator. We can write a preference rule, then, that describes all the above conditions:

Reliable Narrator Rule:
    Prefer to assume that a narrator will (a) provide reliable access to relevant information; (b) define for readers the ordering of values on which their judgments should depend; etc.[8]

Another heavily weighted interpretive rule is the general preference rule of inference. The rule, details of which will be discussed in Chapter Six, requires an interpreter to draw the best inferences possible under the circumstances, with "best" again meaning "satisfying and coherent." The dilemma for Booth, then (the conflict between rules), arises when his best inferences (according to the preference rule for inference) suggest that the narrator is not to be trusted to fulfill the conditions of the Reliable Narrator Rule. He reacts to this dilemma by setting out the conditions from which he finally infers an unreliable narrator. His reasoning here, incidentally, demonstrates how preference rules incorporate gradient concepts. Omniscient narrators are by definition entirely reliable; a first-person narrator might very well be entirely unreliable; however, probably more frequent is the dramatized narrator whose unreliability is chartable as a swerve that the reader can correct for. As soon as the narrator is dramatized within the story, Booth notes, his reliability is to some degree compromised. The reader then has to decide whether the amount of compromise is within the acceptable range of the rule, in which case the narrator will be classified as reliable, perhaps with some qualifications, or whether the narrator has been compromised to such an extent that the rule cannot be consid-

---

[8]Booth describes this rule as a literary rule, with specific reference to novels, but Grice's conversational maxims, applicable to all communicative situations, describe the same phenomenon.

ered fulfilled, so that the narrator is classified as unreliable. A narrator who has a dramatic role in the story must at least now and then be suspected of "interested" narration, and is, furthermore, always limited in what he or she can know. Still, insofar as the author "retains some method of showing what the facts are from which the speaker's interpretations characteristically diverge" (p. 175), the dramatized narrator can perform some of the tasks of an omniscient narrator more or less reliably.

Even after it has been decided that the narrator is more reliable than not, a reader will still have to be alert to the possibilities of indeterminacy and distortion in the narration of a dramatized narrator. The intrusive author as narrator, to use another of Booth's examples, may claim to be omniscient but may nevertheless fail to fulfill his functions. Booth describes three ways by which a reader may know when the narrator is not to be trusted: "when there is a gross disparity between the claims to brilliance of the author and the shoddiness of his presented story" (p. 218); when we perceive "a failure of character in the implied author," who may emphasize his "dulness by claiming to be brilliant" (p. 219); or when we find "a failure of formal coherence" between the ostensible aims of the novel and the effect of the intruding narrator (p. 221). Booth's examples all amount to inference: if the reader infers the narrator's unreliability, he or she cannot keep assuming reliability unless some saving hypothesis is found, perhaps reached by further inference. Thus, for Booth, even though the assumption of a reliable narrator is a heavily weighted rule, the general rule of inference telling him to make the best inferences he can is even more heavily weighted.

Booth now has two choices. He can abandon the interpretive process altogether, concluding that the defects of the narrator will prevent a satisfying interpretation from ever emerging. This is what he does in the case of the novel *Charlotte Summers, the Fortunate Parish Girl*, which was published anonymously about a year after the appearance of Fielding's *Tom Jones*. Here Booth deduces the incompetence of the author in meeting his responsibilities to the reader, and gives up on the attempt to interpret further. The narrator is unreliable unintentionally. But there is a second possibility. To say, as we do, that for Booth the preference rule of inference is weighted more heavily than the reliable narrator rule is to say that he is willing to go to a good deal of interpretive expense to reach an interpretation that, in the face of the inferential evidence of an unreliable narrator, will save his faith in a controlled and intelligent narration. The expense was too great for *Charlotte Summers*, but not too great, apparently, for the seemingly unreliable narrator in Sterne's *Tristram Shandy*. Booth decides that Tristram's unreliability is intentional and that it does not prevent the success of the novel.

He comes to this conclusion by extending the chains of inference that began by identifying the narrator as unreliable. He infers that Sterne had a reason for each of the inferences of unreliability that, as listed above, would otherwise have led a reader like Booth to condemn and dismiss the narration. For example, "the shoddiness of the presented story" is taken to be a sign of the very real problems with time and storytelling that Sterne has his narrator struggle with. Novels in which these problems are not confronted are, by comparison, and to that extent, less rich, less philosophically interesting. Having decided that Tristram, the narrator, is indeed "scatterbrained," Booth finds that this persona provides symbolic coherence in the novel:

The secret of [*Tristram Shandy*'s] coherence, its form, seems to reside primarily in the role played by the teller, by Tristram, the dramatized narrator. He is himself in some way the central subject holding together materials which, were it not for his scatterbrained presence, would never have seemed to be separated in the first place. His double claim—that he knows yet does not know what he is about—simply makes explicit what is self-evident in our experience from beginning to end: that in some ways he is giving us a novel like other novels, and in some ways he is not. [p. 222]

Still in search of a satisfying and coherent interpretation, Booth then goes on (p. 224) to identify three other traditions besides the novel from which he might infer Sterne's purpose in providing a narrator who cannot cope with the task of storytelling: "the comic novel exploded," the "sugar-coated collection of philosophical essays" and the "miscellaneous satire." Tristram, Booth argues, would be the ideal narrator for a work deriving from all three traditions:

On the one hand, since many of Tristram's difficulties are of his own making, his action is like any traditional comic action viewed by spectators who know better than the character. . . . On the other hand, since Tristram is in many respects admirable, we are on his side. He is up against insurmountable obstacles that we all face—the nature of time, the nature of our unpredictable minds, and the nature of human animality as it undercuts all of our efforts to attain to the ideal. [p. 230]

In sum, Booth could not stop with a decision that the book is a failure. Rather, because the rule took precedence which required him to continue making inferences until he reached the best (satisfying and coherent) interpretation, he was finally able to decide (p. 197) that Sterne had indeed provided him with a narrator who could help him set the mood, understand the hierarchy of values, relate them to norms, mold readers' beliefs, and "generalize the significance of the whole work."

Historically, there have no doubt been variations in the point at which readers have decided that the general rule of inference has overridden the Reliable Narrator Rule and have given up on the possibility of finding an intelligence concealed behind a bumbling narrator. Changes in the set of literary texts and conventions over which the reader's experience extends must have some influence on the point at which a reader loses patience and no longer believes that the narrator is providing "reliable access to relevant information." Twentieth-century readers are presumably quicker to recognize a narrator's unreliability than eighteenth-century readers were. At least we can say that for the twentieth-century reader the "novel without a stable narrative voice" is available as a generic category whereas Sterne's original readers would have had to infer the possibility of such a category—invent it.

To generalize from Booth's rules to the rules of a community of readers, we could hypothesize that the Reliable Narrator Rule was more heavily weighted in an eighteenth-century context than in the context of the late twentieth century. Twentieth-century readers, because of their experience with unreliable narrators (including Tristram), do not necessarily assume reliability in reading contemporary literature; having reweighted the rule as a consequence of literary innovation, they also do not necessarily assume reliability when reading earlier fiction (though earlier readers may well have done so). Donaldson (1954), for example, while assuming Chaucer's competence, questions the competence of Chaucer's pilgrim narrator to penetrate the hypocrisies of the other Canterbury pilgrims. Whether such retrospective reweighting is considered to produce a well-formed interpretation requires a separate judgment.

The reader who recognizes an unreliable narrator has acquiesced to the power of the rule of inference, a preference rule that, weighted more heavily than the Reliable Narrator Rule, has overridden it. But overriding is not canceling or suspending; tension is the price paid for whatever resolution is achieved. An unreliable narrator remains a continuing source of tension in a text even after the judgment has been made. Even though Booth is able to continue the interpretive process of *Tristram Shandy* to a satisfying conclusion, he knows that his inferences from the unreliability of the narrator are not a substitute for the assurance an omniscient narrator provides. His appreciation of Sterne, in fact, derives in part from Sterne's helping him to see just this. According to Booth, Tristram maintains that "you may take my word":

> Take his word we do, but only part of the time, and the resulting delightful ambiguities permanently enlarge our view of the possibilities of fiction.
>
> But Sterne enlarges our view of its problems as well. We take his word only part of the time; of all the many problems the reader of *Tristram Shandy* shares with the reader of modern fiction, that of the narrator's indeterminately untrustworthy judgment is most important here.
>
> With his own confusions, he makes our path a troubled, insecure one. The history of unreliable narrators from *Gargantua* to *Lolita* is in fact full of traps for the unsuspecting reader, some of them not particularly harmful but some of them crippling or even fatal. [p. 239]

Conflicts like this are only more or less resolved. When there is a conflict between different judgments and neither is stronger, the ambiguity remains even if a reader makes an arbitrary choice; again, prevailing conditions may or may not value the ambiguity.

We have shown with this example that the way readers use their three competencies to interpret literary texts is not different from the way language is understood in any context. The model suggests the interdependence of the systems that are continuously interacting. None of the three systems (the autonomous, the pragmatic, and the literary) can by itself produce a satisfactory interpretation of more than a small stretch of text. Small interpretive decisions made within one system need further interpretation through the rules of another. Decisions stimulate other decisions, eventually coming to rest at an interpretation sufficiently stable and satisfying to meet prevailing conditions of significance. New information received as the reading continues will force temporary decisions to be reconsidered and recast. The reader engages in a process of hypothesis formation, testing, and modification through which he or she arrives at an understanding of the text. The process is not unidirectional. Expectations are always being met, not met, revised (see Iser, 1972:293). Hypotheses suggested by one system need to be confirmed by information from another system.

Although, as we have said, when mutual confirmations are available a strong interpretation evolves, it is not always the case that this kind of "strength" is valued. A text in which no interpretive hypothesis could be confirmed would be unreadable, but a text that presents too many reinforcing features and too few unexpected features would presumably be considered stereotyped. A community's conditions of significance would describe the balance considered most satisfying according to genres. The description of the balance between given and new in a text, in fact, would be one of the conditions of a genre rule. Stereotyping may be a heavily weighted condition in a liturgical text but not in a lyric poem; a stipulated combination of given features and new features would be a condition in the description of the successful murder mystery.

Although all these systems of interpretation are in principle always interdependent, this does not mean that all the rules or even all the systems are always applied in the interpretation of any given sequence of discourse. Different stretches of text at different stages of interpretation may require different combinations of interpretive strategies. The data from the autonomous system may be interpreted through the appropriate pragmatic subsystems only, and even without literary rules, some of the sequences in a literary text are readable. The rules of the literary system provide additional interpretive power. On the other hand, interpretation of some parts of some texts may be reached through the autonomous and literary systems alone. The transparency of a model that allows the operations of each system to be accounted for independently of the others helps rather than hinders interpretation.

It is our hypothesis that the kind of linguistic theory appropriate to literary theorists is a theory that can show that the choice between a fully determinate, fixed, and objective system of interpretation on the one hand, and a creative, subjective one on the other is no choice. Human beings, as a good language theory must show, manage both in the exercise of their linguistic and literary competence. They make decisions about the well-formedness of structures, and they make judgments about the structure and functions of texts. The combination of their judgments made by the application of preference rules produces maximally stable interpretations.[9]

Chomsky's current Government and Binding Theory, along with his earlier versions of generative grammar, cannot make a major contribution to the basic tasks facing the literary theorist because it cannot describe the ability to categorize along a continuum. Jackendoff's extension of generative linguistics, however, is of great use to us because it ties semantics to a cognitive theory with important claims about how readers manage impure categorization.[10] Its preference rules provide a method of describing how readers in fact make judgments about the nature of the texts to be interpreted. Literary genres, as will become clear in the description in Part II of the various kinds of conditions involved in their categorization, cannot be defined by well-formedness rules alone. The preference conditions that describe them are in turn determined and weighted by a cultural system. "Literature" is ultimately a category in the pragmatic, not the literary, system.

[9] Jackendoff (1983a: 149) suggests the dimensions of the dynamism when he says: "An accumulation of instabilities here and there in a conceptual system may upon occasion be relieved by a more global restructuring—if the organism has sufficient computational capacity to measure relative stability of two or more competing global organizations. Alternatively, one may simply learn to live with local instabilities (or deny them, as in a neurosis). In short, a processing model of cognition must include an active component that continually seeks to adjust and reorganize conceptual structure in an effort to maximize overall stability."

[10] The theory, it is important to note, is not a theory of meaning of things, states, and events, etc., in the real world. As Jackendoff says (1983a: 27, 29), although "we are constructed so as normally to be unaware of our own contribution to experience . . . we have conscious access only to the projected world—the world as unconsciously organized by the mind; and we can talk about things only insofar as they have achieved mental representation through these processes of organization. Hence *the information conveyed by language must be about the projected world.*" This projected world, or world of structured representations, is identical, Jackendoff convincingly argues, with the semantic level of language. If it were not (just to mention one point in his argument), we could not respond to verbal instructions (e.g., "Sit down") by *doing* things (e.g., sitting).

Part II

Categorization

Chapter Three

Determining Structural Genre

The relationship between structure and function, both in the study of material culture and in the study of language and signs, could probably be said to be the major concern of scholarship in humanistic disciplines in this century. The "discovery" of structure by the structuralist movement and the deconstruction of structure in the poststructuralist movement are only two examples of intellectual developments that have had the effect of readjusting or revaluing the relative positions of structure and function in academic models of human activity. Yet it is still far from clear that the words "structure" (or "form") and "function" represent two distinct notions. We assume that a function is a structure for which a purpose has been inferred. Though structure and function may seem relatively easy to separate in the abstract, however, they are not at all easy to study in isolation. The history of recent scholarship, particularly in the language-related fields, is a history of claims for the dominance of one or the other as a governing principle with a growing chorus of voices claiming that separation of the two is impossible.[1] The is-

---

[1] Chomsky's theory is limited in that it is a structuralist theory that defines its domain as linguistics in the narrow sense, i.e., as that which can be studied by observing and describing language structures; language functions, therefore, are either directly derived from structures and thus entirely defined by (subordinate to)

sues are only in part methodological issues, however: exactly what role does function or "purpose" play in the operation of human systems of understanding? In spite of the new vocabulary, the question is at base the old, unanswerable one of free will. Yet we must still ask, Should structure and function be studied together or must investigation necessarily be oriented in one direction or the other?

Furthermore, does a theory need to concern itself with function at all? Since functions cannot be known directly but must be inferred, it would seem to be functions that introduce indeterminacy into systems; it might, thus, be argued that they are prima facie outside the scope of theory. Indeed, the structuralist enterprise in anthropology, linguistics, and literary criticism was designed to achieve greater determinacy by banishing at least some aspects of function. But the structuralists were unsuccessful; they could not banish the effects of functions, which always had to be let in through the back door. Robert Scholes (1974:133), for example, in trying to describe a spectrum of literary genres in terms of their structures is forced to recognize this loophole: "terms like tragedy and comedy . . . are meant to refer to the quality of the fictional world and not to any form of story customarily associated with the term. In this modal consideration, what is important is not whether a fiction ends in a death or a marriage, but what that death or marriage implies about the world."

Since values are of course not structures, Scholes's statement amounts to an admission of the inadequacy of structural categories, even while he proceeds to manipulate his modes as if they were purely formal, making no theoretical or methodological allowances for the differences between structures and functions. The tradition of genre criticism has always recognized both formal and functional categories, although it has, in general, failed to distinguish clearly between them. Aristotle (*Poetics* I. 6–7) recognized that different categorizations group the same texts in different ways, and that structural categories have often been conflated with functional categories.

---

them, or are underivable from linguistic structures. Those that are directly derived account for very few functions, and possibly those of interest primarily to the autonomous system; those that are underivable, by definition, fall outside the scope of linguistics. See Chomsky (1965: 68–74) and Li (1976); for a survey of the variety of meanings for the word "function," see Nagel (1961).

The structuralists are right, of course, in assuming that there is systematic determinacy that can be charted; the functionalists, that is, those nonformalists (including intentionalists and subjectivists) who propose homogeneous systems (systems that do not distinguish structures and their effects from functions and their effects), are wrong to have given up on the attempt. The situation to be accounted for is one in which there is both structural determinacy and functional indeterminacy, and we can at least make a start on understanding their relations by charting the points where they intersect.

We are committed to the methodological advantage of isolating aspects of structure and function in language systems, not only so as to be able to observe them separately, but even more, so as to study how they interact. Language theory is badly in need not just of acknowledgment of this interaction but of a model for it. One of the most formidable tasks now facing students of interpretation is that of understanding how structural and functional aspects interrelate in any given instance to produce an interpretation. Keeping the notion of a structural category separate from that of a functional category has the great advantage of allowing the exhibition of relationships between the two. Moreover, the existence of the distinction between structural literary genre and functional literary genre is crucial to an explanation of genre change.

Roughly speaking, structural literary genres include categories such as play, novel, and poem; functional genre categories include romance, tragedy, picaresque, etc. To assign a text to a functional category type is to judge it according to an inference about its function. We are not talking about two processing stages, nor are we postulating an extra step in the process of understanding functional genre; having nothing to say about how the inference from structure to function is made, we make no claims about how many stages are involved in the making of an inference. From the perspective of a reader's competence to identify them, the structural genre categorization of a text and the functional genre categorization of the same text are qualitatively different. A reader may categorize a text by its structure without making any decision about what function the author intended, or about what the function may actually be in the context of interpretation regardless of the author's intention. A functional genre, on the other hand, is always inferred; in naming the functional genre of a text, one makes one or both of the above-mentioned decisions.

In the preference model, both structures and functions can be primitives—that is, they both have a certain amount of irreducible and uncancelable meaning which is theirs by virtue of long conventional association (some would say by definition). This meaning inevitably has a part in the interpretation of the text, but usually only as a starting point, as a primitive—as in the example of the simple structural category "play," whose meaning is simply the representation by actors of an action, with a beginning and an end. Similarly, "tragedy" defines a functional category on the basis of which a larger interpretation can be derived.

Structures can, and regularly do, serve more than one function at the same time. Let this example of the relationship between structure and function in a nonliterary setting serve to illustrate how widely the distinction applies, and how complex it is. Consider an academic cocktail party. It may function to honor a visiting lecturer while also providing an opportunity for local scholars to exchange ideas informally. It also provides the host with an opportunity to repay social obligations, and it helps to keep the importers of Scotch whiskey solvent. Notice that all these functions could be served by other structures besides the cocktail party. Functions, literary or otherwise, cannot be uniquely derived from structure, or vice versa, and either can serve as a primitive.

Charting the interaction between structures and functions is one of the chief ways in which the preference model displays interaction between meanings that are conventional (and therefore relatively more determinate) and those that are less determinate. It is not the case, however, that these two aspects are homologous with received notions of objectivity and subjectivity in the usual sense; indeed, oversimplifying the question by associating subjectivity with freedom and objectivity with limits impedes understanding. A better principle for defining the limits (fixities or determinacies) that are of interest in literary and linguistic theories is that of systematicity, the use of primitives and axioms to define systematically logical possibilities and relationships among those possibilities.[2] Though systems

---

[2] This kind of limit is not to be confused with the empirical limits that would be described by a performance theory.

can be open or closed, the possible structures of a language are defined by closed systems and therefore provide whatever limits a competence model describes. In contrast, there is no evidence that the possible functions are definable so systematically. Moreover, the limits that have so far been proposed in the description of functions do not appear to have any theoretical justification—only an empirical one. Functional theories in linguistics and literature have in general presented their functions as lists rather than as systems: Jakobson (1960), for example, claims that language has six functions, and Halliday (1973) and Searle (1969, 1976) have also made lists that are closed but not systematic. But if the apparently unsystematic nature of functions has encouraged the association of function with freedom—and thus structure with fixity—in fact structure, too, provides freedom, in which the creativity comes from the recombinatory (i.e. syntactic) potential of the system. Thus, although function and structure do not represent freedom and fixity respectively, owing to the nature of function, fixity (or determinate meaning) can only be described as the conventionalized functioning of structures. Thus, although a presumed contrast between subjectivity and objectivity has been the focus of several literary theories (e.g., Bleich, 1978), we would argue that structure and function are a more useful set of coordinates.

Structure encompasses both the individual structuring mind with its unique combination of furnishings as well as internalized public codes, and the structure of language texts created by individuals working within conventional systems. Function encompasses the freedom to infer a theoretically unlimited number of purposes, many of which are understood by human reasoning, and others of which are understood by reference to shared conventions. The difference between structural and functional genres in the pragmatic system has been variously formalized by, among others, speech act theorists. Their major contribution to language philosophy and to linguistics has been the recognition of the importance of function in a language theory, particularly in a semantics. In spite of the various weaknesses of the attempts at describing how conventional grammatical structures are understood functionally, the explicitly functional orientation of such theories serves our purposes here by helping us to clarify the distinction between structural and functional literary genres.

Speech act theory can be thought of as a reaction to the inability of a sentence-based grammar to explain the functions of sentences in context. The sentence is a structural unit with a "locutionary meaning" that distinguishes it from another sentence. The speech act, however, is a functional unit. The speech act, according to Austin (1962:148) has an "illocutionary force." The illocutionary force is what is done in saying something: to warn by asserting that the ice is thin, for example. It is the function of a structure. Austin regards the performance of speech acts as conventional, and thus the illocutionary force can be discerned and the linguistic event categorized. Unfortunately, as has been widely recognized, things are not so simple. Indeed, the ability to recognize function, that is, to classify illocutionary acts, is crucial to pragmatic competence.[3] It cannot, however, be accomplished entirely on the strength of convention without nonconventional inferences, and thus inevitably introduces the indeterminacy that always accompanies inferences about function. The problem of classifying illocutionary acts and the solutions that have been suggested are parallel, as we will see in the next chapter, to the difficulties of determining functional genres in the literary system.

Among attempts to specify principles for the determination of functional categories, Searle's list (1976) of twelve points of "significant dimensions of variation" between speech acts is perhaps the most sensitive to the multitude of interrelated factors. Although Searle does not specify a system to account for the competence to produce judgments on the basis of his twelve points, Kent Bach and Robert M. Harnish (1979) have made an attempt to describe a system of inferences by means of which a hearer can move from a sentence to an understanding of its illocutionary force. Another way to account for a hearer's competence to make a judgment is to take into account Searle's twelve dimensions of variation by reinterpreting the points as well-formedness and weighted preference conditions for classes of speech acts. They would then be negotiable within the preference model, in which case the model accounts for

[3] Austin proposed a taxonomy of speech acts in his 1957 lectures and in 1976 Searle proposed a revision of his own and Austin's categories and their conditions. Other classifications have been proposed by Vendler (1972), Ohmann (1972), and Fraser (1974) and carefully compared and extended by Hancher (1978). Another version was proposed by Bach and Harnish (1979).

the relative strength of inferences, that is, the judgments identifying speech acts. Searle's three most important points are in fact functional conditions: speech acts are distinguished, he says, according to (1) differences in the point or purpose of the type of act; (2) differences in the direction of fit between the words and the world (does the text aim to describe the world or change it?); (3) differences in expressed psychological states (what is the attitude of the speaker toward the propositional content of the illocutionary act?).

The illocutionary point for speech acts of the representative class, for example, is a gradient condition that "commits the speaker (in varying degrees) . . . to the truth of the expressed proposition" (Searle, 1976:10). "Varying degrees" can be understood as the interval over which variation is allowable, or, for any gradient condition that has a focus, the allowable variation away from its focal point. (Point 3 is a gradient condition but it does not have a focal point.)[4]

Functional literary genres belong in different ways to Searle's representative class (1976). They hypothesize, assert, state, insist, or avow various propositions. To put it the other way around, when a discourse is identified according to the illocutionary force of its proposition, a judgment has been made about the functional genre of that discourse.

In order to explore the interpretive power represented by the crucial task of categorizing texts according to genre, we will examine a structural genre determination first and then a functional one. Let us begin with the example of what was available to prospective the-

---

[4]An assertion is closer than a guess to the focal point of this class. A partial example of the continuum for the illocutionary force of the representative class would look something like the following, with "assert," or perhaps "state," as the focal point:

| Suggest | | | | | | | | | Avow |
| Guess | Hypothesize | Believe | Deduce | Conclude | Assert | State | Boast | Insist | Swear |

The continuum for the illocutionary force of requests might look like this:

									Beg
							Entreat		Demand
Permit	Advise	Invite	Pray	Ask	Request	Order	Defy	Command	Insist	Challenge
								Dare		Plead

These are continua for the illocutionary force of a class, which is not the same thing as continua for membership within a class; the existence of conditions will also influence the class determination.

atergoers in search of an evening's entertainment in New York City during the week of August 17, 1981. In the genre terms of *New York* magazine, they had a choice of a "revival of a classic musical," a "play," a "musical," a "romance," a "musical comedy entertainment," a "comedy thriller," a "saga," a "drama," a "comedy," a "musical comedy," an "operetta," a "musical production," a "peppy, modern-day glamorized version of burlesque," a "mini-musical," an "improvisation comedy," a "thriller," a "show," a "farce," a "comic adventure in anxiety," a "burlesque," a "one-actor," and a "drawing-room comedy." The theater editor, in the three or four lines allotted to her, was able to communicate not only a genre characterization, either structural ("play," "musical," "one-actor") or functional ("comedy," "burlesque"), but also a judgment about quality, along with any particularly interesting or original feature.

The note describing *Children of a Lesser God* (p. 63) is a good example of the compact form: "Phyllis Frelich and John Rubinstein star in Mark Medoff's touching play about a romance between a deaf woman and her non-handicapped lover." This note is what the preference model calls a categorization judgment. The theater editor's judgment about the similarity of the new work to other already familiar works is a judgment about its structural genre (it is a play). Its subject constitutes its difference from other plays (it is about a deaf woman and her hearing lover). The editor also gives an abbreviated value judgment (it is "touching"). Both the similarities and differences would be equally important to prospective theatergoers: though they would not understand something that was in every detail unlike anything in their previous experience, still they would not be looking for entertainment that was entirely stereotyped.

Children of a Lesser God was highly successful by Broadway standards (it was well into its second year of performance by the week of August 17, 1981), and it is clear that those who saw it and knew it as a "play" were readily able to categorize it on the basis of their familiarity with a set of structural conditions associated with the subset of theatrical performances known as plays. This play is indeed a good example of the relative simplicity of structural categorization. It is in some outstanding ways unconventional and it prompted critical hyperbole ("I've never seen anything quite like it," "an extraordinary play," "a play unlike any other"), yet in the reviews and in the publicity for the play (posters, advertisements) none of the reviewers has any hesitation in declaring it a play. Structural genres do not normally seem to be problematic: recognizing and naming them do not depend on subtleties of interpretation. Furthermore, there seems to be little trouble about describing or even naming a new structure that as yet has no name. *New York* magazine of April 1, 1985, for example, names several new structures: "*Queenie* is a sand book, like last summer's *Hollywood Wives*" (a book for taking to the beach on vacation); *The Loves of Anatol* is "a revival of Arthur Schnitzler's memory play with music and dance"; *Tracers* is a "collaborative play, written and performed by Vietnam veterans"; *First Amendment Comedy Theatre* is composed of "audience-suggestion improvisations and musical comedy revues."

A familiar structural category such as "play" names some fairly unambiguous formal features. These features can usefully be distinguished by four different kinds of conditions—two necessary conditions and two typicality conditions. The two kinds of necessary conditions are the well-formedness conditions, and the gradient necessary conditions (GNCs). All necessary conditions of a category must be met if the text is to be placed within that category. Well-formedness conditions help to exclude ill-formed possibilities. Gradient necessary conditions can be exemplified by the general rule of inference, mentioned in Chapter One. The evidence may more or less fit a gradient necessary condition (its gradient aspect), but any such condition cannot go entirely unmet (its necessary aspect). The competent understanding of a play, for example, depends on the ability to separate the playwright from the actors and to draw inferences about the relationship of the people on stage to an assumed playwright. (Children, who at first assume that stage or television characters speak to them directly and in their own voices, have to learn this condition.) This condition is gradient in that it can be fulfilled by inferences ranging from strong to weak about relationships between the playwright and each person on stage. Whenever possible, a gradient condition is expressed in terms of relative closeness to a focal point: a focal point plus a spread function delimits the range over which a token may vary and still unquestionably be judged to be an instance of a type. Whether a focal point and a spread function for the rule of inference could be stated is not clear, but the specification of the allowable interval might make use of the distinction between an entailment as the strongest available inference and a range of weaker inferences. Though it still remains to be determined whether such foci and spread functions are in practice quantifiable or even specifiable, psycholinguistic research on the color spectrum has shown that, in principle, focal points are identifiable within gradient perception.[5]

The rule of inference is considered to be a gradient one because, even though the best inference about the relationship between the author of a play and what the characters say may be a weak inference, yet it is still unquestionably an inference. As we will see in Chapter Six, the rule is also a preference rule, that is, it takes the form: "Prefer the best inference possible under the circumstances." Because people *necessarily* make inferences from language they can make sense of the various typicality conditions of plays. Typicality conditions, as their name implies, are not necessary: they are conditions typical of a given category, or are typically associated with it. If any one typicality condition is not present in the token text, the judgment that that particular text does belong to a particular category is not scuttled. Like necessary conditions, typicality conditions are distinguished as gradient and nongradient (or discrete). For example, one heavily weighted nongradient typicality condition of "play" is that the actors who perform in plays are not understood to be speaking spontaneously, as they presumably do offstage, but are acting in roles that have been specified more or less exactly and have been practiced or rehearsed before the performance. Although an actor may, at the moment of performance, feel total identification with a role (and in certain styles of performance this may be desirable), and although actors may, in other styles of performance ad-lib some dialogue, a play is not a group of actors engaging in spontaneous dialogue in front of audiences. The function that spon-

[5] Research on the color spectrum has been summarized by Roger Brown (1976). In brief, it seems that the spectrum has points of greater and lesser intensity for each color—places where green is more clearly green than other places. Slobin (1979: 187) points out that although languages differ in the number of color terms they have and how those terms divide the spectrum, "regardless of how many color terms a language has, and regardless of the boundaries between the various color terms, there is a physiologically determined collection of FOCAL, or PROTOTYPICAL colors." Where focal points can be determined they are clearly useful in describing what it means to be similar to a type.

taneous dialogue has in some genres of performance (television talk shows, for example, or popular music concerts in which star performers intersperse singing and talking) is precisely to distinguish these genres from rehearsed plays in which this rule of learned dialogue is heavily weighted. The rule of learned dialogue in plays allows these other genres to define themselves as informal and spontaneous because they are not plays, that is, to define themselves in opposition to the category "play."

Even within the genre "play" a playwright or director could not work against the convention, as Pirandello does, for example, in *Six Characters in Search of an Author*, were the condition not a heavily weighted condition, which is always assumed to be in force. (The presence of a heavily weighted condition is not, however, sufficient for classification: the condition of learned dialogue is consistent just as equally with the category "opera" as with the category "play.") In most instances, a sufficient set of conditions must be matched before competing possibilities can be eliminated. We have here another example of a gradient necessary condition: a sufficient number of inferences must be made in order to make sense of the relationship between the language one hears from the actors and the playwright. The gradience of this condition comes from the impossibility of stating how many conditions must be met, the necessity of the condition, from the need for categorization even when insufficient information is available. Both these issues will be discussed more fully later on.

In the New York run of *Children*, Phyllis Frelich played the role of Sarah Norman, and John Rubinstein played her lover, then husband, James Leeds. The typicality condition of learned dialogue described above eliminates the possibility that what the audience witnessed on stage was a spontaneous conversation between a deaf woman and her lover; any interpretation claiming that it was such a conversation would be unsatisfactory. This would be true regardless of the actual relationship between the actors. In the first performances of *Children*, at Las Cruces, New Mexico, in 1979, Phyllis Frelich played opposite her husband, Robert Steinberg. Although one can think of numerous other acting couples in the history of theater, even in those cases, the interpretations have always assumed that the text as a whole makes a statement that is ultimately the author's rather than the actor's—even when, as sometimes happens, an actor is acknowledged to be "interpreting" a role in a very personal reading.

The condition also holds when all or some of the dialogue seems to fit the offstage life of the actors: the additional meaning so provided does not cancel the attribution of intended meaning to its author. Mark Medoff, quoted in the *New York Times* (April 1, 1981), expressed his understanding of his play *Children* as being that "the problems of the deaf somehow provided a perfect metaphor for the difficulty of all human communication." Walter Kerr, in his opening-night review of the play (*New York Times*, March 31, 1980), moves from a judgment based on an assumption that he had heard the author speaking directly to a judgment he finds more satisfying, that is, that he had heard a character speak:

I had a rather complicated experience at the very beginning of the deeply engaging new play at the Longacre, Mark Medoff's "Children of a Lesser God." As the curtain rose on a skeletal classroom in a speech clinic primarily designed to aid the deaf, therapist John Rubinstein stepped forward to offer a brief, sunny, dead-earnest introduction. "In the beginning," he said, "was silence, and out of it could come only one thing—human speech." I promptly felt a stir of rebellion. Because Mr. Rubinstein is an extremely personable performer and because he was speaking with urgent candor, I took the remark at face value, as though the actor were speaking for the author and as though what he was saying was to be accepted as the evening's theme.

However, Kerr goes on to explain, it gradually becomes apparent that Medoff also considers the speech therapist's generalization to be wrong: the character's statement turns out to be a misunderstanding which threatens the romance and marriage to come.

The judgment is further complicated by another condition special to the production—and one that makes it quite different from other plays about a deaf woman, such as William Gibson's *The Miracle Worker*, in which the actress Patty Duke played the deaf and blind Helen Keller. The condition—the actual deafness of the lead actress, Joan Frelich—has to add a level of meaning to her portrayal, making her presence on the stage something like "spectacle" in the Greek or Jacobean theater. It is too simple to assume that the success of *Children* resulted from the exploitation of the human instinct of curiosity about the handicapped. The impassioned actress's deafness refers to itself, inviting the audience to consider the situation of a deaf actress. But it also reminds the audience of the convention that the actress and the role are separate. These extra dimensions of meaning surely contributed to the reviewers' reactions to the play. Not only did they find it "winning," "thoughtful," "beautifully written," and "worth walking to" (it opened during a strike of public transportation in New York City), but also "compelling," "engrossing," "gripping," "vastly absorbing," "fascinating," and "heart-wrenching" (*New York Times*, April 6, 1980).

The active involvement of Frelich—a professional actress and founding member of the National Theater for the Deaf—in the development of the script marks an additional difference between this play and other biographical or autobiographical plays. Medoff's introduction to the printed version of the play tells how he invited Frelich and her husband to his home in New Mexico and how they worked together with him for six months, recalling experiences of their courtship, suggesting, correcting, and generally making him sensitive to the world of the deaf. The wide publicity given to these circumstances made it likely that its audiences knew that Medoff had written the play especially for Frelich. Personal concerns and even autobiographical details in the plot or dialogue of a modern drama are not unusual, but one cannot think of very many examples of this kind of identity between an actress and her role since the Restoration, when Nell Gwyn, the celebrated actress and mistress of Charles II, played the witty and worldly wise heroine in a series of roles created not only specifically for her but also to take advantage of the audience's awareness of her position in court (see Peter Holland, 1979). Frelich tried to clarify her relationship to the play in an interview with Michiko Kakutani that appeared in the *New York Times* two days after the play had opened. Kakutani writes:

Certainly, Miss Frelich's marriage, which bridges the realms of the hearing and the deaf, parallels the one in the play, and during the Playwright's Lab workshop production in New Mexico, Mr. Steinberg, who is currently John Rubinstein's understudy, played opposite his wife. Still, the actress is quick to point out that she does not think the play is autobiographical, that the misunderstandings endured by Sarah and James on stage remain dramatic constructs of Mr. Medoff's imagination.

Neither Kakutani nor her copy editor seems to have noticed the error of suggesting that a play written by Medoff could be an autobiography of Frelich. The interrelations of the principals in the production are indeed complex and possibly without precedent on the contemporary stage. The point here is that although these variations in the usual relationships between author and actor have consequences for the determination of author's meaning serious enough to produce a confusion of fiction, biography, and autobiography, and even to obscure the issue of who is asserting what, yet since these are questions of function and not of structure, they never threaten the very simple and incontestable characterization of this stage production as a play.

That seven other typicality conditions of the structural category "play," several of them heavily weighted typicality conditions, are unambiguously met undoubtedly contributed to the assurance with which critics named *Children* a play. All seven are examples of gradient typicality conditions. The condition that a play be the representation of an action is clearly met by *Children*. It also meets the condition that a play consists of dialogue. In addition to dialogue of the conventional sort, *Children* also has sections of monologue and some unusual combinations of sign language and speech that are different from normal stage dialogue.[6] This particular combination of partial dialogue does not compromise the classification, however, as it would if the condition about dialogue were not a gradient condition. A play can still be judged a play even if much of it is monologue; and even if there is no dialogue at all, a play may still be considered a play if enough other conditions of the category "play" are met, because the requirement of dialogue is a typicality, not a necessary condition. (Recall Beckett's *Krapp's Last Tape*, in which one character talks to a tape recorder.) A dramatic representation in which a heavily weighted typicality condition is not met might prompt a recategorization, if there is one available. A performance with only one character might be categorized (again, depending on other conditions) as a reading rather than a play. If the representation consists of dialogue without action, as when the different parts

---

[6] The actor who plays James Leeds actually speaks two parts. He signs when he speaks to Sarah, who does not lip-read, and he also speaks his lines aloud for the audience. Many of his spoken lines are echoes of what Sarah says (in sign language), but they are the only way an audience that cannot understand American Sign Language or Signed English would know what Sarah says.

are read by actors standing at podiums—a reading of Shaw's *Don Juan in Hell*, for example, which is actually the third act of *Man and Superman*—the performance will almost surely be called a reading, not a play. The presence in a text of structures matching a heavily weighted typicality condition of a category, such as dialogue, is not a sufficient condition for a categorization judgment. Its presence, for example, would be consistent with the category "novel," even though in the novel the presence of dialogue is a less heavily weighted typicality condition.

Children also meets the gradient typicality condition of length by being approximately two hours long. If a Shakespeare production runs longer, or a one-act play shorter, the gradient typicality condition of length is still satisfied. That a play typically lasts two hours plus or minus part of an hour is an example of a gradient condition with a focal point (two hours) and a spread (part of an hour).

All typicality conditions, both gradient and nongradient, can also have absolute exceptions, that is, can be entirely unsatisfied. *Children* consists of two acts of approximately forty-five minutes each. *The Life and Adventures of Nicholas Nickleby* was presented in two sittings totaling eight and a half hours. Eight and a half hours is beyond typical bounds, but *New York* magazine nonetheless described *Nicholas Nickleby* as a play because, in terms of the preference model, it met most of the other typicality conditions. If too many typicality conditions are missing, the categorization "play" may be replaced by something less specific like "theater," but the substitution seems to be resorted to only when, besides the absence of many of the typicality conditions, there is some question about the degree of fit, that is, how closely the text can be said to conform or match up with a particular condition. An example of this could be a case in which actors hold conversations with members of the audience as much as with each other, and/or the sense of an autonomous and coherent action is lost. A performance of this sort might be categorized as "guerrilla theater."

Four other typicality conditions that *Children* meets unambiguously describe plays as typically having actors in costume, being performed on a stage, set with scenery, and specially lighted. The absence of any of these conditions, their absolute exception, would have a less destabilizing effect on the categorization than would the absence of one of the more heavily weighted conditions. A play can be acted on a wagon or a lawn, in a living room or a street and still be a play. It can be acted without costumes, scenery, or special lighting. *Children of a Lesser God* would be no less a play if it were performed in a college quadrangle instead of on a Broadway stage; and though most plays are understood as scripts for performance, *Children* is no less a play when read in one's living room. Since typicality conditions can have absolute exceptions, that is, can be entirely unfulfilled, and the text can still be considered a play (as long as the necessary conditions and some subset of the typicality conditions are met), the absence of one of these less heavily weighted typicality conditions would not be as significant to a judgment as its presence. Absence has some effect on the judgment: there is an interesting difference between a particular condition's being irrelevant and being an absolute exception. The presence of a heavily weighted condition makes more difference than the presence of a lightly weighted one, and the absence of a heavily weighted condition makes more difference than the absence of a lightly weighted one. Also, the absence of a typicality condition can have a more significant effect than the effect on the categorization judgment. Actors typically hear and speak, if not normally, then better than normally. The deafness of the lead actress in *Children* would be important in any interpretation of the play, but it does not threaten the categorization "play."[7]

Children of a Lesser God makes an interesting case for the discussion of structural categorization because, while it is a play in such an entirely unambiguous way, the task of identifying a conventional functional genre for it is much less straightforward. When the theater critic of *New York* described it as a "touching play about a romance between," she was probably not using the word "romance" to suggest the functional genre "romance," for aside from the obviously met typicality condition that *Children* is a love story, it does not readily fulfill the whole set of conditions of romance. It meets certain of the conditions set forth by Frye (1957): the hero must undergo a test, and if he passes, he receives a reward, "usually in-

---

[7] Jackendoff (1983a) suggests the case of a one-armed person. Although such a person is an exception to the condition that people have two arms, the absence of that condition has no effect on the categorization of the person as such and yet the absence of the arm is extremely significant to that person and to one's reaction to that person.

cluding a bride." But if the functional genre must be determined in part by an inference about the text's assertion, about its illocutionary point, then it will have to be said that *Children* declines, in the end, to assert the benign vision of the genre romance.

Can reviewers be assumed to be assessing their readers' interests correctly when they omit a functional categorization? *Children* ends with the separation of husband and wife, although whether that separation is to become permanent is ambiguous. The conclusion, according to Kerr (*New York Times*, March 31, 1980), is "a tantalizing gesture, half-despair, half-promise." Kerr's comments may mean that he is assigning the play to the functional literary genre that we can broadly call "serious." This would mean that the most heavily weighted typicality condition would be a gradient one that identifies the author's purpose as an attempt to investigate a difficult and serious social or personal problem in a way that exhibits both its seriousness and the difficulty of its resolution. "Serious" is not included in the classical lists of literary genres; we could put its recognition as a genre somewhere in the early twentieth century, perhaps alongside the New Critical acknowledgment that great literature was bound to be, to some extent, vague or ambiguous. Such a category, it might be argued, would include nonfiction as well as fiction; fictionality would be a relatively lightly weighted typicality condition of the genre. This genre is an example of the category functional genre. It is the task of the next chapter to describe how functional genres are defined and how they are recognized.

Chapter Four

Determining Functional Genre

The procedures for determining functional genre are similar to those for determining structural genre, but because of the difference in the way functions and structures are apprehended, the determination of functional genre is more complicated and is less likely to result in agreement among readers. Unlike structural genre determination, the determination of functional genre depends on inferences: about an author's intentions and about the functions of the form beyond those controlling intentions. In this chapter we offer an example of a functional genre determination—of Emily Brontë's *Wuthering Heights*—which, not incidentally, also provides confirmation of the example of structural genre determination given in Chapter Three, *Children of a Lesser God*. Although the framework of genre expectations is necessary for interpretation, apparently a clear structural genre categorization is sufficient.

As in the categorization of *Children* as a play, so with *Wuthering Heights* readers have made judgments about genre by finding the best possible match between the various features of the text and conventional generic conditions. The essential indeterminacy of inferences, however, makes this functional categorization much less certain. The determination of functional genre is thus like the categorization of speech acts. Instead of moving from structure to structure, as was possible in the judgment that a representation with actors, stage, costumes, etc. (structures) could be categorized as a play (another structure), an inference about function, that is, about illocutionary force, must be made from a combination of structural and functional conditions.

Wuthering Heights is usually referred to by its structural genre, novel. This is clearly the safest approach, though it was called a romance by at least one reviewer at the time of its publication (Allott, 1974:224f.), and it has also been called a romantic novel (by John K. Mathison, in Sale, 1963:320). Mark Shorer (Sale, 1963:357), making a guess about its intended function, calls it a "work of edification" in "the nature of a grand passion." J. Hillis Miller (1963: 175) says it "carries the tradition of romantic love as far as it can go." Mary Visick (Allott, 1970:208), in contrast, says that it "commands assent of the kind we accord to tragedy," and Derek Traversi (Allott, 1970:174) says it "approaches . . . the severe simplicity of the pagan tragedies." But even these critics do not seem to feel that a conventional functional genre categorization is of pressing importance. For the most part, they call it a novel, and although the term "novel" can be used to label both a structural and a functional category, these critics seem to use it as a structural genre. Thus we can again infer that structural categories can themselves shape the experience of reading.

The apparent sufficiency of a structural determination to many theater critics and readers of novels is counterevidence to the views of some of the major genre theorists of the last forty years who have assumed the distinctions among genres to be primarily distinctions among functions or purposes (see, e.g., Olson, 1952; Crane, 1953; Hirsch, 1967; and Todorov, 1976). An analysis of the decision-making process of a series of readers of *Wuthering Heights* reveals that when the decision about the structural genre of the text is clear, readers can go on to speculate about its functional genre. The security of a strong judgment about structural genre does not preclude speculation about functional genre, but it does allow readers the freedom to be satisfied with a weak functional categorization. Indeed, according to one of the conditions of significance in force since the Romantic period, the ambivalence of the functional genre is appreciated; it is now widely held that a good reading is one that forbears closure and resists unity, either structural or functional. J. Hillis Miller (1982) makes the point about *Wuthering Heights*:

> The best readings will be the ones which best account for the heterogeneity of the text, its presentation of a definite group of possible meanings which are systematically interconnected, determined by the text, but logically incompatible. . . . There is an error in the assumption that there *is* a single secret truth about *Wuthering Heights*. . . . The secret truth . . . rather, is that there is no secret truth. . . . Any formulation of such a principle is visibly reductive. [p. 51]

Miller's admonition is evidence that readers do seek some functional generic categorization, and it may also be evidence that, despite its absence from Aristotle's list, "serious writing" is a functional genre and, according to Miller, the appropriate categorization for *Wuthering Heights*. Let us suppose, then, that the reader, like Mathison, is entertaining the possibility that the novel is a romance. What conditions describe the competence of an experienced reader to recognize a text as a romance? The preference model must propose a set.

The list of conditions we propose as the rule of romance is based on the description of romance that Northrop Frye published in 1957 in *Anatomy of Criticism*. There are several reasons for using Frye's list. The first is simply that Frye has read many of the texts our literary tradition has considered romances and has thought about the subject more than many people. Indeed, most critics since 1957 reflect his influence and more or less accept his formulation— so much so that the rule of romance for many contemporary readers is not only the experience of the texts themselves but the experience of Frye's text of Frye's experience of them: the authority for that rule is the authority that attaches to Frye's text. It is not necessary to accept Frye's guess about the conditions of romance as an ideal set, and we do not do so; Frye's conditions are his own. Nonetheless, using Frye's terms should make it clear that the question of whose rule is the prevailing one, and the precise specification of the rule, is a contingent, community-dependent issue.[1] Different groups of readers have different lists, of course. Few nonacademic readers would base their categorization on Greek romances, and some

---

[1] Claudio Guillen (1971:114) observes that Goethe made this point.

readers of medieval romances who know them only in modernized versions may categorize them as adventure stories rather than as romances: their category, unlike Frye's, includes modern romances, that is, love stories. Within the academic world, however, Frye's rule has been the basis for thinking about the genre of romance for the past quarter-century, and whatever its strengths or weaknesses, it stands alone. The texts on which Frye based his rule are, in large part, still the canonical texts academic readers would call romances. Although few younger scholars are as familiar with the classics as Professor Frye is, as long as those books continue to be read the rule will remain relatively stable.

The second reason for using Frye's rule is the more interesting from a theoretical point of view. Frye's central claim about his system of modes is that it has a psychological reality of the kind we will eventually claim for necessary rules, that is, a human universality. The possible meanings human beings can attribute to human action and character do not seem to be open-ended. Frye's assumption (and apparently Aristotle's also, as we note when we come to his understanding of tragedy later in this chapter) is that human attitudes toward existence are systematic and limited in number and, like the medieval humors, are defined by human biology. This claim for built-in conceptual limits is important, quite apart from any consideration of whether or not Frye succeeded in cutting the human from the cultural "at the joint." [2]

By taking Frye at his own estimation and distinguishing as well-formed, or necessary conditions, those that he considered to be so, we can examine how a system of such conditions works, even if the content of the conditions or their labeling ultimately needs adjustment. In the following version of the rule of romance, with the typicality conditions given in order of weighting from the most to the least important, all the direct quotations are from Frye (1957).

Rule of Romance:

Prefer to categorize as "romance" a text that meets all the following well-formedness and gradient necessary conditions and a sufficient number of the typicality and gradient typicality conditions:

WFC 1: The text is "the nearest of all literary forms to the wish-fulfillment dream"; it is a narrative in which "the virtuous heroes

---

[2] See Krieger (1966) for various arguments that he did not.

*and beautiful heroines represent the ideals [of the society that pro-
duces it] and the villains the threats to their ascendency."*

WFC 2: *"The essential element of plot . . . is adventure."*

WFC 3: *The major adventure is a successful quest involving
conflict.*

WFC 4: *"The central form of romance is dialectical: everything
is focussed on a conflict between the hero and his enemy, and all the
reader's values are bound up with the hero."*

WFC 5: *"The hero of romance is analogous to the mythical Mes-
siah or deliverer who comes from an upper world, and his enemy is
analogous to the demonic powers of a lower world."*[3]

GNC 1: *The text has a "perennially child-like quality . . . marked
by its extraordinarily persistent nostalgia, its search for some kind
of imaginative golden age."*

GNC 2: *"The enemy may be an ordinary human being, but the
nearer the romance is to myth, the more attributes of divinity will
cling to the hero and the more the enemy will take on demonic
mythical qualities."*

GNC 3: *"Romance is naturally a sequential and processional
form."*

GTC 1: *"The complete form of the romance is clearly the successful quest [which has] three main stages: the stage of the perilous
journey and the preliminary minor adventures; the crucial struggle,
usually some kind of battle in which either the hero or his foe, or
both, must die; and the exaltation of the hero . . . using Greek
terms, the* agon *or* conflict, *the* pathos *or* death struggle, *and the*
anagnorisis *or* discovery, *the recognition of the hero, who has
clearly proved himself to be a hero even if he does not survive the
conflict." [Later in the essay Frye proposes a four-stage form, which
makes clear that he considers both structural possibilities typicality
conditions.]*

GTC 2: *This threefold structure is repeated: "The successful hero
is a third son, or the third to undertake the quest, or successful on
his third attempt." Cf. "the three-day rhythm of death, disappearance, and revival which is found in the myth of Attis and other
dying gods."*

---

[3] This list of Frye's conditions largely retains his phrasing and his grouping: as he
sees it, the hero's identity as a deliverer is inseparable from the villain's connection
with the underworld. Subtler distinctions could be made, however, and Frye may be
grouping together a number of conditions that might in fact operate independently.

TC 1: Although the enemy may have connections to a lower world, "the conflict . . . takes place, or at any rate primarily concerns, our world, which is in the middle, and which is characterized by the cyclical movement of nature."

TC 2: "The opposite poles of the cycles of nature are assimilated to the opposition of the hero and his enemy."

TC 3: "The enemy is associated with winter, darkness, confusion, sterility, moribund life, and old age."

TC 4: The hero is associated "with spring, dawn, fertility, vigor, and youth."

TC 5: The enemy may be a beast or a dragon; the dragon may guard a hoard.

TC 6: The lower world (inside or behind the guarding dragon) "is a place of oracles and secrets."

TC 7: Mutilation may be the price to be paid for the attainment of the secrets.

TC 8: "The reward of the quest usually is or includes a bride."

TC 9: This bride may have to be rescued from the "embraces of another and generally older male," from a tabooed place, from sleep, from ugliness.

The association of a text with a particular genre involves comparing the list of conditions of that genre with the text in order to determine the degree of fit. At the outset, a reader's judgment may be based on information given on the title page, previous knowledge, and/or an obvious match between the text and some prominent conditions of one of the genres in the reader's repertoire. Thus, at first the reader may find in *Wuthering Heights* a match between the text and the fourth well-formedness condition (WFC 4), the first and third gradient necessary conditions (GNC 1 and 3), and the eighth and ninth typicality conditions (TC 8 and 9) that is sufficient to suggest the possibility that the genre is romance: the structure focuses on a conflict between the hero and his enemy, there is a persistent nostalgia and search for an imaginative golden age, it has a sequential form, and the reward of the quest promises to include a bride who must be rescued from another man.

On several points, however, the reader finds that the judgment about the genre cannot be confirmed. First of all, certain conditions, including one well-formedness condition and several typicality conditions, not only cannot immediately be met but seem actually to be contradicted by conditions of the text: it is the hero (assuming that Heathcliff is to be considered a hero) and not the enemy, as the well-formedness condition says it must be, who seems to be "analogous to the demonic powers of a lower world," and it is the hero and his home (Wuthering Heights) that are "associated with winter, darkness, confusion," while the enemy seems to have "spring, dawn, fertility, vigor, and youth." The reader also has difficulty determining the degree of fit between the text and the other conditions. Can it be said, in *Wuthering Heights*, that the beautiful heroine represents the ideal of society? If society is represented by the narrators Nelly and Lockwood, then the answer must be no. But if the stolid bourgeois virtues of these two are interpreted as comic (as in Knoepflmacher, 1971:89) on the inference that Emily Brontë disapproves of their limited understanding, then the reader may see the intensity of the passion shared by Catherine and Heathcliff as a wish-fulfillment, and perhaps also as the fulfillment of a social ideal in the pride, passion, and utter honesty and loyalty of Heathcliff.

Substituting Emily Brontë's approval for "society's" ideals is one way of saving the romance categorization, because it is only in this way that WFC 5 can be said to be fulfilled. (Remember that a well-formedness condition must necessarily be fulfilled to allow the categorization.) If *Wuthering Heights* is a romance, it must be posited that Heathcliff is the deliverer who comes from an upper world—a world that may look savage but is in fact noble. The same interpretation would allow the "attributes of divinity" of the second gradient necessary condition to apply to Heathcliff. This last example shows that the reader can confirm or reject an original hypothesis by noting mismatches that signal the need to move beyond matching procedures; the reader must also apply transformations and make various kinds of inferences that, like the above example, have the effect of reinterpreting aspects of the text so that they are sufficiently tractable to count as instances of conditions of the type under consideration. Since the conditions themselves are also susceptible to transformations, suggesting their own extensions, the details of the text can be understood as more or less matching them.

According to Frye, the ninth typicality condition (TC 9) can be met by saving the woman from a monster, from a man, from a place, etc., and any of these would count as the required danger. In principle, this appears to mean that any token text can, with enough patience, be adjusted to fit the conditions of any type. But the infinite deferral may be halted for several reasons. First, there is a cost to inferences. The reader presumably wants to make as few as will be satisfying according to the conditions of significance under which he or she is reading the text. Patience enough to match *King Lear* to the type of comedy would, under prevailing conditions, be perversity, but of course there are interpretive circumstances in which perversity is highly valued. On the other hand, a change in a single heavily weighted condition, or enough changes in the weighting of several typicality conditions, may alter the balance and make recategorization not only possible but desirable. The difficulty of interpreting Donne's lyrics as love poetry by nineteenth-century standards disappeared when the standards of what counts as love poetry changed.

A second factor mitigating against unending transformations is that when a token cannot be fairly easily matched to a type, another type is very likely waiting in the wings with which a match may be attempted, making the cost of a long chain of inferences and transformations an expenditure to which the reader has no motive to agree. The reader will, all things being equal, find it more satisfying to investigate these other possibilities than to extend the chain of inference. The decision to investigate other possibilities rather than to extend the chain of inference is itself a preference judgment. Further analysis of our case study, *Wuthering Heights*, shows how these decisions are made.

Notice, for example, that the second well-formedness condition ("the essential element of plot is adventure") can be said to be met only if the various trips Heathcliff and Catherine undertake and the marriages they contract are considered adventure. Are misalliances adventure, or must adventure mean that one's life is in danger? Catherine certainly seems to feel that her adventures—specifically her abandonment of Heathcliff—are the cause of her death. Just before she dies, she tells Heathcliff that she is dying for her mistakes. But her admission of guilt does not solve the problem in Frye's terms, under which, one assumes, the hero undertakes the adventure and the heroine is the reward. *Wuthering Heights*, a romance written by a woman, suggests that Frye's condition may not be as universally applicable as he thought it was. His list may be unnecessarily limited by the texts he considered representative of the genre. Always a champion of the underlying seriousness of folk and popular literature, Frye might today want to reconsider his conditions in the light of the enormous popularity of love stories (called romances) written by women and for women which fulfill many of his conditions.

Another way of solving the genre categorization problem would be to consider Heathcliff's vengeful machinations an adventure insofar as they are designed to rescue himself and Catherine from the danger of compromise in bourgeois marriage. Once it is agreed that Heathcliff's scheming is adventure, it should not be too difficult to see it as a quest, thus fulfilling the third well-formedness condition.

With each additional element of the token text that readers can interpret as satisfying one of the given conditions a stronger interpretation develops, or an earlier categorization hypothesis is confirmed. Matching the text to typicality conditions (in contrast to necessary conditions) need not require great ingenuity in making inferences and applying transformations since some of the typicality conditions can remain entirely unmet without weakening the judgment. Linton, for example, may be the dragon guarding the treasure (Catherine herself), fulfilling TC 5. He does not, however, seem to be guarding any secrets that were not already known to Heathcliff. If this putative match seems farfetched, it can simply be forgotten, as long as a sufficient number of other typicality conditions do match.

The evidence about *Wuthering Heights* collected so far, and at a not unreasonable price, works to confirm it as a romance. When Catherine dies in the middle of the book, however, the case is dealt a severe blow. This plot event weakens the arguments made earlier which allowed the romance categorization to proceed in spite of doubts about how closely the text fits the conditions of the type. Ideals, represented by Catherine and Heathcliff, are supposed to triumph, not die. It is true that Frye allows for the temporary eclipse of the hero (GTC 1), but Catherine, in Frye's terms, is not the hero, although this is the second time she has been caught looking like one. The talk of forgiveness in the scene before her death might be considered a metaphoric transformation ("displacement" in Frye's vocabulary) of the stage of *anagnorisis* in which the true heroism or virtue of the hero is revealed, but on Catherine's death, Heathcliff seems to be plunged into a world far from romance. When he learns of her death he cries: "May she wake in torment!" (Sale: 139). The motif of revenge, not new to Brontë's narrative, now makes tragedy seem a much more likely categorization. At this point the reader may think it would be easier to switch categories than to invest any more effort in applying transformations so as to fit the text to the original category. As long as other categories suggest themselves— either well-known ones like tragedy, or new ones like supermarket junk romance—the economy of interpretation will suggest that re-categorization is easier than the continued use of transformations in an effort to make the token match the preconceived type. The type of tragedy is ready to step in.

The rule of tragedy in the Western tradition is identified with the authority of one critic, Aristotle. Even so, Aristotle's word is not the only law. As understood by experienced readers today, the rule of tragedy derives not only from Aristotle's descriptions of Greek plays but also from Shakespeare's tragedies, from classical French trage-dies, and from the rich body of criticism on all three sets of texts. Moreover, as time passes, conditions of a type tend to drop out completely. Contemporary readers no longer consider verse and song to be a condition of the general category of tragedy, for ex-ample, although both were necessary to Aristotle; now they are considered conditions of Greek tragedy. Other conditions may be reweighted: a chorus is no longer considered necessary or even typi-cal, although readers can recognize a character who fulfills the function of the Greek chorus. The list that follows includes all of Aristotle's conditions, so that contemporary readers may note the attrition. In addition, we have appended Frye's explanations (1957) of Aristotle's conditions at points where Frye demonstrates the way twentieth-century readers have expanded or revised the original conceptions. This layering is a way of summarizing an inherited tra-dition of tragedy. Undoubtedly the rules are oversimplified in some places and overspecified in others, but they serve to suggest how an experienced reader judges the genre of a text: on the basis of read-ing experience, both immediate and inherited, rather than on the basis of a platonic ideal.

Rule of Tragedy:
Prefer the designation "tragedy" for a text that meets all of the following well-formedness and gradient necessary conditions

and a sufficient number of the typicality and gradient typicality conditions:[4]

WFC 1: *The text is a dramatic form of imitation written in verse.*

WFC 2: *The text has six parts, which parts determine its quality—namely, Plot, Character, Thought, Diction, Song, Spectacle. [Aristotle acknowledges that these are the conditions of all plays, including comedies.]*

WFC 3: *The text falls into two parts—complication and unraveling or denouement.*

Frye refers to the binary structure of tragedy, calling the two parts "original act" and "revenge." Tragedy, he notes (pp. 208–9), "seems to lead up to an epiphany of law. In its most elementary form, the vision of law operates as *lex talionis* or revenge. The hero provokes enmity, or inherits a situation of enmity, and the return of the avenger constitutes the catastrophe." Frye infers (p. 210) what seems to him to be a significant contradiction in this two-part structure: it exhibits "the omnipotence of an external fate," yet "the act which sets the tragic process going must primarily be a violation of *moral* law" (Aristotle's *harmartia* or flaw):

The tragic hero is very great as compared with us, but there is something else, something on the other side of him opposite the audience, compared to which he is small. This something else may be called God, gods, fate, accident, fortune, necessity, circumstance, or any combination of these. [p. 207]

At the same time, however,

the great majority of tragic heroes do possess hybris, a proud, passionate, obsessed, or soaring mind which brings about a morally intelligible downfall. Such hybris is the normal precipitating agent of catastrophe. . . . The hero's act has thrown a switch in a larger machine than his own life, or even his own society. [pp. 210–11]

Note that Frye is here proposing that Aristotle's conditions imply a heavily weighted functional condition. He continues:

[4]Although Aristotle's desiderata and his absolute requirements are not always clearly distinguished, certainly some of the conditions he found necessary are no longer considered so. Aristotle clearly thought that all tragedies were plays, but some modern readers have been willing to consider Thomas Hardy's novels, for example, as tragedies. We list Aristotle's conditions in the order he discusses them, and we assume that the order he presented them in corresponds to the weighting he gave them.

All theories of tragedy as morally explicable sooner or later run into the question: is an innocent sufferer in tragedy (i.e. poetically innocent) . . . not a tragic figure? Tragedy, in short, seems to elude the antithesis of moral responsibility and arbitrary fate, just as it eludes the antithesis of good and evil. [p. 211]

Although, as Frye notes, this question is the crux of modern thinking about tragedy, there is no sign that it concerned Aristotle. It might be argued that Aristotle's failure to mention it may be proof that he—and his audience—took it for granted and considered it entirely obvious.[5] Aristotle may be touching on the question when he speaks of "poetic justice," but his claim (see TC 2 below) that surprise events which seem to follow as cause and effect are a good way of producing terror and pity suggests, on the other hand, that his failure to mention the contradiction Frye notes was also his failure to notice it.

WFC 4: *The parts of the text are the Prologue, the Episode, the Exode, and the Choric Song, this last being divided into Parade and Stasimon.*

GNC 1: *The text is an imitation of one action (i.e. a dramatic action).*

GNC 2: *The action of the text is serious (terrible and pitiful).*

GNC 3: *The aim of the action is to produce through pity and fear "the proper purgation of these emotions."*

GNC 4: *The action of the text is complete (has a beginning, a middle, and an end).*

GNC 5: *The action is "of a certain magnitude."*

GNC 6: *The text is written in "language embellished with each kind of artistic ornament" (rhythm, harmony, and song). "Song holds the chief place among the embellishments."*

GNC 7: *"The incidents and the plot are the end of a tragedy . . . character comes in as subsidiary to the actions."*

GNC 8: *Within the action there must be nothing improbable or irrational.*

GNC 9: *The tragic character is "a man who is not eminently good and just, yet whose misfortune is brought about not by vice or*

[5] Perelman and Olbrechts-Tyteca (1969:8) note that a society's most fundamental assumptions are never mentioned; they need not be since they are universally presupposed.

depravity, but by some error or frailty. He must be one who is highly renowned and prosperous."

Frye's understanding of the tragic character, derived from Hamlet as well as from Oedipus, is not inconsistent with Aristotle's, but it emphasizes an inner frailty as opposed to a frailty exposed through an error in judgment or action (p. 208): "From the urbanity of Hamlet to the sullen ferocity of Ajax, tragic heroes are wrapped in the mystery of communion with that something beyond which is the source of their strength and their fate alike. . . . The center of the tragedy is the hero's isolation, not in a villain's betrayal, even when the villain is, as he often is, a part of the hero himself."

GNC 10: The change in the hero's fortune is from good to bad. The change comes about as the result not of vice, but of some great error or frailty in a basically good character.
GNC 11: The ending is unhappy.

Frye adds that tragedies do not always end in disaster, though they *do* always "end in serenity" and are predominantly somber in mood.

TC 1: "The most powerful elements of emotional interest in tragedy—the Peripeteia or Reversal of Intention and Recognition scenes—are parts of the plot."

Aristotle only occasionally admits any of his conditions to be merely typicality conditions. We know that this one is because he says that in a simple plot the change of fortune can take place without the reversal and without the recognition. In each of the following typicality conditions, however, there is a word or a conditional verb tense (in Butcher's translation) which invites the inference that the condition need not necessarily be present.

TC 2: The effect of terror and pity "is best produced when the events come on us by surprise; and the effect is heightened when, at the same time, they follow as cause and effect."
TC 3: The characters may or may not be historical figures.
TC 4: The subject can be legendary, but need not be.
TC 5: The tragic action (e.g., murder) that most inspires pity and terror is that which happens between "those who are near or dear to one another" (i.e., family members).

TC 6: "Tragedy endeavours, as far as possible, to confine itself to a single revolution of the sun."
GTC 1: Characters should be good: "better than in actual life."
GTC 2: Characters should have virtues appropriate to their sex.
GTC 3: Characters should be true to life.
GTC 4: Characters should be consistent.

Earlier, *Wuthering Heights* seemed to match some of the conditions of romance immediately, but now it appears that the story of Heathcliff's childhood, love, rejection, revenge, and death may also match several of the conditions of tragedy (according to either Aristotle or Frye) without recourse to transformations. The story can be said, for example, to be an imitation of one action that is terrible and pitiful, complete, and of a certain magnitude (GNCs 1–5). Heathcliff fulfills many of the conditions of the tragic hero: he is isolated and seemingly fated in some way to his tragedy (Frye's version of GNC 9); he is surely possessed of hybris, having "a proud, passionate, obsessed mind" (Frye); his actions can be said to inspire terror and pity both in the characters in the story and in the reader (GNC 2), often by their surprising nature (TC 2). The scene between Catherine and Heathcliff immediately before her death may be seen as the recognition and reversal of intention which Aristotle considers the most powerful elements of emotional interest in the tragedy (TC 1). Finally, the tragic action takes place between people who are closely related.

As in the effort to satisfy the categorization of romance, the reader may now consider some transformations and inferences so that additional matches may be made in an attempt to strengthen the judgment "tragedy." For example, one could note that the story falls into two parts: the complication is the separation of Heathcliff from Catherine, and the second part is his revenge (WFC 3). The same inference that made Heathcliff into a romantic hero—that Emily Brontë must have approved of his larger-than-life capacity for passion, honesty, and loyalty—can now make him the tragic hero who is basically good: "better than in actual life" (GTC 1) but flawed (GNC 9). Terry Eagleton (1975) reads *Wuthering Heights* as a tragedy in which Catherine rather than Heathcliff is the tragic figure. Catherine is "proud, passionate, obsessed" and, according to Eagleton, she brings on the tragedy:

Wuthering Heights . . . confronts the tragic truth that the passion and society it presents are not fundamentally reconcilable. . . . The primary contradiction I have in mind is the choice posed for Catherine between Heathcliff and Edgar Linton. That choice seems to me the pivotal event of the
novel, the decisive catalyst of the tragedy; and if this is so, then the crux of
Wuthering Heights must be conceded . . . to be a social one. In a crucial
act of self-betrayal and bad faith, Catherine rejects Heathcliff as a suitor
because he is socially inferior to Linton; and it is from this that the train of
destruction follows. [pp. 100–101]

Readers, of course, regularly attempt to make inferences about
an author's "confrontations" or assertions, and they will, when necessary, rely on what they consider to be the less indeterminate aspects of the text to disambiguate a crux and derive an authorial assertion. This is not a specifically literary choice, but a pragmatic
one. Todorov (1976:169) suggests that a literary genre is identifiable with "the speech act . . . at its base." The accumulation of satisfied structural conditions allows the inference of functional conditions just as the fulfillment of the conventional conditions for the
performance of a speech act allows the inference of the essential
condition or illocutionary force. A hypothesis about the illocutionary force, in turn, allows the recognition of additional structural
features that strengthen the judgment.

Functional conditions within the set of conditions of a genre,
perhaps because they are less amenable to secure judgment, have
been the focus of interest for much of the history of literary criticism. Unlike conditions that can be fulfilled by matching structures
alone, functional conditions must always be inferred. Therefore in
order to represent the reader's recognition of functional as well as
structural conditions, the sets of the conditions of romance and
tragedy taken from Frye and Aristotle need to be supplemented by
adding some functional conditions derived from inferences about
the essential condition or illocutionary force of the genre to the predominantly structural conditions already listed.

Since the power of functional conditions depends in great part on
their complexity, it is not easy to state them in a way that commands
widespread assent. Nevertheless, in order to call attention to exactly how different these conditions are from structural conditions,
we may cite at length Clayton Koelb's recent formulation (1980) of
a very heavily weighted functional typicality condition of tragedy.

Koelb's interest, the growth of an idea of "the tragic" as distinguished from the classical notion of tragedy, corresponds closely to the difference between functional and structural naming. Koelb argues that the German romantics first articulated this concept as a version of "the sublime": the tragic is "a metaphysical notion emphasizing the poet's attitude and the philosophical impact of his play." Paraphrasing Schlegel, Koelb says (pp. 278–79): " 'The tragic' is chiefly characterized by its depiction of human greatness and human destiny, by its exposing us to the paradox of man's limitations and his boundless freedom."

It is easy to see how many varieties of this condition could be suggested, how many views of the illocutionary force of tragedy might compete. We have seen Frye's attempt at formulating this condition. Koelb also quotes A. C. Bradley's view of "the center of the tragic impression":

Everywhere, from the crushed rocks beneath our feet to the soul of man, we see power, intelligence, life and glory, which astound us and seem to call for our worship. And everywhere we see them perishing, devouring one another and destroying themselves, often with dreadful pain, as though they came into being for no other end. Tragedy is the typical form of this mystery, because that greatness of soul which it exhibits oppressed, conflicting and destroyed, is the highest existence in our view. [p. 281]

Although all the conditions of a genre contribute to the formation of the inferences represented above as a heavily weighted functional condition, its source can be seen particularly clearly in the structural conditions that Aristotle calls the "parts" of the genre. In a tragedy, the original conflict (Part One) brings on further suffering (the tragic action, the denouement), and that is the end of the play. In romance, however, at least according to Frye, the successful quest (adventure) with a three-part structure is a necessary condition. The third part in romance is understood as granted by the power of grace, which gives the hero another chance and rewards him in this world for the maturity and understanding he has gained through suffering. The tragic hero also gains understanding through the tragic action, but the only reward for him is what Frye calls "serenity," usually just before death.

The range of possible inferences from structural conditions is broad, though not infinite. The possibilities of variation are illustrated nicely by the distinction between the functional conditions of the genre of romance as described by the scholars who consider that the tradition is continuous from classical through medieval romance and including the Romantic poets, and Harold Bloom's description (1971:13–35 *passim*) of the functional conditions of the poets he calls the High Romantics. Frye, for example (p. 186), considers romance a search or a quest: the "perennially child-like quality of romance is marked by its extraordinarily persistent nostalgia"; the hero is in search of "some kind of imaginative golden age in time or space." John Stevens, in his book *Medieval Romance* (1973:28) argues that a heavily weighted functional condition of romance is the experience of "a supreme aspiration." Romance asserts the reality and the significance of such ideals as romantic love (the idealized sexual relationship) and honor (idealized integrity). Stevens (p. 21) quotes Shelley's phrase "beautiful idealisms of moral excellence" in partial explanation of his notion of idealization, and he also (p. 17) quotes Henry James, explaining in the New York Edition Preface to *The American* that the concern of romance is "experience liberated, so to speak; experience disengaged, disembroiled, disencumbered, exempt from the conditions that we usually know to attach to it."

Bloom reaffirms the connection between the genre of romance in Stevens's view and the poetry of Blake and Wordsworth, Shelley and Keats. He believes that romance is something permanently human, and accepts Frye's suggestion (WFC 1) that romance is necessarily a wish-fulfillment dream. He sees the quest motif as an internal quest, and considers it a central structural condition from which inferences about meaning derive. Bloom's Romantics, like James's, strive toward ideals that are liberated from "death-in-life" reality (Bloom, 1971:32). But since the quests and idealizations of the Romantic poets are all internal struggles, the antagonists are neither dragons nor other men, but instead "everything in the self that blocks imaginative work" (p. 19). Bloom posits an additional condition, which he claims does not apply in earlier romances. The quest in the Romantic poets, he argues, results in a solipsism, the result of which is that the fulfillment of one ideal threatens another ideal:

The movement of quest-romance, before its internalization by the High Romantics, was from nature to redeemed nature, the sanction of redemption being the gift of some external spiritual authority, sometimes magical. The Romantic movement is from nature to the imagination's freedom (sometimes a reluctant freedom), and the imagination's freedom is frequently purgatorial, redemptive in direction but destructive of the social self. The high cost of Romantic internalization, that is, of finding paradises within a renovated man, tends to manifest itself in the arena of self-consciousness. The quest is to widen consciousness as well as to intensify it, but the quest is shadowed by a spirit that tends to narrow consciousness to an acute preoccupation with self. [p. 16]

While any one of these conditions—of Schlegel, Bradley, Stevens, James, or Bloom—especially when reduced to a few sentences, seems less than adequate to the description of the essential conditions of either tragedy or romance, they all make the point that structural conditions must be given inferred meaning, and, for them, meaning that makes a claim to universality. We are assuming that an experienced reader of tragedy or romance will internalize among the conditions of the rule at least one functional condition that describes the illocutionary force of the genre. However complex this formulation may be, it may be presumed to take the form of Searle's essential condition on classes of speech acts (1969:65ff.): "the text as a whole counts as a representation of. . . ."

The condition that distinguishes a romance from an anti-romance or a tragedy from a parody of a tragedy would be a version of Searle's sincerity condition (1969:65), which would take the form of a heavily weighted gradient typicality condition:

GTC: The author of the text believes the representations made by the functional conditions of the genre.

In interpretive communities in which this functional condition is heavily weighted by an authority granted to the author's intention, this gradient typicality condition might seem to be as important as a well-formedness condition. If it were possible to match the condition to the text unambiguously, this would be heavy weighting, but the conditions cannot serve an arbitrating function in the genre categorization because, being inferred, they can never be unambiguously matched and can have only indirect authority. Normally, gradient typicality conditions of this indirect sort would not carry any more weight than any other conditions. Among readers who attribute greater authority to archetypal or mythical meaning, for example, this gradient condition will carry little weight. When a text contains conditions of significance that outweigh the authority of the author's "sincerity condition," the reader can categorize the text within the genre or as a parody of that genre.

From the readings of *Wuthering Heights*, and from the various formulations of tragedy and romance suggested above, we can conclude that when a text is classified by the functional genre "romance," the functional well-formedness condition suggests the power of benign forces to effect some kind of redemption, whether of the protagonists themselves, or in the generation of the children of the protagonists, or in the society that encompasses them all. In tragedy, on the other hand, one of the functional well-formedness conditions describes the powers in the world that defeat the heroic human being striving for freedom. Any serenity that comes to King Lear or to Hamlet comes late and has very little to do with the way order is restored after they die. In *Wuthering Heights*, the recognition scene between Heathcliff and Catherine results not in Heathcliff's serenity but in his swearing to revenge, and therefore it hardly can be said to be redemptive. Perhaps, then, *Wuthering Heights* is a tragedy after all; so a reader might feel at Catherine's death.

The categorization "tragedy" becomes less probable, however, as the story continues into the second generation. Indeed the second half of the book sets before the reader a narrative that may be said to start from the beginning again with a new child named Cathy. Joyce Carol Oates (1982:447) points out that of all the characters in the novel "only young Catherine undergoes a change of personality and, in willfully altering her own fate, transforms the Heights itself." She argues that the new generation (specifically Cathy) can make the compromises that her elders could not—can, in fact, abandon tragedy and grow up. Here we have the third stage of romance in which good has the power to redeem and maturity is achieved:

Young Catherine . . . soon exhibits an altogether welcome instinct for self-knowledge and compromise—for the subtle stratagems of adult life—that have been, all along, absent in her elders. Where Heathcliff by his nature remains fixed and two-dimensional, a character in a bygone drama, until his final "change" draws him so unresistingly to death, Catherine's nature is bound up with and enforced by the cyclical motion of the seasons: her triumph over him is therefore inevitable. . . . For suddenly it becomes possible at Wuthering Heights, as if for the first time in human history, that one generation will not be doomed to repeat the tragic errors of its parents. [pp. 447–48]

Having considered the categorization of tragedy, a reader may now reject it. In any case, the structural features that continue to accumulate until the end of the book continue to be matched up with the list of conditions as they were in the first half. The reader continues to use new information to confirm whatever judgment is momentarily in the forefront. If the book is being read as a romance, the marriage between Hareton and the second Catherine can be seen as Oates sees it, that is, as a sign of maturity, of reconciliation. If it is being read as a tragedy, as Eagleton reads it, "the future lies with a fusion rather than a confrontation of interests between gentry and bourgeoisie."

Wuthering Heights does, after all, end on a note of tentative convergence between labor and culture, sinew and gentility. . . . But this is a consequence rather than a resolution of the novel's tragic action; it does nothing to dissolve the deadlock of Heathcliff's relationship with Catherine. . . . The antinomies of passion and civility will be harmonised by the genetic fusion of both strains in the offspring of Catherine and Hareton, effecting an equable interchange of Nature and culture, biology and education. But those possibilities of growth are exploratory and undeveloped, darkened by the shadow of the tragic action. [pp. 118–19]

In either case, the judgment a reader makes about the functional genre of *Wuthering Heights* will be a weak one, and the shadow of the other possibility will be very strongly present. But a weak judgment about functional genre does not necessarily mean either that the novel is itself weak or that the aesthetic experience it provides is weak. The combination of a stable structural genre determination and recognition of theme has apparently provided sufficient unifying force for critics to appreciate the book even without a strong determination of a functional genre. Indeed, the evidence demonstrating the widespread functional condition of significance favoring ambiguous endings suggests that a strong determination of functional genre may work to reduce the pleasure. As Knoepflmacher (1971:108) points out: "By fusing pessimism and hope, tragedy and comedy, Emily Brontë was able to resist the formulas by which her characters want to reduce reality. It is a tribute to the reality of *Wuthering Heights*, as well as to the novelist's integrity, that she was able to control the polarities on which her vision is built."

Since a clear functional genre is not a necessary condition of a successful text as long as there is a clear structural genre, an author has considerable freedom to combine, contrast, and re-create functional genres. This freedom is constrained only by the necessary presence of familiar structures in sufficient strength to guide the process of making and testing hypothetical interpretations. The invention of new conditions or the recombining of conditions of one functional genre with those from other genres is possible because of strategies of inference, which help the reader to infer a functional genre from the reworking of the conventional conditions of previously familiar ones as well as from his or her experience with particular nonconventional situations.

To the extent that conditions of a structural genre are present in sufficient strength to create unity, the readers' failure to understand all the implications of an unfamiliar functional genre will not affect their feelings of satisfaction with the recognizable unity. The reverse is also true: if the function of a text can be made clear by an unwavering recourse to the conditions of a conventional functional genre (presumably a pragmatic genre, since conditions outside the token text would be available to confirm the inferences about function), major re-formation at the structural level should present no problem. The birth of the essay form in the Renaissance is an example of this. Where the intentions of Montaigne and Bacon were sufficiently clear (Montaigne, taking no chances, stated his explicitly in a Foreword to the 1580 edition), the introduction of the new form presented no problems of interpretation to an audience that had never read an essay before. But when the function of the text is unclear, it is not so simple to play with the conditions of form. The original reception given by theater audiences to the early plays of the theater of the absurd is an example of the difficulty. Since the functions were not obvious, audiences were upset by the seemingly unmotivated abuses of the structural typicality conditions of plays.

The possibilities of change show that, to some extent, structural and functional genres operate independently. A reader who has a clear notion either of the conventional function associated with a structural genre, or of the author's intention, will have enough secure information to permit inferences about the unconventional conditions of the text in its other aspects. Since both structural and functional genre types are in principle open to experimental redefinition, we must conclude that none is in any sense universal or permanent in all its conditions.[6] It would seem that we need genres, but the evidence does not lead us to believe that understanding is dependent on the kind of total system Frye, Todorov, Scholes, Guillen, and Brooke-Rose have proposed, that is, a system of theoretical genres. The functional and the structural genres of a text cooperate to allow innovation, by leaving a reader with ground to stand on while he or she learns to understand the meaning of the unfamiliar. The evidence of Frye's rereading of Aristotle, leaving out what he no longer finds relevant and enriching where he feels the need, seems to show that tokens within the reader's experience are the real basis for the types against which unfamiliar texts are matched. Frye finds no difficulty ignoring Aristotle's rules about songs and the chorus and can easily find room for tragedies that lack those classical elements.

Readers do not seem to require ideal genre types. Ideal genre types, like any idealized category names, would require definition by necessary and sufficient conditions. Attempts have been made along these lines, but the history of genre scholarship shows that such definitions have not been attained, and the recent study of the problem of definition suggests that they are in principle not attainable. Instead, we propose a set of types in the form of preference rules. Since these do not specify an absolute set of necessary and sufficient conditions, but rather one constituted by necessary and typicality conditions, they can reflect readers' familiarity with historical types and with the tradition of those types. In contrast to ideal genres, these generic types describe the matching and inference process well and are theoretically possible to construct; ideal genres have so far been elusive.

[6]Of course, if the claims made for theoretical genres as archetypes could be sustained, their meaning would be universal and unchangeable, but as Hardin (1983) points out, most of the anthropological evidence on which such claims are based has been challenged, although news of these challenges has not filtered through to literary scholars.

Chapter Five

New Genres
and Historical Change

The account in Chapter Four of the behavior of structural and functional genres in relationship to each other should have made clear why new subgenres or new varieties of previously familiar genres proliferate. Since a genre is defined by a set of conditions, the kinds of changes that are possible in the different conditions and their interrelationships describe the kinds of changes that are possible in the genre system. A change in any member of the set of conditions changes the balance of conditions away from an already established type. If the condition is a heavily weighted one, its change is more disruptive; if it is a lightly weighted one, the change is less so. In any functional genre, for example, a change only in the gradient condition that describes the author's attitude toward the illocutionary point of that genre can create a parody of that genre.

The existence of parody is itself proof of the limits of a description of a genre that depends entirely on structural conditions. Searle has argued, for speech acts, that the performance of an illocutionary act counts as an expression of a related attitude toward the propositional content of the speech act, even if in fact the speaker is insincere. Thus it is "linguistically unacceptable" to say "It is raining but I don't believe it is raining" (1976:4). When a representation is made, Searle claims, it is taken to express not only the propositional content but also a belief in the truth of that content. But the necessity of the identification that Searle's conventionalist position insists on cannot be maintained. The possibility of distinguishing as two separate conditions the illocutionary force (i.e. the representation) and the belief about the illocutionary force is what allows a text to be read as a parody. For example, it is a functional condition of romance that the author idealize, among other things, romantic love. (This would be Searle's "expressed psychological state.") One of the conditions of an anti-romance, or a parody of a romance, is to represent that belief while simultaneously rejecting it. When Gabriel Josipovici (1971) reads Vladimir Nabokov's *Lolita* as a parody, he is inferring a disparity between its illocutionary point and the belief in it: it is, he says (p. 207), "a critique of Romanticism: it shows what happens when the Romantic imagination is placed in the real world." Searle is nevertheless correct in noticing that whether or not a speaker is committed to his or her speech act, a speaker may be understood, *ceteris paribus*, as being committed to it, but that is because the assumption of sincerity is often a heavily weighted condition. Hypocrisy is possible and parody may certainly go undetected.[1] It is the functional aspects of communication, the inferences a reader draws, that allow parody or hypocrisy to be recognized, and these inferences are what a speaker must be careful to avoid evoking, or must explicitly cancel, in order to lie successfully.

One of the hallmarks of the deconstructionist critical position is its exploitation of the separability of the "expressed psychological state" from the functional condition of a genre that is its illocutionary force. The separation allows for a reweighting, a foregrounding, of ironic reflection on the heavily weighted typicality conditions of a genre: the deconstructionist position entails the simultaneous presence of both the expressed psychological state of a genre and the denial of that psychological state, that is, the expressed psychological state of its parody. The very fact that these two points (the illocutionary force and the expressed psychological state) are not conventionally separated but are separable creates a situation in which the possibility is always open to a reader to reject the conventional link

[1] See Schauber and Spolsky (1983).

and take up an ironic perspective. As Culler put it (1975:145), "nothing can resist irony except complete innocence."

In the example of parody, all the conditions of the genre on which it is parasitic remain the same except for the condition of the expressed psychological state. Changing a condition can change the genre categorization, and so, too, can adding an entirely new condition and weighting it heavily. New categories can be made from old types with new conditions. A "bedroom" comedy makes fun of sexual mores, an "urban" romance involves hypersophisticated urbanities. When a feature is so heavily weighted as to become a defining feature, a new category type is available: Doris Lessing's *The Golden Notebook* became the type of the women's book. The new condition is the expression of an awareness of what is considered a specifically woman's point of view. That the book is written by a woman turns out to be a typicality condition subject to exception: John Irving's *The World According to Garp* and John Fowles's *The French Lieutenant's Woman* have also been considered to be women's books.

Just as new categories can be added to one's repertoire by the addition of necessary conditions, unused categories ("theodicy," "anatomy") may be dropped or just as easily called back. In principle, the list of genres available to writers and readers has no limit and is always open to additions. Changes may also occur in the existing conditions of genre categorizations while the category remains the same. Alistair Fowler in his discussion of nineteenth-century literary forms (1982:141) points out that "Romantic and Victorian writers were fond of returning to earlier labels for historical authentication of their generic novelties." He speculates that it would be difficult to say how much remained the same while new writers were "all the time adding further extensions, new transformations, etc." The novels that outnumber all the other genres in the current pages of the *New York Times Book Review* are both recognizably similar to the nineteenth-century novel and recognizably different from it in ways that are describable by changes in the typicality conditions. Josipovici, a sensitive reader of modernism, describes ways in which the modern novel reacts against "Renaissance norms of verisimilitude" (p. xi), that is, revises or deletes typicality conditions of nineteenth-century fiction. He argues, further, that the anti-realist novel revives important typicality conditions of medieval fiction; modern literature has more in common with Langland and Chaucer than with Dickens and Eliot. Not only can typicality conditions be added or deleted, but what counts as satisfying a condition can also change: Aristotle said tragedies must have "spectacle" but the scenery that plays now typically have is of a kind that might not have satisfied Aristotle.

The set of genres or categories that makes up the reader's set of expectations is an open-ended component of the interpretive system equivalent to the lexicon of a grammar. But open-endedness does not mean lack of structure. As new information is added to the lexicon, it is assimilated into the old structures: if a new word is categorized as a noun, it participates in derivational morphology or syntactic transformations the way any other noun does. Similarly any one of the new genre names fits into the pattern of the established genres and participates in the system as they do. A critic can read and write about a new book in a way that names a new genre. A single *New York Times Book Review* (June 7, 1981) in addition to categorizing books in the traditional genres of "true life adventure," "manifesto," "bestseller," "memoir," "whodunit," "study," "family saga," "biography," "history," "novel," "diary," and "spy novel" also found examples of the "lightweight novel," "first novel," "bigtime commercial sex novel," "novelization," "pretentious junk novel," and "novel of exile." All these more or less ad hoc noun phrases are immediately clear, and they are useable categories available to function as a genre designation, either structural or functional. They are a good example of the way in which a token can take on the additional feature "-hood," thereby becoming a type (Jackendoff, 1983a) that provides the same pattern of expectations as more conventional genre names do.

Like any other social institution, the institution of literature is embedded in the larger culture that is its context, and changes in the preference rules for literary genres cannot be independent of changes in the larger culture. Readers' competence in drawing inferences outside literary texts is therefore part of their sensitivity to understanding changes in the purpose or effects of genre, or to what might be called new genres. In theory, the experienced reader has sufficient competence for all the literature he or she reads. In practice, the competence of even experienced readers is limited to a partial set of subsystems, and only readers who are familiar with a particular subsystem can really interpret innovations within it. The innovations of James Joyce and Virginia Woolf, for example, were readable within their immediate circles, but puzzling to the broader contemporary literary world. As experienced readers drew inferences, and as the authors themselves and the members of their circles published explanations of the motivations of the formal changes, the number of those who felt they understood the new forms increased until the connections between form and function that were originally inferred with difficulty are now conventionally made even by readers of relatively limited experience. The stream-of-consciousness technique, for example, which at one period labeled a new genre, is now diffused through many kinds of prose narratives. The rule describing stream-of-consciousness narration not only is a heavily weighted condition for a particular kind of novel that was prominent in the first quarter of the twentieth century but is now also a typicality condition of the broad category "novel," which may or may not be present in any given novel.

We may conclude that the genre competence of an experienced reader is both nimble and creative, and has both historical types and ahistorical types available for use and adaptation. The fact that the genre of romance or tragedy has changed (and as a result a nineteenth-century novel can be judged a tragedy or a twentieth-century narrative can be judged a romance) does not cancel the historical type: an experienced reader can distinguish between a romance and a medieval romance, for the difference between the two is a matter of a few conditions. The addition and deletion of conditions and the redefinition of terms within conditions do not threaten the stability of the system, which by its nature not only accommodates but welcomes change.

CONDITIONS AND RULES

With the examples of a structural and a functional preference decision behind us, we are now in a position to summarize what can be said about conditions and rules, and to describe the working of conditions of significance. We have used the word "rule" to talk about a set of conditions. A *condition* is that which, as a member of a weighted set of conditions, contributes to the emergence of a judgment. Any condition will itself have conditions that describe it (e.g., describe its terms), and any rule can be seen as a condition of a rule with a broader scope, that is, as describing a term in a higher-level rule. Whether a descriptive statement looks like a rule or a condition is a function of the context of discussion. From a systemic point of view, there is no structural difference between rules and conditions, only a functional one. *Category types* are defined by either structural conditions or a combination of structural and functional conditions: both can be necessary in some cases and typical in other cases. The definition of a functional category in the preference model will include functional as well as structural conditions, and for the determination of a functional category in any given case, the preference model requires at least one of the functional conditions that is met to be a heavily weighted typicality condition.[2]

It should be clear at this point how the preference model explains why it doesn't really matter that no one has ever been able to suggest a principle on the basis of which the minimum number of conditions to be met could be determined:[3] the more typicality conditions that are met, the stronger the judgment; the fewer, the weaker. There is no one functional condition that is necessary, and thus, in principle, no single condition is necessary and sufficient for the genre determination. A convention, that is, a conventional association of a particular structure with a function, is one type of functional condition that might seem to serve in a functional category decision as a gradient necessary condition. Thus,

GNC: *Some typicality conditions must be met.*

The possibility of extraconventional communication, however, and therefore of change, means that a reader's familiarity with any specific convention will never be sufficient to ensure an entirely determinate connection between the condition and a meaning. No matter how exhaustive the list of typicality conditions for any judgment, additional factors, non-necessary and non-typical, in the

---

[2] The alternative would be for the set to include a subset of functional typicality conditions at least some of which must always be met. All the conditions of the category per se would be typicality conditions, and the applicable necessary condition is that at least some of them be met. This condition would then be a gradient necessary condition of the general rule of categorization rather than a condition of the specific category. This arrangement would describe definition in a way consistent with Wittgenstein's theory of "family resemblance" (1953:I. 67).

[3] But see Searle (1958) and Jackendoff (1983*a*:135).

propositional content and its context may influence the interpretation of the function.

Typicality conditions in an entirely autonomous structural system are by definition structural. If the interpretive system had no history of its own, the conditions in the pragmatic and literary systems would also be structural, and from them, in the presence of propositional content and other context, functions would be inferred. But the rules of the interpretive system describing complex functional types (which many of the units of the pragmatic and literary systems are) include both structural and functional typicality conditions, because functional inferences that have already been made over smaller domains and from other texts in the reader's experience have been incorporated into the conditions. The fact that many of these functional inferences are conventionalized and the inference is not made again for every judgment in which it participates may obscure the inferential basis of all functions. This opacity does not necessarily prevent the structural conditions from being available for reanalysis, in which case different inferences may be drawn at other points in a derivation,[4] but the conventionalized inference will not be canceled by a new one. On the contrary, the continued presence of old inferences is one of the factors that allows for irony, or comedy, or any effect that seeks to play off an old association against a newer one. In sum, the set of conditions constituting a rule in the pragmatic or literary system includes both structural and functional conditions.

In addition to describing the four types of conditions as two kinds of necessary and two kinds of typicality conditions, the preference model cuts the same four conditions another way, distinguishing three preference conditions from the one well-formedness condition. Gradient necessary conditions, typicality conditions, and gradient typicality conditions are all called *preference conditions*. Unlike well-formedness conditions, which are binary and can only eliminate ungrammatical possibilities, preference conditions describe variability. *Well-formedness rules* consist only of well-formedness conditions.

---

[4] It could, though, prevent a child from learning the steps of the historical inference in the first place, leading to a change within one generation. What once seemed reasonable would in this way come to seem arbitrary.

Preference rules consist of a combination of well-formedness conditions and preference conditions. They account for variability by virtue of the fact that at least one of their conditions is a preference condition—a condition that can describe a variable situation. The four kinds of conditions are thus accounted for along two axes: necessary/non-necessary, and discrete/gradient.

Well-formedness Conditions:
  WFCs are necessary and discrete.
Preference Conditions:
  GNCs are necessary and gradient.
  TCs are non-necessary and discrete.
  GTCs are non-necessary and gradient.

The three preference conditions (the non-necessary and gradient conditions) describe the indeterminacy in the interpretive system. Well-formedness conditions are the only conditions that are neither non-necessary nor gradient, so that for a rule to be totally free of indeterminacy it would have to be based entirely on well-formedness conditions. But three types of conditions will introduce indeterminacy whereas only this one type represents determinacy. This may help to explain why indeterminacy is so pervasive. It also demonstrates that indeterminacy, while covering much of the interpretive field, does not cover all of it. A judgment that can be made on well-formedness conditions alone, with no preference conditions, is a determinate judgment. Not a lot of judgments can be made this way. Even so, a good many scholars within the humanities and social sciences have tried very hard to narrow the decision-making processes to make more determinate judgments possible. From the perspective of the preference model, these attempts to make those fields more "scientific" involve efforts either to rewrite preference conditions as well-formedness conditions (Frye's effort to discover and describe the archetypes, i.e., the universals of literature) or to eliminate the need for preference conditions by narrowing the subject matter to that which can be described by well-formedness conditions alone.

In the preference model, well-formedness conditions appear primarily in the phonological and syntactic components of the autonomous system. They therefore account for very little of what is specifically literary in a literary competence model. No literary judgment, regardless of how complex, can be made without autonomous linguistic competence, and so no judgment can be entirely indeterminate. The existence of some points of determinacy will not eliminate the points of indeterminacy, but it also does not necessarily follow that points of determinacy disappear as smaller judgments contribute to the construction of larger judgments. The role of well-formedness conditions in a model composed mostly of preference rules is small but crucial. For an example of the place of well-formedness conditions in interpretation we may look at the by now familiar example of the debate between Cleanth Brooks and F. W. Bateson about the Wordsworth poem "A Slumber Did My Spirit Seal."[5] While the two readings are different in important ways, both readers propose descriptions of the speaker's reaction to a woman's death, that is, they read the "she" as referring to a human female, and they base their assumption that she is dead on the shared pragmatic knowledge of Western burial customs. Their differences are what most interest critics, but their agreements are what make discussion possible.

CONDITIONS OF SIGNIFICANCE

In our discussions of *Children of a Lesser God* and *Wuthering Heights* we referred to typicality conditions that were more important than others in making a judgment as relatively heavily weighted. The weighting or importance of a condition is not an intrinsic characteristic of that condition but is a value associated with it in the social contexts in which the text is created or read. It reflects the weightings that a society imposes on interpretive activity independent of the text at hand. Walter Kerr in reviewing *Children of a Lesser God* did not find the lack of resolution of the ending a weakness. Open-endedness in the theater is now accepted as conventional, so that a structure that may be said to imply a blurring at the boundaries of fiction (the text of a play) and its context (the world) is presumed to confer additional value on the text.

Nancy Armstrong, in a recent article (1982) on the genre of

[5]Brooks (1951:736); Bateson (1950:33, 80–81). See also Hirsch (1967), Appendix 1.

Brontë's *Wuthering Heights*, demonstrates how the lack of clarity about the functional genre that upset many of the original readers of the novel is now a valued ambivalence. Armstrong believes that Emily Brontë was torn between a dying romanticism and a yet-to-be-born realism:

Out of this dilemma . . . came Heathcliff, who, in participating in both literary traditions, actually reveals the limitations of each. This is why he remains an enigma to readers, then, not because he is both noble savage and entrepreneur, but because he is ultimately neither. He only prefigures a time and discourse in which the boundary between self and society is no longer so necessary to the making of fiction. [p. 245]

Armstrong gives up the attempt to categorize *Wuthering Heights* either as romantic or as realistic and suggests a new genre, "the novel which illustrates the unresolvable dilemma," in this case, a rhetorical dilemma. In so doing she demonstrates that she is living with the same condition of significance that allowed the New York theater critics to admire *Children of a Lesser God*: namely, the heavy weighting of the representation of ambiguities without resolution.

The set of *conditions of significance* is the set of preference conditions of a rule of significance.[6] Such rules delimit, as we have seen in our examples, the use of the preference model in any given interpretation. It follows that a set of conditions of significance will determine which texts are considered worth reading and studying at the time when and in the community where those conditions are considered to hold. Texts that can be understood as meeting the conditions of significance in force will be the more highly valued texts. They will be considered to reward a reading that mobilizes the rules of the literary system. So-called popular literature is presumably a class of texts that meet some of the conditions of significance, but not all, or not the ones more heavily weighted by aca-

---

[6]Culler wrote an early version of the rule of significance (1975:115). Barbara Herrnstein Smith has argued (1981:11) that literary theory must ultimately consider the "variable and contingent" conditions that influence whether a particular text is considered "good" "not as 'biases' to be *discounted* in the investigation of literary value but, on the contrary, as the fundamental variables of which literary value is a function and therefore as the very phenomena to be *counted* and *accounted for*." We support her call "to discover their limits and the principles that govern them, and to clarify both their individual dynamics and the dynamics of their relationship to one another."

demic readers. Different categories of marginal literature would then be defined by the kind of conditions of significance they meet or do not meet.

We would formulate the rule of significance as a functional preference rule in the pragmatic and literary systems. It has one well-formedness condition: "A set of conditions of significance is always in force." The other conditions that describe significance in all its dimensions are functional typicality conditions. Like all sets of conditions, they are weighted, and when one typicality condition of significance conflicts with another, unresolvable tension is created. In a given context, however, a heavily weighted typicality condition may be indistinguishable from a necessary condition: it may seem so natural as to be actually attributed to "human nature." Whereas the absence of a typicality condition cannot in principle eliminate an interpretive possibility, the absence of a condition of significance can de facto block a transformation or an inference because its presence is necessary as part of the trigger. The value of ambiguity and paradox in the interpretive rules of the New Critics led them to identify subtle paradoxes in earlier English poetry that had been unidentified or, as they saw it, undervalued, for generations. The set of typicality conditions of the general rule of significance in the literary system will be different from the set in the pragmatic system, but the two sets will overlap and the values in the latter will clearly influence those in the former. The weightings of conditions that appear in both systems may be expected to be different, but could in some places be identical.

The conditions of significance interact with and determine the weighting of other conditions in the interpretive system, thereby affecting the interpretation from several directions at once. Exactly as their name implies, they are attributions of significance to different aspects of a literary work and to the interpretation of that work. They are the vehicle for the operation of value judgments, both individual and communal, within the interpretive process. Although weightings are sometimes so widely agreed upon as to seem "objective," these common standards do not function in the system differently from highly subjective or local prejudices. Shared or idiosyncratic, they are not open to debate within the preference model (though certainly debatable elsewhere), which must simply account for them. Their influence on the system needs to be charted. Inter-

preters who share a set of conditions of significance are usually recognized as a subcommunity within a larger literary community.

The conditions of significance in force for an individual or for
a community define what interpretations will be considered best in
the preference model. They describe what will count as a significant
and a coherent interpretation in that community or for that individual. They provide the circumstances under which preference decisions will be judged strong or weak.

In the preference model the best categorization (or transformation, or inference) is the best under the circumstances where circumstances include the text, the conditions of significance, and the
preference model. The conditions of significance, as a set, describe
the factors external to the text that effect the preference model at
specifiable points. The set of parameters according to which significance is described derives from the philosophy or politics of contemporary cultural context, including, of course, what that culture
considers its historical context. Conditions of significance are
weighted relative to each other. Conventional weightings provide
stability over time in the reading community; nonconventional
weightings account for originality on the part of both readers and
writers. Different weightings produce different judgments because
they constitute different definitions of "best."

Wherever a preference condition exists, a judgment is being
made about what is best. Because preference conditions involve
conditions of significance, and conditions of significance may involve idiosyncratic as well as culturally sanctioned weightings, the
introduction of preference conditions introduces a subjectivity that
will be carried through the system. Much of the weighting of rules is
culturally sanctioned conventional weighting and as such does not
create the indeterminacy that subjectivity can. The conditions describing a genre, for example, are conventionally weighted within a
specified context. Nevertheless, the greater the number of preference conditions, the more possibilities there are for introducing
indeterminacy.

Whether a descriptor is called a rule or a condition depends on
the focus of discussion. Each decision about whether or not a given
condition is fulfilled in a token text is itself a preference judgment in
a regression that is theoretically infinite. An additional source of indeterminacy in a preference judgment is the indeterminacy of the

decisions about whether or not conditions are fulfilled. Much of this indeterminacy is eliminated by the weight and number of the conditions considered to be fulfilled, but the strength of the judgment is also affected by whether or not and to what degree the conditions that are present reinforce each other.

Reinforcement seems to depend more on the content of the conditions than on their relative weight. The rule of romance, for example, specifies (WFC 1) that the narrative presents "virtuous heroes and beautiful heroines." Typically (TC 8) "the reward of the quest . . . includes a bride." If the bride reward is the same character as the beautiful heroine, as she is in *Children of a Lesser God*, the conditions may be said to reinforce each other. If the heroine is not the reward, as in *Wuthering Heights*, even though the hero receives another reward (money and property) and even though it is true that typicality conditions can have absolute exceptions (the model stipulates that Heathcliff's not marrying Catherine would not be fatal to the categorization of "romance"), still, the lack of reinforcement where the propositional content of the conditions suggested there could be some does somewhat weaken the preference judgment. At least, it does not provide a reinforcement where one was possible. But where mutually reinforcing typicality conditions do exist, an interesting phenomenon occurs: two conditions that are both, in principle, indeterminate to some degree, reduce indeterminacy by reinforcing each other.

One last characteristic of a preference rule model, as opposed to a system of necessary and sufficient conditions, is that it describes a judgment that is made whether or not all the conditions of a text are checked against the rule. Often there are conditions that cannot be checked against the text at hand. As long as a judgment can be reached, unused or uncheckable (or subconscious) preference rules are assumed as default values. Jackendoff (1983a: 142) points out that this use of preference rules to supply default values "is an extension of the principle of the syllogism to less fully determined cases. For example, a typical person has kidneys; you are a person; therefore, you probably have kidneys and I will act as though you do until I have evidence to the contrary."

The most widespread reliance on default values of text interpretation is the inference of functional genre from structural conditions. Wayne Booth (1961 : 198) points out that in novels where no one character (including the narrator) understands enough about the meaning of the whole to provide a general view of events, the job of generalizing may be left entirely to the reader: "It is interesting to note how much more importance titles and epigraphs take on in modern works, where they are often the only explicit commentary the reader is given: *Portrait of the Artist as a Young Man, The Sun Also Rises, Vile Bodies, A Handful of Dust, Brave New World, Antic Hay, The Sound and the Fury.*" In default of evidence to the contrary (an assertion from a reliable narrator), the reader may infer such an assertion from the title or epigraph.

The preference model describes such drawing of inferences as one of three discernable operations by which categorization is accomplished. Identifying references and applying transformations also contribute, in grossly specifiable ways, to the interpretation of texts in which categorization is not automatic and unambiguous. The extensions of the categorizing operations described in Part II will be the subject of Part III.

Part III

Interpretive Operations

Chapter Six

Reference, Transformations, and Inference

Part II dealt with genre categorization as the basic operation by which readers understand language texts. Successful categorization, in the terms stated there, is the matching of sets of conditions that have a conventional, though not necessarily arbitrary, relationship to each other. A relatively conventionalized set of conditions was called a rule. A reader is said to understand a text when he or she is able to match a sufficient number of the features of that text to a similar set (i.e. the rule) in his or her experience. "Relatively" and "similar" are words that present more serious theoretical than practical difficulties: readers not only seem to manage to interpret texts that cannot be matched exactly to their experience but even seem to prefer the challenge of such texts. A preference theory is needed because of the theoretical difficulty of accounting for the relativity and similarity, which seem to be part of the nature of the interpretation of language data. In spite of the efforts of the early generative grammarians, semantic systems continue to resist description within a well-formedness system. A generative grammar is designed to account for how it is that speakers of a language produce and understand new sentences and texts; a grammar allows a combination of units (already categorized) in an (in principle) infinite number of ways.[1] The potential for creativity in such a grammar, however, is unacceptably limited if it cannot deal with fuzzy categorization. Not only does a grammar need additional rules to account for a reader's ability to understand literary texts, but it also needs the different kind of rule embodied in the preference rule so that it can account for the understanding of all sorts of language texts.

We have already proposed a set of preference rules called conditions of significance to account for judgments about what is to count as a literary text, as well as judgments about what counts as a satisfying interpretation. Part III will discuss some additional sets of preference rules by means of which readers interpret texts that do not fit their experience and cannot be automatically and unambiguously categorized.

Here again, the emphasis is on literary texts. The interpretation of any language text of course requires a competence in strategies that deal with ambiguity and nonconventionality; literary theory is concerned with the interpretation of texts whose value is derived in part from their ambiguity and nonconventionality. Under current conditions of significance, to be so valued is a very heavily weighted typicality condition of a text that is characterized as literary. An understanding of these texts depends not only on a reader's previous experience but also on an awareness of certain rules relating specifically to texts that a reader or a community has already characterized as literary. Literary texts both promise and demand something more than other texts; the "more" is available by way of additional sets of literary preference rules or patterns. All texts, of course, are interpreted as patterned, and interpreters of different genres of texts are schooled to formulate patterns that have different meanings according to the conditions of each field. Applying the pattern-formation rules of one discourse to the texts of another results in the familiar subvarieties of literary criticism: psychological criticism, historical criticism, and so on.

In our discussion of *Wuthering Heights* we made the point that, just as speakers of a language can understand sentences never heard

[1] Fodor (1979: 31) explains that to argue the ability of a grammar to generate an infinite number of sentences "is not, of course, to argue that the *practical* possibilities are *literally* infinite. . . . The infinite capacity of the representational system is . . . an idealization, but it is not an *arbitrary* idealization. . . . The essential point is the organism's ability to deal with *novel* stimulations."

before, so readers apparently do understand texts, even when the text needs interpretation in terms of some conditions that do not match their experience exactly. Readers are not dependent on a set of types that are platonic ideals; on the contrary, when the rules of those types fail to provide a satisfying interpretation, their grammar allows them to fall back on other rules—rules that combine the three theoretically separable but functionally interactive operations of identifying references, applying transformations, and drawing inferences. Experienced readers of literary texts will, naturally, have a larger stock of these supplementary rules available, but the interpretive operations in which these rules function are essentially part of a general language competence, the ones that all speakers of a language use to understand any language string they have not heard before. Most of these rules are probably either universals or are constrained by universal principles and therefore can be described by necessary conditions or principles constraining a possible necessary condition (e.g., human beings make inferences); some others may be language or culture specific (e.g., descriptions of what counts as an acceptable inference). These rules are not just a list but, together with categorization, they seem to make up the field of understanding. In any case, whether or not this list is in fact exhaustive is, in principle, open to empirical confirmation.[2]

Reference is in some aspects set apart from the operations of applying transformations and drawing inferences. Reference includes those mental operations that might be described as involving movement through time and space, which make it possible for a reader to apply memories of past or distant meaning, derived from either actual or literary experience, to the current interpretive effort. *Transformations* and *inference* manipulate the various parts of the text at hand in relation to each other and to the imported references. These operations are not sequential: inferences can be made from imported references, and inference can be used to choose an external referent. Transformations, in the most general sense, are operations by which the reader recognizes similarity and in that way understands the meaning of substitutions or changes. Transformations are relational: they make partial matches meaningful, "x is *like* y"

---

[2]See Fodor (1979) and Jackendoff (1983b) for a more detailed and complex picture.

(not necessarily "x *is* y"), and are thus useful for finding new meanings when direct attempts at categorization fail. Inference is a bridging process, involving reasoning in order to understand relationships such as the relationship of cause and effect, or of a part and the whole. The two strategies are fundamentally different, because the determination of some similarity between two units that are not identical, that only partially match, is not a formal logical operation even if it involves reasoning.

Roman Jakobson's distinction (1956) between metaphoric and metonymic relationships perhaps captures the distinction we propose between transformations and inferences. He refers to "a well-known psychological test" in which

children are confronted with some noun and told to utter the first verbal response that comes into their heads. In this experiment two opposite linguistic predilections are invariably exhibited: the response is intended either as a substitute for, or as a complement to the stimulus. In the latter case the stimulus and the response together form a proper syntactic construction, most usually a sentence. These two types of reaction have been labeled substitutive and predicative. [pp. 76–77]

Jakobson provides examples of responses to the word "hut": substitutive responses were "cabin," "hovel," "palace," "den"; predicative responses were "burnt out," "is a poor little house." The distinction here, and in other distinctions Jakobson makes between schools of poetry and between different kinds of brain-damaged aphasiacs, is not without some ambiguity, but it does seem to reinforce our suggestion of the possibility of two quite distinct sets of interpretive operations.

It is quite possible that the operations of interpretation we separate into three may ultimately be shown to be fewer, or to depend on many more distinguishable operations. References and inferences, for example, might turn out to be the structural and functional versions of the same process. Our claim is not a processing claim, however, but a methodological one—that separating these operations in the model aids the understanding of each of them, and therefore of the whole. In literary interpretation, certainly, the two distinctions of special interest are those between memory or already categorized meaning and the new interpretive situation, and another between a bridging kind of operation (inference) and a substitutive kind of operation in which partial matches are recognized as in some way similar (transformation).

By means of these interpretive strategies, the reader finds meaning in a text by understanding its patterns. Whether or not the author was aware of these patterns is not relevant here. From the point of view of a competence model, there is no reason to think that readers cannot both find patterns consciously presented by an author and recognize others that the author did not or could not have intended. Using the rules that are available to him or her, the reader manipulates the text until a satisfying pattern emerges. The prevailing conditions of significance determine what counts as satisfying. The reader has understood a text when he or she has identified its units as similar to familiar patterns and recognized their relationship to one another: which match necessary conditions and which typicality conditions, and how the latter are weighted with respect to one another.

The interpretation of a text is, one can say, the description of the patterns that constitute the reader's understanding of the text: pattern and interpretation are both defined in terms of a "set of conditions." A pattern is a set of instantiations allowed by the rules with respect to a given text. As such, a pattern can function as a rule: a pattern familiar from one text acts like a rule when another text is read (that is, becomes a possible way of organizing that other text). Nonetheless, the methodological distinction between pattern and rule is crucial. By preserving the distinction between a conventionalized (already available) set of conditions (a rule) and an unfamiliar, nonconventional, possibly unique set of units (a pattern), we focus on the competence of the reader to understand creatively, to deal with new information and new stimuli according to rules that not only incorporate prior experience but also, most importantly, do not limit the understanding to what he or she already knows or understands.

Critics who collapse the distinction between the two on the grounds that a text is never not organized, never not already interpreted, are recognizing the power of previous experience and already-in-place commitments to shape the experience of interpretation; but in doing so they are foreclosing the possibility of understanding how it is that texts that are like earlier texts but also not like them can be appreciated for their novelty. They are foreclosing, so to say, the possibility of learning. The terminological distinctions our model makes between rules and the output of those rules (patterns) and between the parts of a rule (its conditions) and the parts of a pattern (its units) are not intended to deny the perception that through the power of history a text can be understood as embodying the rules for its own interpretation. The model does not at all deny the power of any pattern to be a rule for a subsequent text (or for the same text read subsequently), or for any unit of a text to be encoded as a condition of a rule in a subsequent reading. Rather, it is designed to prevent the collapse of a distinction that is necessary for the explanation of creativity and change even in the face of the conservatism of interpretive systems.

The way in which experienced readers use their interpretive strategies for nonconventional interpretation, by finding references, applying transformations, and drawing inferences, can be illustrated by examples from the autonomous and pragmatic systems as well as from the literary. In Chapter Seven, using specific examples, we will demonstrate the role of these systems in the interpretation of literary texts as a way of showing how the interpretation of literary texts is similar to the interpretation of all texts. Here, we will discuss the details of the separate parts of the interpretive process.

IDENTIFYING REFERENCES

Reference might be described as the ferrying into the interpretive purview of information needed for patterning. A reference, that is, information known about the referent, then becomes available to transformations in the same way as the other conditions of the text are. Like any structural unit, a reference itself does not specify its function; the function of a reference must be derived through combinations of transformations and inferences. While any specific reference is dependent on the situation, the competence to determine the relevant features of the referent and to use them in a pattern is rule-governed and is therefore accounted for within the preference model. The general preference rule for reference takes the form of a gradient necessary condition:

GNC 1: Prefer the best reference possible under the circumstances.

Two gradient necessary conditions describe "best reference":

GNC 1: *The best reference is that which allows the most coherent interpretation to emerge.*

GNC 2: *The best reference is that which allows the most satisfying interpretation to emerge.*

The first lines of George Eliot's *Middlemarch* (Hornback, 1977: 1) offer an example of a text whose interpretation depends on autonomous linguistic, pragmatic, and literary reference: "Miss Brooke had that kind of beauty which seems to be thrown into relief by poor dress. Her hand and wrist were so finely formed that she could wear sleeves not less bare of style than those in which the Blessed Virgin appeared to Italian painters." The name that begins the novel, "Miss Brooke," creates a reference: though it cannot be said to bring in information, since the words "Miss Brooke" do not themselves refer, by virtue of its linguistic category it is understood to act like a reference, and therefore produces a new unit. It creates a fictional character who can then be referred to and further described. The words "her" and "she," according to autonomous linguistic rules of anaphora, refer back to "Miss Brooke," and the phrases to which they belong fill out the fictional picture of the referent. This kind of reference within a text (endophoric reference) operates both within and across sentences (Lyons, 1977: *passim*).

References to nonlinguistic contexts (exophoric references), such as the references to "the Blessed Virgin" and "Italian painters," bring into the text whatever information the reader may have about those referents. New units of interpretation, that is, conventional and nonconventional associations with the referent, are thus created. According to the conditions of significance in some interpretive systems, new units (imported ones) have less weight than units that are viewed as having been "in" the text (cf. the conventional distinction between "denotation" and "connotation"). In other systems, cabalist interpretation, for example, the opposite weighting prevails, and in some places, deconstructionist interpretation, for example, this distinction between exophorically determined units and textually determined units is not given any weight. Whichever way, it need hardly be argued that literary competence depends on knowledge of the systems of the world, whether one's access to that world is direct or mediated.

One of the major tasks of exophoric reference in the preference model is that of providing a basis for the importation of nonfictional references into fictional texts. What is specifically not at issue here is the question of the truth values of literary texts. Reference is one of the ways of importing new units into the interpretive arena whether the whole of the text counts as fiction or as nonfiction or whether the genre of the text is a pragmatic or a literary one. There is no difference *qua* reference between Eliot's reference to Italian painters and *New York*'s reference to the Longacre Theatre.[3] The difference between fiction and nonfiction is a functional issue whereas reference is basically a structural one (even when pragmatic or literary factors are necessary to the recognition of the structures). To the philosophical issue of whether there are two kinds of texts, one with a specifiable connection to the real world and one without, reference, as we have described it, has nothing to say. Units created by exophoric reference act like any other units of the text. Readers may conventionally infer truth from fictions or may apply transformations in ways that allow them to infer truth if the conditions of significance value such inferences. Different genres provoke different expectations about the relations between the references in a text and a world external to it. A parable, for example, is conventionally a fiction that makes a nonfictional point not by direct reference but by a conventionally expected inference.

APPLYING TRANSFORMATIONS

Sometimes the surface of the text itself displays the similarities from which a structural pattern is made: the repetition of words forms patterns of symmetry and dominance, a headline dominates a news story, a couplet ends a Shakespearean sonnet. But not all structural patterns are immediately available; many more result from transformations. The notion of a transformation is familiar both in formalist literary criticism, where its use is loosely "change," and in Chomskyan grammar, where it has a technical definition. Although a competence model does not aim to specify what transformations in-

---

[3] From a different perspective, Kempson (1984*a*, 1984*b*) argues that all types of reference can be given a unitary characterization. She demonstrates that intrasentential reference (anaphora) exhibits the same characteristics as discourse anaphora and thus must be understood in part through the pragmatic system.

volve in the way a processing model would, we will nevertheless specify our use of it in the preference model in order to increase the explanatory power of the term for literary theory.

In autonomous generative theories a transformation is a rule that describes a possible relationship between two syntactic trees (phrase markers). In the Standard Theory (Chomsky, 1965), for example, the rule has two parts: the *Structural Description* is a description of the conditions a tree must meet in order to be an appropriate participant in the *Structural Change*, and the Structural Change, the second part of a transformation, is the description of the changes between a possible first tree and a second tree. A set of pairs of syntactic trees related by transformations constitutes a derivation. At one end of the set is the tree that represents the underlying form and at the other end is the tree that represents the surface syntactic form. In the Standard Theory, as in revisions of it, each term in the transformation is structurally defined. Whether as part of the transformation itself, as in the Standard Theory, or as conditions on applications of transformations (added in the Extended Standard Theory; Chomsky, 1972*a*) or as principles constraining possible variation, now in Government and Binding Theory (Chomsky, 1981, 1982), what counts as a possible structural change is strictly delimited.

The word "transformation," though somewhat different in its use in literary theory, still seems to suggest a basic conceptual principle with different manifestations in different systems. Furthermore, while the actual transformations in the autonomous system are specific to that system, the transformations in the pragmatic and the literary systems differ only where different conditions of significance in the different systems control the applications of transformations. The single set of transformations in these two systems is consistent with (and is in fact an account of) the claims that there is no structural difference between literary and nonliterary language.

Modifications of the definition of a possible transformation within the field of theoretical linguistics give evidence by their developments from the Standard Theory definition that the term does represent a fundamental cognitive concept, and as such can be reasonably extended without such distortion as would render the term meaningless. An early relaxation in the notion of transformation came, for example, from the theory of Generative Semantics in which the definition of a possible transformation was changed, both by enlarging it to include semantic factors in the set of possible terms that could be transformed and by increasing the types of possible changes transformations could make.[4] Recently, Chomsky (1981) has relaxed the notions of Structural Description and Structural Change in a different direction. He now views transformations as still purely syntactic but very general rules without all the specific restrictions of his earlier theories. Many of the conditions on any specific transformation are now relegated to general principles of each of his six subtheories that define well-formedness; some of what had been described syntactically in earlier versions of his theory is now accounted for by principles of semantic interpretation. But he still retains the basic concept that there is a syntactic underlying form distinct from the semantic structure and that this form differs from the surface structure in ways that are best described by transformations (in combination with the phrase-structure component and, as a later development, surface filters). Put the other way around, not all the syntactic information needed for interpretation is visible in the surface form, and transformations are necessary to describe the relationship between visible form and what a competent speaker knows about syntax in interpreting the sentence. Transformations, that is to say, make explicit the structures that are used in interpretation.

Chomsky's basic concept remains in our use of the term in the pragmatic and literary systems: each transformation is a description of a possible relationship between structures. There are structures in the text that are reorganized in the process of interpretation, and the term "transformation" in the preference model refers to a large number of these operations. Transformations are the rules that relate the opaque surface forms of some texts or parts of texts to rearranged structures in order to render their patterns available for interpretation. Although the basic concept remains the same, the parameters that define possible transformations are different in the autonomous system from those in the pragmatic and literary systems. There are three significant differences. First, in the pragmatic and literary systems, although the structures undergoing transfor-

---

[4] See, for example, McCawley (1976) for a variety of essays that represent his particular position and changes in it over time.

mations are occasionally syntactic, they are very often semantic. Second, the context that triggers a transformation in the pragmatic and literary systems is not necessarily formal, though it always is in the autonomous system. Third, the possible outputs of any derivation in the pragmatic and literary systems are not structurally limited. The output of any transformation can be the input to the reapplication of that same transformation or to another transformation. The derivation continues until some condition is satisfied.

PRAGMATIC AND LITERARY TRANSFORMATIONS

Transformations serve a wide variety of functions in the pragmatic and literary systems. The general impetus behind them is the desire of a reader or hearer to understand a text as satisfying and coherent. Since the concepts of satisfaction and coherence are gradient and contingent, the outcome of transformations that satisfy one person at one time and place may not satisfy another or even the same person at another time. This is another way of saying that most conditions of significance are typicality conditions. The non-fulfillment of one of them will not necessarily vitiate an interpretation; neither does the addition of new typicality conditions change the system. The point at which a particular interpreter will decide to stop applying transformations is therefore neither fixed nor arbitrary but determined by the conditions of significance in force for that interpretation.

On the simplest level, transformations in the pragmatic and literary systems mediate between two language structures just as those in the autonomous system do. They are the steps by which images acquire metaphorical meaning. When someone says, "The policeman was an angel and tore up the parking ticket," the possible relationship between "angel" and "policeman" is described by a set of transformations that allows for the creation of a structure in which the relevant features of one unit ("angel") are combined in a pattern with those of another ("policeman"). The new, figurative meaning is not made a substitute for the old—both continue to be available for interpretation.

Transformations also express the relationships between the world of abstractions and concrete images, that is, between aspects of a text and aspects of the context of the text. Elliot L. Gilbert (1983) proposes a dazzling series of transformations from Tennyson's *Idylls of the King* to abstractions about female monarchs which, he argues, would have had significance to a contemporary audience. The opening paragraph of Gilbert's analysis asserts the existence of transformations for which he will then argue:

> Sooner or later, most readers of the *Idylls of the King* find themselves wondering by what remarkable transformative process the traditionally virile and manly King Arthur of legend and romance evolved, during the nineteenth century, into the restrained, almost maidenly Victorian monarch of Alfred Lord Tennyson's most ambitious work. . . . I will argue here . . . that such a metamorphosis was inevitable, given the nineteenth-century confluence of what Michel Foucault has called "the history of sexuality" with what we may call the history of history, and that Tennyson's Arthurian retelling, far from being weakened by its revisionary premise, is in fact all the stronger and more resonant for depicting its hero as a species of female king. [p. 863]

Notice that Gilbert ascribes the need for transformations to what seems to be a failure of categorization: Tennyson's Arthur does not fully match the ideal set by Malory. Indeed, the "manly King Arthur of legend" appears in Tennyson's *Idylls* as an "almost maidenly Victorian monarch." There is, however, a partial match in that both Malory and Tennyson claim to be describing the same King Arthur of Camelot, both are using the same reference as a trigger for their transformations. Gilbert goes on to specify a series of transformations that justify the characterization of Arthur as overly feminine by asserting a reference to "one of the central problems of Victorian society: the growing assertion of female authority" (p. 865) and matching it to the destruction of the society of the Round Table as a result of the treachery of Guinevere. Gilbert's analysis gives meaning to this partial match by applying transformations until he identifies a category into which both Tennyson's character and Malory's fit, one that is more satisfying than that already available.

Gilbert's transformations depend on a good many complex references, (e.g., to the Victorian sense of history, itself inferred, and to the events of the French Revolution), some of which must undergo transformations before they can be used in his argument about Victorian England. Gilbert argues, for example (p. 869), a partial match between Arthur's mythical ascent to the throne of Britain (by removing the sword from the stone) and the regicide of the French Revolution, claiming as a common feature the denial of legitimacy to patrilineal hereditary authority. Instead of being a king because he is the son of a king, Arthur becomes king by receiving his sword (by transformations, his authority) from the Lady of the Lake (by transformations, one's own inner energy): "To the extent that such derivation of power from the deep symbolizes access to one's own interior energy, Arthur's kingly mission is ultimately self-authorized; and in particular, it is authorized by that part of himself which, associated with creative, ahistorical nature, is most distinctly female." Note the embedding here: in order to argue that self-authorization is feminine, Gilbert asks acceptance of two preliminary transformations: (1) the lake is feminine because of its association with the Lady of the Lake, and (2) the lake, or the "deep," is "access to one's own interior energy." He then continues the derivation to his conclusion (p. 875): "In the end—Tennyson summarizes the central theme of the *Idylls*—all certainty is impossible for a man who rejects the stability of patrilineal descent and seeks instead to derive his authority from himself, to build a community on the idealization of nature and female energy." By these and many other transformations, Gilbert has moved from a partial and unsatisfying match, a seeming failure of categorization, to a satisfying categorization of Arthur, the Prince Alfred-like Victorian, weakened, as Malory's Arthur ultimately is also, by "female energy."

The conventions of pragmatic and literary genres that describe the kinds of meaning readers are likely to expect in given contexts are conditions indicating when and where transformations are required. Both pragmatic and literary systems allow for various levels of satisfaction, similarly described by genre conditions and conditions of significance. A psychiatrist, for example, seeks a level of coherence in a patient's discourse that has some explanatory power beyond intelligibility within the immediate context. Similarly, news analysts, political scientists, and historians each have sets of conditions of significance that determine the transformations required by the genres of discourse they study. Genre requirements also determine the choice of transformations, showing that possible patterning is not always considered the best patterning. The conditions of the genre may not be satisfied, even though the text may be coherent as a narration or as a pattern. Grice's (1975) often quoted example of the letter of recommendation that describes the applicant for a position as a lecturer in philosophy as being prompt and having a good handwriting demonstrates this point. The text is coherent, but it does not satisfy as a letter of recommendation for an academic position, so that, in order to understand it as such, the reader must apply transformations and make inferences. The decision to read a text as literature is a decision to search for transformations whose applications provide a specific level of satisfaction. Gilbert's reading of Tennyson's text may be seen as a genre reclassification: if the text fails to satisfy as romance or adventure literature, he will read it as a particular aspect of cultural history and make it satisfying and coherent as such. It is, furthermore, not just any slice of cultural history, but one that is particularly interesting to Gilbert, which forms the framework from which a partial match (in this essay between the views about "feminine energy" Gilbert attributes to Tennyson's context and his own such views) will be noted that is sufficient to trigger transformations.

Culler (1975) in a sustained critique of structuralist semantic theory points out that Gerard Manley Hopkins's poem "The Windhover" is perfectly intelligible as a poem about a falcon. He asks why readers are not satisfied with this interpretation and concludes (p. 90) that "the reader of poetry knows that when such metaphorical energy is expended on a bird the creature itself is exalted and becomes metaphor." This is a reasonable argument, but perhaps more complex an explanation than is needed: the verse form alone would lead the reader to expect more than a description of a bird. Having decided the text is a lyric poem (on the basis of the strictly structural characteristics of length and line arrangement), the experienced reader would not be satisfied with a reading that is no more than a metrical dictionary entry.

Transformations may also be called upon within the literary system to add strength to a genre determination that is tentative or weak. Using again the example of *Wuthering Heights*, we suggest that an experienced reader might notice a partial match between the text and the first gradient typicality condition of romance:

GTC 1: *The complete form of the romance is clearly the successful quest [which has] three main stages: the stage of the perilous journey and the preliminary minor adventures; the crucial struggle, usually some kind of battle in which either the hero or his foe, or both, must die; and the exaltation of the hero.*

A quest, it seems, requires a journey. The meaning of "journey" itself includes the heavily weighted condition of physical movement from one place to another and the slightly less heavily weighted typicality conditions of being long and arduous, and of arriving at a goal. These are the conditions of journeys in stereotypical romances. In *Wuthering Heights*, the only journeys that fit all these conditions are the journey by Lockwood to Wuthering Heights in the beginning of the novel and the journey made by the elder Earnshaw from which he returns with the child, Heathcliff. Neither of these journeys can fulfill the condition since according to the conditions by which we identify heroes, neither Lockwood nor Earnshaw can be one. However, there are several short trips between the Heights and Thrushcross Grange that seem to match parts of the conditions for the quest journey. They fulfill the condition of physical movement from one place to another, though not all the above-mentioned typicality conditions. It should now be clear that, although it would not be impossible to categorize this novel as a romance with the absolute exception of the typicality conditions of a journey, having a type in mind (in this case a literary genre) encourages applications of transformations toward an interpretation in which as many as possible of the conditions of the rule are fulfilled. Since the heavily weighted condition of quest—journey—is fulfilled, experienced readers attempt to reinterpret the other conditions by using transformations. By applying transformations to "long" and "arduous," deriving something like "effecting critical changes," the reader can make Catherine's journey to Thrushcross Grange, from which she returns altered and ready to marry Linton, a candidate for fulfillment of this typicality condition.

The historical contingencies of the period in which a text was composed as well as the generic systems within which the author worked are parts of the literary context that triggers the application of transformations. Another part is the set of literary or pragmatic conditions of significance that are in force for the interpreter, that arise from the context at the time of reading rather than at the time of writing. When a text is remote from the reader in time or when the culture in which it was produced is very different from the one in which it is read, the reader may apply transformations deriving drastically modified units in order to make the text signify. Morton Bloomfield (1972:302) calls such fundamental rereading allegory, which, he says, "conquers time . . . perpetually renews the written word. The age that does not need, or thinks it does not need, the past does not need this kind of allegory."

One of the most remarkable rescues by an allegorical transformation of an old and remote text was performed by J. R. R. Tolkien on the Old English poem *Beowulf*. Before 1936 when Tolkien's "*Beowulf*: The Monsters and the Critics" was published, *Beowulf* was studied primarily by philologists, for whom it was a mine of information about the Old English language, and, secondarily, about the life and manners of the Anglo-Saxon peoples among whom the poem was presumably popular. Nineteenth-century scholars did not consider it to be serious literature because it told of impossible monsters and superhuman exploits. Insofar as it suggested that people of the period were so much less sophisticated than themselves, the story seemed obsolete. Tolkien argued for the necessity of transformations. "A dragon," he wrote (pp. 64, 66), "is no idle fancy" but "a personification of malice, greed, destruction (the evil side of heroic life), and of the undiscriminating cruelty of fortune that distinguished not good or bad (the evil aspect of all life)." He made inferences, and convincingly showed (p. 68) that the poem was about Man fighting Evil, giving it his best, and, inevitably, losing: "Beowulf . . . is a man, and that for him and many is sufficient tragedy." He specified (p. 88) how the poem was connected to the English heritage: "It was made in this land, and moves in our northern world beneath our northern sky, and for those who are native to that tongue and land, it must ever call with a profound appeal—until the dragon comes."

The effect of Tolkien's argument in 1936 was heightened by a shared knowledge of the growing power of fascism in Europe. Beowulf's battle with the dragon's malice was a battle Tolkien's readers could understand. But Tolkien's choice of transformations was more than just timely. The strength of his interpretation lies in its general applicability, as well as its adaptability: the inferred referent of the dragon can change without significantly altering the interpretation, or his interpretation itself can be the input to a new transformation as the referent changes.

In this light the history of twentieth-century literary criticism can be viewed as a series of promises to deliver more: more detail, more tension, more ambiguity. Interpretive studies having in some quarters worn themselves out, the academic reader is promised more (again) from metatheoretical studies ("poetics"); the metatheory (structuralism) having been reread and rewritten, the reader is forced to irony (deconstruction) to provide more—this time more "fun" (Schaefer, 1978:179), or more freedom. It is of course the open-ended nature of pragmatic and literary derivations that gives them their enormous power, that allows this recurrent relocation of the boundaries of satisfaction. Transformations are, along with inference, the major source of creativity in the interpretive system. They are also, obviously, a major source of indeterminacy.

The pragmatic conditions of significance separating an acceptable from a heretical interpretation are as present among literary interpreters as among clerical ones. There will always be an attempt from outside the literary system per se to enforce a specific standard on the application of transformations. In fact, there are almost always competing attempts being argued simultaneously. One familiar argument about which transformations are to be permitted derives from the question of whether or not readers are bound to attempt retrieval of the transformations authors had used. Because the use of transformations is so near the very heart of creativity, wherever an understanding of an author's intention is valued there will be a serious attempt to recover derivations that may be attributed with some probability to the author.

The preference model describes literary and pragmatic transformations by well-formedness and preference rules. The general preference rule for transformations takes the form of a gradient necessary condition:

GNC 1: *Prefer the best transformation possible under the circumstances.*

Like the other general rules, best is described by two gradient necessary conditions:

GNC 1: *The best transformation is that which allows the most coherent interpretation to emerge.*
GNC 2: *The best transformation is that which allows the most satisfying interpretation to emerge.*

Transformations are further described by the following rule:

WFC 1: A transformation is a description of a relationship between two structures as described by a Structural Description and a Structural Change.

A structure participates in a transformation when one of its units satisfies the conditions of the Structural Description. A unit of the text participates by itself or as one of the terms in the Structural Description of a transformation when it is partially matched with a condition in one or more of three contexts, each described by its own typicality condition:

GTC 1: A unit of a text counts as a term in a Structural Description when there is a partial match between that unit and another part of the text.

GTC 2: A unit of a text counts as a term in a Structural Description when there is a partial match between that unit and any conditions conventionally associated with the genre of the text.

GTC 3: A unit of a text counts as a term in a Structural Description when there is a partial match between that unit and a prevailing condition of significance.

Notice that transformations are themselves dependent upon the general categorization rule, "Prefer the best categorization judgment possible under the circumstances." Categorization accomplishes the matching called for by the typicality conditions for transformations—that is, it describes the competence to recognize part of a text as a unit satisfying a Structural Description. A successful categorization certifies the felicity of the transformations. While syntactic transformations rely only on well-formedness rules and thus are exceptions here, the match described by the conditions must be only partial: a complete match would be a successful categorization, and no transformations would be needed, whereas a partial match points to the possibility of applying particular transformations and thus suggests a possible derivation.

The Structural Change referred to in the above well-formedness condition describes the new and larger unit formed from the Structural Description. The larger unit is a reorganization of or a joining of a unit or units of the Structural Description with new material and is itself now available to participate in further transformations.

In contrast to the small number of possible relationships allowed in the autonomous system between a Structural Description and a Structural Change, the relationships described by the literary and pragmatic systems are in principle unlimited. A description of all the possible relationships between a Structural Description and a Structural Change would probably turn out to look much like a classical catalogue of structural rhetorical tropes (metonymy, simile, apostrophe, personification, etc.). This list would be, in principle, open-ended; new tropes could always be invented. For these reasons, the number of transformations that a text can participate in is limitless. Tolkien's allegory of *Beowulf*, for example, does not preclude other allegorizations of that text, nor does it preclude the interpretation of the text or part of the text by a transformation other than allegory.

These rules offer a perspective from which to view the interpretation of structural patterns. Instead of conceiving a transformation loosely as change, it is now possible to see it as a complex of two structures whose relationship is specified. All the information that is specified is available for making inferences. A transformation thus describes a pattern that, in accordance with the well-formedness condition of patterns (see below), is either a symmetrical relationship or one of dominance and subordination. The pattern as a whole or any of its structural units participates in larger patterns that form a hierarchical structure. This hierarchy, in principle, accounts for all the details of an interpretation of a text to the extent that the interpretation is coherent. When any of the structural units already analyzed as terms according to the Structural Change of some transformation then participates directly in another transformation (as one of the terms in a new Structural Description), the rest of the former pattern comes along with it and is thus part of the new structure.[5] Nothing disappears. Literary metaphor is a clear example of this. The transformation, according to the Structural Change, adjoins into a pattern both the image itself and whatever meaning has been attributed to it. A reader who has understood or interpreted a metaphor has not changed or substituted one thing for another, but has specified a relationship among terms. Thus Elliot Gilbert, having

[5] This is not the normal case in the autonomous system but is equivalent to the special case of what Ross calls "pied-piping" (1967: 144–53), excerpted in Harman (1974: 181–88).

identified masculinity with history and femininity with myth in the Arthurian legend, argues the importance of all four terms to a satisfying interpretation of Tennyson's *Idylls*.

The category label for the entire pattern may be the name of the transformation, in this case, metaphor, or symbol. We are now in a position to make an important claim about figurative language: literary transformations, or patterns, as the preference model describes them, are intelligible without the introduction of the notion of deviance. Deviance is a concept that structuralist literary criticism and much recent theory of metaphor depend on, but it has the disadvantage of making the language of literary texts seem like a nuisance that has to be undone. A transformation in the preference model is not triggered by ungrammaticality or incoherence, as it is in so many theories of metaphor,[6] but is rather the result of a partial match, of fitting, to some extent (rather than not fitting), into patterns reflecting more complex concerns. Since the categorization of any condition with respect to another inevitably involves the relativity of degrees of fit, transformations involve deviance, but not more than any other categorization judgments.[7]

DRAWING INFERENCES

Inference is the process by which functions are understood from collocations of structural or functional conditions. It is also one of the ways new structures are added to those already in the text, one of the ways readers and hearers fill in gaps between what is given and what is needed to interpret a text satisfactorily. An inference, once created, acts as a unit of the text and becomes available for patterning just as other units are. We use the term in a broad sense to include the competence to understand the variety of implications that have been described under the headings of logical inference, pragmatic presupposition, invited inference, and conversational im-

---

[6] Max Black, in Ortony (1979), is a classic and influential statement, from a philosopher's point of view, of the position that understanding metaphor begins with an attempt to understand, or correct for, a mistake. Miller, in the same volume, states the same position from the point of view of a psycholinguist. These are only two, and perhaps the clearest, of a very large number of statements of the position that understanding figurative language depends on undoing a mistake.

[7] The exceptions are technical (stipulative) definitions, that is, rules with only well-formedness conditions.

plicature, as well as implications derived from word order, and from assumptions about appropriateness. Inference is also involved in every kind of indirect language use: metaphor, irony, indirect speech acts, etc. Understanding an inference is determining a bridge between units or patterns.

One of the most stimulating nonformal models of inference in the pragmatic system has surely been Grice's theory of conversational cooperation or "implicature." The theory has limitations and some serious theoretical difficulties, but nonetheless it offers interesting applications in the literary system.[8] Grice's theory of conversational cooperation describes how one kind of inference—or implicature—functions as a connective between sentences. In this theory, Grice uses the term "implicature" to refer to the general event of implying, and "implicatum" to mean the information that one must assume in order to make one unit (in this case either a sentence or a phrase) follow from another.[9]

Grice's conversational implicatures are nonconventional; they must be inferred anew in each case. Indeed, the importance of this claim to a literary theory is clearer if it is stated as an assertion of possibility: on the strength of the maxims of conversational cooperation, nonconventional inferences *can* be made. Grice explains a hearer's competence in inference as the ability to recognize that a maxim has been violated or exploited. Grice does not mention it, but maxims can also be invoked (cf. Hancher, 1978). Having recognized the invocation or exploitation, the hearer uses the maxim that has been flagged, as it were, to reconstruct an inference or a pattern of inferences. Presumably the hearer can always state the content of an implicatum directly rather than by invoking or exploiting a maxim; thus part of what may be recovered from an implicature in

[8] The attempt by Bach and Harnish (1979) to detail this system is too limited in scope to be helpful to the complex field of literary theory, and furthermore it retains intact all the difficulties of Austin's theory that Derrida (1977) has pointed out. Not only does it not resolve the problem of unintended meaning but it fudges again the problem of how meaning can be the result of both conventional association and nonconventional inference. For further comments on the treatment of these and other problems, see Green (1983).

[9] Monroe Beardsley (personal communication) has suggested this definition of Grice's "implicatum." Strictly speaking, an implicatum is "what is implied," whereas the more general noun referring to the whole event is "implicature" (cf. "implying") (Grice, 1975:44). Since Grice talks about "conversational implicatures," however, the more general term is normally used.

constructing an implicatum is an inference about the motivation for the indirection. It is not hard to imagine the social circumstances of an utterance that would favor a structure with cancelable implications. The hearer may "choose to ignore" implications; the speaker may want to allow the hearer exactly this way out. Either may claim "[I, you] never said that."

Grice believes that making and understanding inferences requires a framework of assumptions within which participants operate, and he makes the Cooperative Principle the center of his theory. The principle as stated (1975:45) is: "Make your conversational contribution such as is required, at the stage at which it occurs, by the accepted purpose or direction of the talk exchange in which you are engaged." Pratt (1981) argues that the principle forces Grice to make assumptions that are appropriate only to some of the situations in which implicatures arise. A more accurate and complete statement of a cooperative principle would include the expectations of the hearer, would allow for gradience, and would be relevant to written as well as oral discourse. It would also be general enough to cover situations in which only one person is talking (when there is no "exchange") and also those in which the participants have different purposes or directions. Pratt also challenges Grice's four maxims (Quantity, Quality, Relation, and Manner) as situation particular rather than, as he claims, all-inclusive, and she suggests the addition of new maxims as required by other situations: for example (1981:13), "a logic of hostility . . . would give rise to different principles of interaction, such as a maxim of quality that says 'exaggerate the other person's faults' or a maxim of quantity that says 'try to get in the last word.'"

Grice, however, correctly recognizes that there is necessarily one superordinate principle governing language use that controls communication through inference. The problem with his formulation is that he associates that principle exclusively with rational talk exchanges. Cooperation need extend only so far as to include staying to talk, read, or listen rather than walking away, closing the book, or turning off the television. As Grice recognizes, a discourse may serve a set of purposes, and appropriate inferences can be made only if the hearer can guess the speaker's purposes. But that does not require purposes to be shared. In fact, "purpose" is not the best word since some of the functions a discourse serves will normally be unintended at least at the conscious level. That is, even if making inferences requires a judgment about the speaker's purpose, the purpose may not have been agreed upon (even tacitly) as Grice suggests it always is to some extent, and therefore the hearer's judgment of the purpose may not agree with the speaker's conscious or unconscious intention. Often, for example, hostility is recognized—though it may be, at some level, unintended—because a hearer is capable of applying a transformation to construct a derivation that brings together the text of the current situation with conditions conventionally associated with that text. Recalling GTC 2 of the rule specifying possible terms for a Structural Description of a transformation, describing a partial match between a unit and any conditions conventionally associated with the genre of the text, one can imagine a child who when asked by a parent "Have you cleaned up your room yet?" reasonably responds, "Stop yelling at me." Here a transformation joins these two units into one structure, which then is used in drawing the inference of the parent's anger.

In sum, we would argue that a more general version of Grice's Cooperative Principle can describe the necessary condition that allows inference in all discourse without legislating a "normal" or "ordinary" type of situation. Further, the variety of situations in which language is used necessitates a variety of sets of maxims, each set being the necessary and typicality conditions for a different genre of discourse. The preference conditions for the rule of inference are thus the conditions for each genre. There will be necessary conditions that describe a modified version of the Cooperative Principle and a set of typicality conditions, accounting for each of Pratt's principles (e.g., "the conflictive principle," p. 15). We may conclude, then, that inferences are made according to the general preference rule of inference taking the form of a gradient necessary condition.

GNC 1: Prefer the best inference possible under the circumstances.

Two conditions describe the best inference:

GNC 1: The best inference is that which allows the most coherent interpretation to emerge.

GNC 2: The best inference is that which allows the most satisfying interpretation to emerge.

The following conditions describe this picture of inference modified from Grice: [10]

GNC 1: *The participants all have some interest that makes each more or less committed to keeping the discourse going.*

GNC 2: *Each discourse chunk is such as is required for that stage of the discourse.*

GTC 1: *"Quantity." (a) Prefer to assume that a token contribution is as informative as is required; (b) prefer to assume that a token is not more informative than is required.*

GTC 2: *"Quality." Prefer to assume that a token contribution is true: (a) that the speaker does not say what he or she believes to be false; (b) that the speaker does not say that for which he or she lacks adequate evidence.*

GTC 3: *"Relation." Prefer to assume relevance.*[11]

GTC 4: *"Manner." Prefer to assume that the speaker is being perspicuous: (a) is avoiding obscurity of expression, (b) is avoiding ambiguity, (c) is being brief, (d) is being orderly.*

Pratt's "conflictive principle" and associated maxims suggest the following partial list of the conditions for a hostile exchange:

GNC 1: *The participants feel a degree of hostility but still have an interest in keeping the discourse going.*

GNC 2: *Each discourse chunk is such as is required for that stage of the discourse.*

GTC 1: *Faults are exaggerated.*

TC 1: *The person who says the last word wins.*

In the two examples, each GNC 1 counts as a claim that it is possible to make inferences only because of an assumption that each participant has a reason both for continuing the discourse and for saying what was said. This condition introduces the necessary modifications to the Cooperative Principle as discussed above. GNC 2 accounts for the rest of Grice's Cooperative Principle.

---

[10] Lerdahl and Jackendoff (1983 : 310–11) suggest that Grice's maxims can be appropriately rewritten as preference rules.

[11] Sperber and Wilson (forthcoming) have argued that relevance is a superordinate category. In their system, GTCs 1, 2, and 4 would be typicality conditions embedded in GTC 3 instead of coordinated with it. Likewise, Horn (1984) argues for a reduction in the number of maxims, but would reorganize the conditions differently again.

Inference, like transformations and weighting, is, of course, a major source of indeterminacy in the system. It is a source of freedom within the preference model because it allows scope to the influence of the conditions of significance that weight the conditions of the genres of discourse. The process of forming inferences implies a creative reader who makes or does not make inferences according to his or her own knowledge and interests. Creativity on the part of the author involves structural innovation, the ability to generate an, in principle, infinite number of different structures. But the reader's creativity is expressed by functional innovation: the ability to imagine what a text could mean. It is precisely the looseness of the link determined through inference between structure and function, the nonnecessity of any one possible link, that allows creativity and change. In combination with the similar variability in the strategies for identifying references and for applying transformations, this looseness allows the range of interpretations that comparably experienced readers produce for the same text. The building of the patterns from these operations, which are either interpretations or parts of interpretations, is the subject of the next chapter.

Chapter Seven

Patterning

The three operations of finding references, applying transformations, and drawing inferences usually work interactively in the task of understanding the patterns of a text that does not match a reader's experience. They do not only "lead to" or "discover" patterns, they may themselves form patterns—of reference, transformation, or inference—that are in most cases tightly interwoven. Except within the autonomous linguistic component, it is hard to find a transformation that does not depend on an inference or an inference that does not depend on a reference or a transformation. Occasionally, in small patterns, one or the other operation appears predominant. Elliot Gilbert in his study of Tennyson, for example, sets up a pattern of opposition between Malory and Tennyson by referring to Swinburne's criticism of the latter (1983:864): "Swinburne, for one, condemned what he felt was the reduction of Sir Thomas Malory's virile tales of chivalry to a sordid domestic quarrel. . . . In the same essay [he] refers to the *Idylls* as 'the Morte d'Albert' [referring to the recently deceased Prince Consort]." Then Gilbert applies transformations (p. 869)—"In Tennyson's remarkable vision . . . Arthur's coming fulfills that revolutionary law of the French National Convention which declared 'natural children absolutely equal with legitimate'"—and constructs a pattern of inference

(p. 875): "Tennyson was participating in an elaborate symposium with his fellow Victorians on the troubling state of their world." But all these patterns are also units, which have a part in the building of other patterns.

Patterns, like the units of which they are constructed, may be either structural or functional. The general preference rule by which both kinds of patterns are made takes the form of a gradient necessary condition:

GNC 1: Prefer the best pattern possible under the circumstances.

Two gradient necessary conditions describe the "best pattern":

GNC 1: The best pattern is that which allows the most coherent interpretation to emerge.
GNC 2: The best pattern is that which allows the most satisfying interpretation to emerge.

As was the case with categorization judgments, any structural pattern can function in more than one way so that the function of a structure (the functional pattern) is not directly and unambiguously available but must be inferred. For example, the structural pattern of deleting final consonants could function to indicate informal speech, illiterate speech, or lower class speech. But from the same (structural) speech pattern, if repeatedly combined with failure in a variety of situations, failure might (habitually) come to be inferred.

Patterns are thus also described by three well-formedness conditions:

WFC 1: Patterns are continuous or noncontinuous strings of text. [N.B.: References, inferences, and transformations are thus considered units of the text.]
WFC 2: Patterns are combinations of (a) units into patterns, (b) patterns into larger patterns.
WFC 3: A pattern acts as a unit.

As is the case with conditions and rules, the difference between units and patterns is, of course, not absolute. There are not currently extant any theories of basic units that can make such a distinction. Theories that postulate semantic atoms like platonic essences do not fit with anything else known about meaning. Nevertheless, just as conditions and rules differ from each other only functionally, so it is that the same phenomena can, in different contexts, be understood as units or as patterns. While there is some sense of the greater stability and conventionality of units, and of the uniqueness or originality of patterns, this sense is presumably specific to the contemporary context of linguistic description and literary criticism. Further, it seems that within a given context the list of unit categories is at any given moment finite, though easily changed. On the other hand, patterns can also function as units in the preference model, and the units themselves can be further analyzed to reveal the patterns of their derivation. It can therefore be inferred that decisions about what is best understood as a unit and what is best understood as a pattern are preference decisions. In principle there cannot be a necessary condition or set of necessary conditions sufficient to differentiate units from patterns. In some contexts it will be most useful to consider something a unit, in others, a pattern.

Whether built from continuous or noncontinuous strings, patterns are patterns either because the units are in some sense similar, as in groups of couplets, or because the units are in a relationship of dominance and subordination, such as exists between a noun and its modifiers. These alternatives are described by the fourth well-formedness condition for patterns:

WFC 4: The relationship between units within a pattern is one of (a) symmetry, or (b) dominance.

To students of literary interpretation, dominance patterns are probably the most interesting of the patterns studied within the autonomous linguistic system. Grammatical coordination (e.g., of strings of adjectives or adverbs) is a symmetrical pattern. Patterns involving dominance are more varied. Syntactically, any headed phrase can be thought of as a dominance pattern describing the relation between the head and its elaboration. Complex noun phrases, such as relative clauses ("When I have fears that I may cease to be") or stacked prepositional phrases ("Silent, upon a peak in Darien") fit into this category. Semantically, the various notions for which the term "foregrounding" has been used are probably connections in a pattern of dominance and subordination.[1] Semantic dominance can

---

[1] The concept of foregrounding goes back at least as far as the Prague School (see, e.g., Mukarovsky, 1940). For a review of some more recent work with similar notions, see Schauber (1979:229–308).

be created in a syntactically subordinated structure by emphatic stress, by interjections, by semantically complex verbs (e.g., "mumble" instead of "say"), or by adverbs that express the speaker's attitudes rather than the attitude of the subject of the sentence.

An interesting example of a pragmatic pattern of dominance leading to inference is the relation of an assertion to its presupposition. Erteschik (1973:22) claims that it is natural to comment on the dominant part of the sentence only: "A clause or phrase is semantically dominant if it is not presupposed and does not have contextual reference," that is, reference in the previous discourse. The hypothesis holds for all cases in which the presupposition can be separated from (is not part of) the assertion. Several different kinds of assumptions and implications have been discussed as presuppositions, and the weighting between the presupposition and the assertion is likely to be different in different cases. Since these differences would be available for exploitation in the pragmatic and the literary systems, it is crucial that the preference model not mask them.[2]

Gilbert's argument about the feminization of Arthur (discussed in Chapter Six) is built on a symmetrical pattern in which the driving force of the French Revolution is equated with the force of

---

[2]E. L. Keenan (1971), for example, has proposed a separation between "logical presupposition" and "pragmatic presupposition." Logical presupposition, he argues (p. 45), rests on "basic semantic concepts used in mathematical logic: truth and logical consequence": "A sentence S logically presupposes a sentence S′ just in case S logically implies S′ and the negation of S, ~S, also logically implies S′ ." The logical presupposition of a sentence remains constant under negation, so that "Marc likes the puppy he found" and "Marc doesn't like the puppy he found" both logically presuppose that Marc found a puppy. The notion of logical presupposition is here restricted to the autonomous linguistic system and in principle does not depend on knowledge of the world and its cultures. In pragmatic presupposition, on the other hand, the correctness of the presuppositions rests on factors in the context of utterance. Keenan proposes that the definition of pragmatic presupposition depends on our being able to specify the particular relations that obtain in the situation in which a certain presupposition can be said to be appropriate. He defines pragmatic presupposition (p. 49) thus: "An utterance of a sentence pragmatically presupposes that its context is appropriate." Grice makes a distinction between conventional implicatures, which are understood solely by virtue of the meaning of the words uttered (1975:44) and nonconventional implicatures (conversational implicatures being a subclass of these) that are "essentially connected with certain general features of discourse" (p. 45). Karttunen and Peters (1977, 1979) argue that Keenan's logical presuppositions are in fact not logical presuppositions but conventional implicatures. The debate is not over. See Levinson (1983) for a survey and Oh and Dinneen (1979) for a bibliography of works dealing with presupposition and articles taking various positions.

Queen Victoria's reign: both were antipatriarchal and therefore antihistorical in that they threatened the masculine line of inheritance. Gilbert suggests that Tennyson, like Matthew Arnold (another symmetrical pattern), was unhappy with that state of affairs and rewrote the Arthurian story to warn against the dangers of the power of women. Guenevere is patterned symmetrically with nature and myth, in opposition to another symmetrical pattern, civilization and history. The ostensible justification for Gilbert's article is the conventional one: if readers can agree to see things this way, they will have "rescued" Tennyson's poem from the charge of Swinburne and later critics that it trivializes the old and virile stories. (That claim, of course, would rest on patterning "feminine" symmetrically with "trivial.") But the interest of a reader in Gilbert's article, surely, is not in the "saving" of a Victorian text; it is, rather, in the argument for his patterning: in the originality and boldness of the claims for a symmetrical pattern linking the peaceful reign of Queen Victoria to the bloody regicide in France.

LITERARY PATTERNING:
UNCONVENTIONAL METAPHORS

Even a superficial glance at a series of readings of Wallace Stevens's poem "The Emperor of Ice-Cream" can illustrate the rules we have been writing. It should reveal the ways in which understanding unconventional metaphors depends on identifying partial matches between the text and the contexts specified by the typicality conditions: between the different parts of the text, between the poem and pragmatic information (about emperors, wenches, ice cream, etc., and between what a reader may know of other Wallace Stevens texts, both poems and letters), and between the text and the conventions of twentieth-century poetry and literary criticism. The critical comments we quote here are not judged or ranked: we take their appearance in published works on the shelves of major university libraries to be ipso facto evidence of the competence of their authors to produce readings acceptable in one or another reading community.[3] We have made no attempt here to survey a range of opinions about the poem, nor even to present complete arguments

---

[3] Pratt (1977:116ff.) explains how publication is crucially involved in what is certified by the community as acceptable.

for those readings we do cite. Nor is it our intention to produce yet another reading. Our claim is simply that even in their present state of overgeneralization, the rules we have been writing do seem to describe what readers do with poems.

The Emperor of Ice-Cream

Call the roller of big cigars,
The muscular one, and bid him whip
In kitchen cups concupiscent curds.
Let the wenches dawdle in such dress
As they are used to wear, and let the boys
Bring flowers in last month's newspapers.
Let be be finale of seem.
The only emperor is the emperor of ice-cream.

Take from the dresser of deal,
Lacking the three glass knobs, that sheet
On which she embroidered fantails once
And spread it so as to cover her face.
If her horny feet protrude, they come
To show how cold she is, and dumb.
Let the lamp affix its beam.
The only emperor is the emperor of ice-cream.[4]

Ronald Sukenick (1967) ultimately concludes (p. 63) that the power of the emperor who rolls big cigars and whips up the ice cream ("concupiscent curds") is to provide commonplace pleasures in the face of death, "pleasure" being "the only force that has dominion over the commonplace." He seems to have begun his reading by identifying a partial match between the idea of power (a condition of the words "emperor," "muscular," and "whip") and the absolute power of death. From this, he applies the synecdochal transformation: the condition "power" is separated out of these words and the words themselves together with the condition "power" form a pattern of which "power" is the head. The words are subordinate: made to stand for one of their conditions. Other contributory transformations are forming patterns simultaneously. There is a partial match among "ice-cream," "big cigars," "wenches," "curds," etc., which forms a pattern dominated by the condition "pleasure." Where "pleasure" is not a necessary or typical condition, as for ex-

[4] *The Collected Poems of Wallace Stevens* (New York, 1976), p. 64. Reprinted with permission of the publisher, Alfred A. Knopf, Inc.

ample, in "curds," it may be inferred as the transformational pattern emerges. The condition "pleasure" is a new unit that becomes the head of the pattern under which the other units are conjoined. Another subset of words in the poem, in large part but not entirely overlapping the first, forms a pattern of words in which the dominant condition is ordinariness: "kitchen cups," "last month's newspapers," "ice-cream," "cigars," "wenches," etc. For all these the condition of ordinariness must be derived through inference, except perhaps for "kitchen cups," which may have the condition "ordinary" as a typicality condition distinguishing kitchen cups from china too expensive to be used in the kitchen.

This is a good point at which to notice the nature of the boundary between pragmatic and literary competence. The inference of the pattern dominated by "ordinariness" is more likely, it may be granted, to suggest itself to a reader who is aware of the history of the literary debate about suitable topics for poetry. It may also be granted that an experienced reader is more likely to be familiar, even if indirectly, with Aristotle's opinions on the appropriate subjects for poetry, with the controversy about "metaphysical" imagery, and with Stevens's own statement (in H. Stevens, 1966:263) about the deliberate yoking together of what he called, with specific reference to this poem, the "essential gaudiness of poetry" and a "deliberately commonplace costume." But this does not necessarily make such familiarity literary competence. It is, in fact, a good example of the ways in which literary competence is a subset of pragmatic competence. The operation of inference here is presumably no different from pragmatic inference, but the references necessary to make the inferences are ones likely to be familiar within a limited, literary sphere.

For Sukenick to claim that the emperor provides "commonplace pleasures," both patterns ("pleasure" and "ordinariness") are needed. Then the condition of power from the word "emperor" is analyzed as a term of the Structural Description of the transformation that relates power to commonplace pleasures. Another inference and a transformation are required to relate these two. Because its own negative can always be inferred from a word, powerlessness can be inferred from power and identified with the powerlessness similarly inferred from commonplace pleasures. A symmetrical pattern is then formed from the contrast between the conditions "power" and powerlessness, which between them dominate a large number of the units of the poem.

The household items have "power" because the entire unit in the Structural Description remains as part of the new term formed according to the instructions of the Structural Change. The two now exist in a contradiction, for it is the nature of the literary transformations that they retain their original condition of powerlessness, which is now juxtaposed to powerfulness in the newly derived pattern. This larger pattern can now form the basis of a further inference from "emperor" to "oriental splendor," which also contrasts with the commonplace pleasures. (Although Sukenick does not apply this last transformation, at least one other reader, as we will see, has.) In the pattern consisting of the unit "emperor," including power and the commonplace, there is a partial match between the expectations of what a powerful Eastern potentate should be able to provide and what the poem seems to say he does provide, that is, the commonplace pleasures of the other unit of the pattern. Two possible inferences present themselves, both of which appear in other critics' readings: since emperors have the power to provide things more splendid than ice cream, the emperor of ice cream is a paltry emperor indeed. Alternatively, since the emperor is providing it, ice cream and the simple pleasures it represents must be splendid and powerful. Several readers, in deciding between these conflicting readings, have considered Stevens's own statements on the issue to be heavily weighted. Stevens says in a letter, for example, that "ice-cream is an absolute good" (H. Stevens, 1966: 341). But this sentence cannot decide anything since it is not only open to but even seems to beg for an ironic reading: John Enck (1964: 202) provides the ironic perspective when he suggests a possible connection between Stevens's comment, in a letter to R. P. Blackmur, that his daughter liked ice cream, and the "sheeted corpse [which] could be a girl's" (H. Stevens, p. 341). Stevens also says that "the poem is obviously not about icecream, but about being as distinguished from seeming to be." This statement invites further inferences and applications of transformations, including inferences in which the commonplace itself becomes a unit in the larger pattern of things that unpretentiously and commonly *are*, not just "seem" to be.

Blackmur (1932) concurs with Sukenick in seeing "power" as the heavily weighted condition of "emperor" that will lead to a coherent and satisfying pattern, as opposed, to take any example, to "wearing a Franz Joseph moustache," which, while it might conceivably be a typicality condition of "emperor" (even this is doubtful), does not lead, in any reading of the poem we have been able to uncover, to a satisfying interpretation. Both Sukenick and Blackmur may have been reacting to a partial match between the condition of power and contemporary conditions of significance: power is a conventional subject for modern poetry whereas facial hair patterns are not. Blackmur, having hit on "power" as the condition worth patterning, applies transformations somewhat differently to "newspapers," "cigars," and "ice-cream," and therefore arrives at a conclusion slightly different from, but not inconsistent with, Sukenick's. Blackmur concludes (pp. 59–60): "'The only emperor is the emperor of ice-cream' implies in both stanzas that the only power worth heeding is the power of the moment, of what is passing, of the flux." But he also reads an ironic version of that inference:

> The less obvious sense of the couplets is more difficult to set down because, in all its difference, it rises out of the first sense, and while contradicting and supplanting, yet guarantees it. The connotation is, perhaps, that ice-cream and what it represents is the only power *heeded*, not the only power there is to heed. The irony recoils on itself: what seems *shall* finally be; the lamp *shall* affix its beam. The only emperor is the emperor of ice-cream. The king is dead; long live the king. [p. 60]

James Baird (1968) also reads the lines ironically, but he arrives at that reading by means of a derivation involving different parts of the text. The dead woman in the adjoining room is Venus, known by the sign of her attendant birds which she embroidered on the sheet. The mythic rites of longing and courtship are at an end: "the myth belonging to modern girls and boys is ice cream from an 'emperor' who rules . . . at the counter of a drug store" (p. 223).

Enck derives another pattern of symmetry and dominance from the same transformations as Sukenick's, that is, that ice cream is commonplace, routine. "The dead and the living," he claims, are equivalent. Both "exist under a single dispensation: an emperor of ice-cream" (p. 202). This pattern, in turn, requires an inference: "'The Emperor of Ice-Cream' transcends a report about poverty and death. It implies that nothing can be ascertained about the end of life but, likewise, that one cannot wish away a certain mystery."

The mystery that fascinates Enck seems to have to do with the asymmetry between "power" and "ice-cream." He tentatively concludes (p. 203): "The use of *horny* focuses on the passing of pretense. Inadequate illusion in disguising the sordid makes the Emperor a sinister power." To be the emperor of ice-cream isn't enough: death still remains overpowering. Joseph Riddel (1965 : 87) approvingly quotes a pattern first described by Richard Ellmann (1957) that would seem to suggest an answer to Enck's mystery: "The emperor is neither life nor death alone but the 'force of being understood as including life, death, and imagination.'" If the emperor has power, in this reading, it is sufficient only because it is not simply the power to provide pleasure in the face of inevitable death but also the power of the imagination, the power of poetry. This reading might well have been suggested by its partially matching a condition of significance to which Stevens more than once declared himself dedicated, that is, the supremacy of the life of the imagination, and the necessity of the creation of fictions. Needless to say, this ostensible self-dedication itself requires interpretation. Lucy Beckett (1974) is among those (see also, e.g., Buttel, 1967) who has provided a reading of Stevens's other writings that could reinforce the Ellmann-Riddel inclusion of "imagination" as a symmetrical term with "death" and "life." Beckett believes (p. 1) that Stevens spent his whole poetry career "attempting to find or make . . . some kind of answer to the . . . problem of belief." She infers this from, among other places, a statement made by Stevens in 1954: "The author's work suggests the possibility of a supreme fiction, recognized as a fiction, in which men could propose to themselves a fulfillment. In the creation of any such fiction, poetry would have a vital significance." A "fulfillment," in Beckett's reading, is transformed to something like "a satisfying but unsentimental answer to the finality of death." A poet can be, the derivation continues, an emperor dominating both life and death.

It seems at least possible that it was a partial match between contemporary conditions of significance and the concerns of the text that suggested to Ellmann, Riddel, and Beckett that the poem might be about poetry. Jonathan Culler, a reliable reader of literary conventionalities, claims (1979 : 177) that "the convention that poems may be read as statements about poetry is extremely powerful." Stevens thus was participating in a convention, not inventing a new one.

In the context of twentieth-century criticism, both the convention that poetry is a suitable topic for poetry and Harold Bloom's theories of belatedness (1972) may have suggested the partial match Maureen Kravec (1979) sees between Stevens's poem and Spenser's "Epithalamium." Like Blackmur and Baird, Kravec finds the praise of the emperor ironic, but she takes the object of the irony to be courtship poetry rather than courtship rituals. According to Kravec (pp. 8–11), "The Emperor of Ice-Cream" is "a poem about modern poetry . . . which tolls the knell for traditional, outmoded form and declares its own succession." Stevens's poem, Kravec says, exposes the sham of Spenser's poem. In her reading, the transformations relate the commonplace and the "sleazy sham" of a modern "arcade," which itself patterns with the final debasement of the image of Arcadia which reigned over the Renaissance genre of commissioned and conventional marriage poems.

LITERARY PATTERNING: CHARACTERIZATION

The understanding of characterization in fiction depends on sets of rules according to which patterns of speech are understood as characterizing. That such rules exist has seemed to most literary critics to be a truism that does not need to be argued. Critics who studied characterization in the mid-1960's assumed it was (see, e.g., Harvey, 1965: 52, and Walcutt, 1966: 5). Stanley Fish (1976) challenged the assumption, arguing that specific patterns of speech cannot be assigned characterizing meaning outside of or previous to the contexts in which they occur. Fish is right to the extent that structure does not entail meaning: whatever patterns are found must be interpreted by inferring their functions in context. However, as already has been discussed, such inference is possible, and therefore speech is characterizing. In addition, if it is granted that Austin was right to understand speech as action, the assumption that speech is characterizing is safely within the Aristotelian tradition in which an important part of character is defined as the actions a character chooses or his responses to actions.

The complexities of characterization, in and out of literature, demand an accounting of both idiosyncratic and communal patterns of language. Even when speech is individuating, it is still the language of a community. Speech patterns, therefore, can only be characterizing to the extent to which readers are familiar with the speech patterns of the communities that the text implies. Readers of literary works must also be familiar with the conventions by which recognizable communal speech patterns are transformed into literary patterns. By examining the conditions under which the patterns that produce literary characterization are understood, we will show how experienced readers construct patterns from the units of text and context and infer a set of functions from those patterns.

In broad terms, a literary audience must have three separate kinds of information from the pragmatic system in order to draw inferences from speech patterns in a text. At the most general level, a reader will recognize the patterns of a person's or a character's speech that connect him or her to a specific community and mark the social class within that community. At this level, characterizing involves a symmetrical grouping of similar patterns. In addition, patterns of contrast that are not necessarily symmetrical mark the speaker's social roles within the community. This identification, like the first, distinguishes as well as groups, delineating role relationships—showing that the speaker is an older sister, not a younger, or a priest, not a parishioner, or a teacher, not a student. Speech functions also mark the individual within a role—mark an older sister, priest, or teacher as different from a stereotypical one. Individuality is a matter of the degree of fit between the set of expectations evoked by conventions of the rule and the characteristics of the individual.

Any given speech pattern will not necessarily be understood as performing all these functions. It is hard to see how it could not perform the first, but it is not hard to imagine casual speech contact that might not reveal role identification. Speech patterns that truly identify individuality beyond social role are much less obvious and perhaps rare, rarer in life than in literature. When the language serves only the first two functions, those of identifying the speech community and the role of the speaker within that community, the character is not individuated but remains more or less a stereotype, identified primarily as the representative of a group. Speech patterns do individuate characters, separating each from a group and from others in similar roles in the group, and helping to create "round characters," in Forster's terms (1927), rather than "flat" ones. Since these pragmatic conditions work in life and in literature to define the participation of a character in patterns of similarity and difference, a reader could produce a coherent interpretation of the characters of certain kinds of realistic fiction with pragmatic competence alone, at least insofar as the reader limits the field to texts produced within his or her own culture.

The experienced reader can reach a different understanding of a text by controlling additional literary patterning rules about characterization. A character recognized as the hero, for example, has a place in a pattern of characters. The hero or heroine is placed in opposition to an antagonist and participates in a hierarchical pattern within a range of secondary characters. References, transformational rules, and rules of inference sort the *dramatis personae* according to matching or contrasting terms. The rules may match two characters of equal importance or may pair the protagonist with a foil. David Daiches (1963) reads the pair of sisters in *Middlemarch* according to these rules, focusing on the incident in which they discuss dividing the jewelry inherited from their mother:

> [Dorothea] treats Celia with an almost patronising affection . . . but it does not take us long to discover that she is really the more vulnerable. . . . The devices which she employs only half consciously to keep her high moral tone with respect to Celia . . . indicate a moral consciousness continually on the stretch. And the deep sensuous awareness which she possesses is fought down or transmuted to religious feeling with almost pathetic contrivance. . . . Which of these two sisters sees more clearly? And what is the relation between clear-sightedness and virtue? [pp. 15–16]

Daiches sees the pattern of contrast between these characters functioning to express a pair of attitudes toward the thematic material of the novel. Similarly, readers of Hemingway's *For Whom the Bell Tolls* have understood the group of Spanish partisans whom Robert Jordan works with by reference to the Spanish politics of the time. Pablo and Pilar, Joaquin and El Sordo were understood as exhibiting a range of possible attitudes toward the Spanish civil war that correspond to a set of political attitudes familiar to the readers' experience. The assemblage of characters in a plot modeled after the archetypical "ship of fools," the World War II bomber crew, for example, would be understood this way, as would a group of advisers to a main character, for example, the parliament of devils in Milton's *Paradise Lost*.

An experienced reader of literature will be able to understand fictional characters by the references they may make not only to historical figures or attitudes but to other fictional characters. Such a pattern would join the features described in the preference conditions of a rule, such as the rule describing an archetype or a classic literary figure, to the feature of the token character in the text. Thus a young man in a war novel, in the absence of evidence to the contrary, will be granted the characteristics of innocence, honesty, and sensitivity by the structural similarities of his situation to a generic rule. The reference to Prince Hamlet in T. S. Eliot's "The Love Song of J. Alfred Prufrock" and to the Blessed Virgin in the first paragraph of *Middlemarch* are read as providing contrast and some irony to the characterizations of Prufrock and Dorothea respectively.

These and other rules in the literary system describe both the patterns by which the character exemplifies a rule (e.g., the rule describing the conditions under which a character is categorized as a hero), and the ways in which he or she is not typical of it. These functions are very difficult to separate from each other, but they may be examined as they are embedded in Stephen Booth's reading of Act I, scene ii of *Hamlet,* in which the new king, Claudius, reveals to the audience his version of the pattern that should obtain at court. As Booth points out, one of the patterns against which the main characters are matched is a cultural pattern of kinship and inheritance, a pattern described by pragmatic rules specific to the culture and historical period of the play. Because of underspecified recent upheavals in Denmark, the partial matches between cultural roles and literary types and the characters in the play create tension. Is Claudius Hamlet's uncle, or father, or both? Is Gertrude Hamlet's mother, his father's widow, Claudius's queen, or all the above? Why hasn't Hamlet inherited his father's throne? Is Hamlet a revenge tragedy hero?

Booth argues (1969:149–50) that in the face of these ambiguities, Claudius's first task is to stabilize the situation. He seeks to establish a clear social pattern, naturally one of his own choice and one of which he is unambiguously the head: "Scene two presents [a] kind of double understanding in double frames of reference." Claudius, because of his rank and because of the inevitable staging of a court scene, is visually the "focal figure" while at the same time "the genre and the particulars of a given performance focus the audience's attention on Hamlet." A pattern of competition for head position is thus set by the simultaneous presentation of one pattern in which Claudius is the head and another in which Hamlet is the head.

To know that the king is the head does not, of course, require inference. He is head by virtue of his title, that is, by convention. An audience's pragmatic competence is thus sufficient to comprehend that Claudius's regal entry, which begins this scene, and the fact that Claudius does all the orchestrating and most of the talking, count as reminders of the privileges of a king and refer to our knowledge of the pattern in which the king is dominant over his subordinates. Booth's case for the competing pattern of which Hamlet is the head is more complex. Various literary conventions in scene i, including the opening dialogue between two sentries, suggest the genre of revenge tragedy, and in this genre Hamlet, as the revenger, is the protagonist, the head. Booth says (p. 140) "when a work of art focuses on sentries, it is usually a sign that what they are guarding is going to be attacked." Literary convention here allows for an inference that could not be made pragmatically: pragmatic competence is sufficient to discern that sentries guard places that are potential foci for attack, but only rarely is attack expected imminently. Booth claims that such an inference would be preferred here, however, because the literary genre rules weight as significant the presence of sentries more heavily than pragmatic rules do.

The major element in scene i that determines the genre categorization is, of course, the presence of the ghost asking for revenge. In scene ii the presence of an actor dressed in black, a character, the audience is told, whose father has just died, refers back to and patterns with the elements of threatened attack and revenge in scene i, and invites the inference that Hamlet wants to revenge his father's death. Hamlet is thus positioned as the dominant character in opposition to the king by the genre and by the staging even before his first lines are spoken, and before he himself has seen the ghost. This contrast between the king and Hamlet is reinforced for an audience that recognizes the actor in black as the company's chief actor.

The first exchange of lines between Claudius and Hamlet clinches the pattern of opposition formed from the two separate patterns with different dominant heads. Claudius, finishing up his other conversations in an orderly fashion, turns to Hamlet ("But now, my cousin Hamlet, and my son," l. 64),[5] with a phrase that Booth notes

---

[5] References to Shakespeare are from Craig and Bevington (1973).

(p. 150) "is typical of [Claudius's] stylistic unifications of mutually exclusive contrary ideas (cousin, son)." Claudius, whose language has already shown him to be a reconciler and a diplomat, is here trying to enforce order in his domain by reconciling by fiat, as it were, seeming contradictions. As Booth points out (p. 148), noting that Claudius's "first sentences are unifications in which his discretion overwhelms things whose natures are oppugnant," Claudius offers Hamlet the terms for a relationship:

> Therefore our sometime sister, now our queen,
> Th' imperial jointress to this warlike state,
> Have we, as 'twere with a defeated joy,—
> With an auspicious and a dropping eye,
> With mirth in funeral and with dirge in marriage,
> In equal scale weighting delight and dole,—
> Taken to wife. . . .
>
> [I.ii.8–14]

Pairs of oppositions form a new, larger pattern, which can be understood through a transformation that relates all these pairs as patterns the head of which are the conjoined pair of words "delight" and "dole."

Booth points out (p. 149) that while the king is busy trying to unify opposites, smoothing them over "by rhythm, alliteration, assonance, and syntactical balance," Hamlet (l. 65) sets himself in opposition by disunifying ideas: "A little more than kin, and less than kind," he remarks in an aside. That is, while the king has tried to unify semantic opposites, has tried to overshadow the meaning with phonological and syntactic patterns of unification, Hamlet insists on the continuing presence of ambiguity. He flouts Grice's maxim of manner, which requires the speaker to avoid obscurity of expression and ambiguity. His response is obscure, in terms of the autonomous linguistic and pragmatic systems, because it does not make clear whether the two parts of the utterance are meant to have different referents (a syntactic phenomenon), or, for either part, who should be the reference or references for the subject. If speculation is limited to inferences that the response might evoke were it within the pragmatic system, it could be said that Hamlet is not impressed by the King's attempt to be conciliatory, and is not making a very great effort to be obliging to the King and Queen. Given their status roles in his society as parents and rulers, Hamlet might well be expected to make such an effort. This interpretation, which comes through the pragmatic system alone, would not lead a play-goer wildly astray. However, to the more experienced, such as Booth, who are familiar with the rules of the literary system and to whom the text is well known, a still more complex interpretation is available.

As the play goes on, Booth continues, the conflict between Claudius and Hamlet cannot be covered over by fair speech, and it becomes clear that Hamlet cannot play a part in a society whose values he cannot accept. At this point the pattern of characterization interacts with the other patterns of the text, including plot patterning. Ultimately the tension arising from the competition between two dominance patterns is resolved by a plot pattern that is typical of the genre. The tension resulting from the claims made by both Hamlet and Claudius to be the head of a pattern of dominance is resolved by the tragic plot structure that leads them both to their deaths. Hamlet has refused to participate in the language games proposed by the arbiter of all social rules in Denmark, the king.

Many literary texts have been read as capitalizing on the conflict between heroism and the conventional nature of language. Insofar as languages are conventional social systems, their functioning depends on that part of the social contract in which members of a society agree to cooperate in the accepted language games of that society. Montaigne says as much in his essay on lying:

Since mutual understanding is brought about solely by way of words, he who breaks his word betrays human society. It is the only instrument by means of which our wills and thoughts communicate, it is the interpreter of our soul. If it fails us, we have no more hold on each other, no more knowledge of each other. If it deceives us, it breaks up all our relations and dissolves all the bonds of our society. [Frame, 1963:286]

The ordinary language philosophers have tried to explain how these bonds operate. Grice posits his overarching Cooperative Principle as the governor of (successful) conversation. Searle (1979:78) argues that one trusts people to mean what they say because "the performance of the speech act is *eo ipso* an expression of the corresponding intentional state." The inherent irony of the Cooperative Principle and of the identification of speech act and intention is that each is, like every law, the basis for its own abuse. While Grice and

Searle are right to claim that the assumption of an identity between speech and intention is a basic principle on which conversation proceeds, the two are not, as we argued in Chapter Six, as inseparably joined as Searle claims they are. Indeed, it is their possible separability that allows Umberto Eco (1976:7) to say that "semiotics is in principle the discipline studying everything which can be used in order to lie." Obvious abuses of social norms may be dealt with openly; covert abuses, hypocrisy, for example, may be insidious and destructive. A liar or a hypocrite "palms off counterfeit linguistic currency," Barbara Herrnstein Smith says (1978:100), and thereby commits "a social transgression of the first order precisely because [he or she] undermines the community's confidence in that verbal medium of exchange so basic to social transactions."

In fact, it is not lying per se that is difficult for society to handle. The language behavior of some well-known literary protagonists demonstrates that it is quite possible for speaking the truth to be as problematic as Montaigne assumed lying to be. What is important for the maintenance of social equilibrium is not truth but the accession of the speakers to the language games of the society in which they find themselves actors. The iconoclast can be more disruptive than the liar.

From the point of view of a society naturally dependent on a high degree of conformity for its smooth functioning, literature is something of a rogue's gallery. The Prufrocks, even the Claudiuses, are less disruptive than the Hamlets. A high degree of linguistic nonconformity should be expected in the speech of literary protagonists. In fact, protagonists are defined in part as heroic, villainous, or tragic by the way the patterns of their speech and actions fit or do not fit the patterning of the world the text creates around them.

Literature from the Middle Ages until the present provides examples of the ways societies can ostracize characters who refuse to meet their language obligations. A hypocrite, for example, is rarely welcome. Of the large number of hypocrites among Chaucer's Canterbury pilgrims, critics have generally found the most irritating to be the Pardoner, who preaches excellent sermons with no genuine interest in the souls of his audience, thinking only of how he can separate them from their money. While he brags about what a wonderful speaker he is, he at the same time refuses to argue for or account for his sins, and in the context of his relationship to his fellow pilgrims this refusal to show any contrition by even a lame attempt to justify himself is an even greater offense against propriety than his hypocritical sermons. If he presented some mitigating reasons for his corruption or hinted at some regret for his evil (as the Wife of Bath most ingratiatingly does, for example), his audience of fellow pilgrims, few of whom are free of sin themselves, might be inclined toward some sympathy for him, might be willing to share his joke, to join him in looking down on the gulls he swindles. As it is, his total disregard for his audience's pragmatic genre expectation that confession be accompanied by some indication of contrition is maddening to them, and he is so out of touch with expected social patterns that he fails to understand the reason for their anger. The Pardoner's inability to meet his audience's genre expectations is a failure to carry on social intercourse with them and is reflected in the suggestion Chaucer makes that he is castrated: "a gelding or a mare."[6]

Shakespeare's *Coriolanus*, as Stanley Fish has shown, demonstrates that refusing to submit to the conventions of language use can be just as destructive to society when the motivations are high-minded honesty as when they are greed and dishonesty. Coriolanus, Fish says (1976:989), "spends much of the play trying desperately to hold himself clear of . . . commitments and obligations." He cannot make requests, or receive praise. He "is always doing things (with words) to set himself apart" (p. 995), and he gets his way; he is banished from the Roman State. Banishment, enforced physical separation, is the perfect punishment for a person who will not accept the responsibilities of living in society, will not accept the responsibilities of a cooperative principle.

Linda Brodkey has shown how William Dean Howells, in *A Modern Instance*, similarly prescribes banishment. The news reporter protagonist, Bartley Hubbard, commits a string of increasingly serious language crimes against his wife and against the public trust in his role as a reporter. He is accused of his most serious deception and called "a dangerous person" by his boss (Gibson, 1957:267). He is forced to resign his job. Fairly soon after, he abandons his wife and child to move west, away from the society

---

[6] F. N. Robinson, ed. (1957), *The Canterbury Tales*, I, 691. For a fuller discussion of the Pardoner's offenses see Schauber and Spolsky (1983).

whose language rules he has abused. He commits perjury in order to obtain a divorce and finally dies, the result of still another public abuse of language: this last time, in his weekly newspaper "he unfortunately chanced to comment upon the domestic relations of 'one of Whited Sepulchre's leading citizens' . . . and he is shot for his indiscretion" (Brodkey, n.d.).

What is the difference between the Pardoner, Coriolanus, and Bartley Hubbard? Their motivations are not equally admirable, but they would share equally the opprobrium of Montaigne for threatening social structures. The survival of societies seems to be a result of cutting out the abuser one way or another: from a pragmatic point of view, the stability of society suffers no less damage from the words of heroic challengers of the status quo like Coriolanus than from the verbal abuses of hypocrites like the Pardoner and cynics like Bartley Hubbard. But in the literary system there is a difference. That difference is distinguished by the heavily weighted typicality conditions of the literary genre rules that frame the action of the fiction by means of value judgments about the outcomes of the plot. Language abuses and misunderstandings may end in death, as in *Coriolanus,* or in multiple marriages, as in *Twelfth Night.* Coriolanus, like Hamlet, refuses to participate in the language patterns of his society, and he is forced to leave the state. Bartley Hubbard's abuses are considered "dangerous," so he is ostracized by separation from his job (he is fired), and from his wife (he is divorced). The Pardoner, a eunuch, who is thus sexually separated, by the end of his tale, "so wrooth he was, no word ne wolde he seye."[7]

The pragmatic system by itself may punish abusers with a sense of frustration at being misunderstood, but it is by the force of the literary transformations and inferences that the language abuses of these characters function as metaphoric separations. The easiest way to see that this is a literary genre convention is to look at some texts in comic genres in which necessary conditions require a different pattern. Somber consequences do not result from the same kind of language abuses and misunderstandings. On the contrary, misunderstandings are cleared up and the end is happy. Shakespeare's *Twelfth Night* (or indeed any of several hundred years of romantic

[7] F. N. Robinson, ed. (1957), *The Canterbury Tales,* VI, 957.

comedies) displays flagrant language abuse. Viola, dressed as a male servant, answers Olivia who has been taken in by the disguise and has fallen in love with her. She responds with this "truth," counting on being misunderstood:

> By innocence I swear, and by my youth,
> I have one heart, one bosom and one truth,
> And that no woman has; nor never none
> Shall mistress be of it, save I alone.
>
> [III.i.169–72]

The play is full of similar speeches and deliberate misleading. But in the genre of comic romance, "this is very midsummer madness." The passage of time is trusted to undo the tangles and restore the social balance by correcting the misunderstandings, and indeed it does. The marriages that end the play are new connections, metaphorical opposites of the patterns of separation and exile that result from the same kinds of abuse in tragedy.

The rules that describe patterning, like those that describe categorization, are derived and have been exemplified from the work of experienced readers whose interpretations have been accepted within the Anglo-American academic community of the last fifty years. It is this communal acceptance that accords them the designation "well-formed." "Ill-formed" interpretations do not usually appear in print, although teachers of literature are familiar enough with them. The challenge is therefore not only to distinguish well-formed from ill-formed interpretations but to distinguish between stronger and weaker well-formed interpretations, and to distinguish communities producing competing well-formed interpretations. When is a critic working within the same system as other critics and when has the system been changed? What counts as a change? These are the issues and questions of Part IV.

Part IV

The Spectra of Interpretation

Chapter Eight

Interpretive Communities

The main obstacle to attempts to distinguish competing well-formed interpretations both from weaker ones and from ill-formed ones, and thereby to understand what kinds of variation an interpretive system permits and what kinds it does not, has been the seemingly unarguable and unchartable influence of the conditions of significance on any interpretation. The preference model demonstrates that, although conditions of significance are indeed unarguable within a literary theory, it is possible to chart their impact on the system of interpretation as a whole, and thus possible to indicate where these conditions can legitimately influence judgments and where they cannot. By encoding the relative weighting of conditions (including conditions of significance), the preference model accounts not only for the differing interpretive interests and goals of different readers but also for their differing literary experience.

Interpretive competence includes the knowledge of where conditions of significance influence the system and how variously weighted conditions produce a range of interpretations. What is at issue here is more than just describing a well-formed interpretation in terms of its consistency with some preference rule system, including a set of conditions of significance; perhaps more important is accounting for variations in interpretation both because of differences in individual systems and because of individual differences in ability to make use of a system. The preference model, being a competence model, does not, by definition, produce ill-formed interpretations; these are produced only when the model is not fully operating. However, the smooth functioning of the model does not ensure uniformity of interpretation. Disagreement among interpreters is built into the system at the places where the conditions of significance and their weightings influence the references that will be found, the transformations that will be applied, and the inferences that can be drawn. And though the partial or insufficient operation of the model resulting from an interpreter's lack of experience with the model itself, or with a sufficiently broad range of literary texts, may be of little theoretical interest, it does explain how the system can produce well-formed but weak interpretations, that is, interpretations that are not satisfyingly coherent.[1]

A well-formed interpretation, of a sentence, a paragraph, or a narrative, is a well-formed pattern. The best pattern that can be proposed is the strongest, that is, the most satisfying and coherent interpretation, "satisfying" and "coherent" being determined by the conditions of significance. A strong pattern is one in which details that have not been explicitly considered would, if considered, form a coherent pattern with the rest of the interpretation; in a weaker interpretation such unconsidered patterns would be incoherent. For a given well-formed interpretation, "best" may not seem good enough. A community generally judges a text to be weak when the best interpretation available under its conditions of significance is not satisfying or coherent. The best interpretation available, a well-formed interpretation, may thus be a weak one. Consider, for example, any of the standard interpretations of the character of Hamlet's mother, Gertrude: that she is easily managed, that she conspired with Claudius in old Hamlet's death, that she is unnaturally

---

[1] We have discussed elsewhere (Schauber and Spolsky, 1981) how inexperienced readers may apply pragmatic rules where the model requires literary ones. Inexperienced readers of Shakespeare's comedies, for example, may be unacquainted with the genre rules that would help them transform and infer meaning from the conventions of multiple and transsexual disguises. Recognition scenes with their symmetrical pairings may leave such readers without a literary interpretation. And so they fall back on a pragmatic one in which they as readers seem themselves to be more perceptive than the apparently overly gullible sixteenth-century audiences. This is a coherent and satisfying interpretation, but it is not a literary one.

attached to her son, or that she is governed by sexual appetite. None of these has been considered an entirely satisfying, coherent, and strong interpretation because conflicting as well as supporting evidence can be brought forward for each of them. Some of these interpretations are compatible and some are competing, but they are all equally weak and none is, by itself, preferable to the others. Any one of them is well-formed and can stand with a strong interpretation of the larger text that does not conflict with it. A strong interpretation can show a text thought to be weak to be, when different conditions are patterned, strong. This is what we saw as one of the results of Elliot Gilbert's reading of Tennyson's *Idylls of the King*.

When an interpreter explicitly disagrees with one or more of the conditions of some particular preference rule system whose conditions have been defined and weighted to account for a set of contemporary interpretations, we may well ask whether we are in the presence of a different interpretive community. David Bleich (1978) and Stanley Fish (1980) propose the notion of interpretive communities in an attempt to deal with the varieties of interpretation that can arise within a single interpretive model, and to distinguish those readings from those that might arise when critics disagree about basic principles.[2] Neither, however, specifies how membership in an interpretive community is determined, leaving readers to assume that such classification is self-evident. Fish's references to interpretive communities point to the inherent weakness of the notion in its current underspecified form. He claims, for example (1980: 304), that he and M. H. Abrams can understand each other despite their very serious disagreements because they address each other *within* "a system (or context, or situation, or interpretive community) and that the understanding achieved by two or more persons is specific to that system and determinate only within its confines." He tells the title story of the book: a student asked a colleague of his "Is there a text in this class?" Fish's colleague replied, "Yes, it's the *Norton Anthology of Literature*." The student was unsatisfied, because what she wanted to know was the theoretical orientation of the teacher. Did he regard a literary text as autonomous from its con-

---

[2] Fish apparently adapts the notion of speech community or social network from sociolinguistic usage. Bleich has an earlier discussion of the notion of communities of interpretation.

texts and readers? Fish claims that he himself would have understood the question in the way it was intended; and his colleague too, he says, was immediately able to switch his interpretation and recognize his error.

In telling this story, Fish unfortunately hedges the crucial issue: he does not specify whether he is or is not a member of the same community as the colleague who, though he at first understood a potentially ambiguous question differently from the way Fish himself would have, was quite capable of seeing the second possible reading the moment he was given a hint of it. If we generalize from Fish's statement about himself and Abrams, we have to assume that Fish and his Johns Hopkins colleague are in fact in the same community because both could (ultimately) understand both interpretations of the question with no great difficulty. Thus we draw two conclusions from Fish's example: first (a point that he has often made), that the first response one has to a statement depends on the context in which it is embedded; second, that since a teacher in a college English department might at first understand things differently from a colleague but can be brought to see things as that colleague sees them, teachers in college English departments must form one community. But as Fish well knows, putting people who disagree as fundamentally as Abrams and Fish in one community robs the notion of "community" of much of its usefulness and interest. One will merely have come back to the starting point, needing some way to describe the differences between Fish and Abrams. The determination of subcommunities within the community of academic literary scholars is therefore hardly a minor problem. If, on the one hand, every variation in interpretive perspective or strategy indicates a new community, then the notion of community loses its force. If, on the other hand, major variations in perspective do not mark community boundaries, then again the notion has little use. It seems that in Fish's use, membership in a community is a new way of talking about point of view: it determines the first context in which one interprets, but it does not prevent understanding in other contexts.

What is needed is a specification both of the ways in which Fish and Abrams are in the same community—that is, a description of the kinds of things (not the things themselves) they agree about—and also of the ways in which they differ (not the points of difference). Clearly, some kinds of variation are significant and indicate that a new community is forming, but some others are variations that the old community permits, even encourages. These latter are described by the preference model as typicality conditions. These types of variations are in fact intelligible because they are rule-governed even though variable, that is, they are *both* constrained *and* allowed by the grammar that defines the possibilities for interpretation within a community. Fish's claim that the academy sanctions a certain number of subcommunities at any one time is true but not nearly so interesting as the question of how to know when one is in the presence of a new community. Certainly it is not the number of communities that is of interest but how difference is allowed at all and what counts as a significant difference.

As a model of categorization, the preference model should, of course, be able to distinguish among communities just as it can distinguish among genres. Therefore the attempt to define literary communities by sets of conditions is just one more test of the model. But it is also important at this point that we investigate whether the preference model can distinguish between those communities whose interpretive methods it describes and those whose interpretive methods it does not. It must, that is, defend itself against the charge of being too powerful, of being so flexible that it can co-opt any attempt to challenge it. A model that is to answer the kinds of questions a theory of literary interpretation must answer has to have limits. It should be able to specify where it can accommodate originality and change, that is, freedom for individuals or for groups of readers with historically determined interests, but it must also be able to recognize an external challenge. If the model cannot specify these limits, then it is either claiming a permanence inconsistent with our knowledge of the history of interpretation or aspiring to a level of generalization so great as to make it uninteresting as a literary theory. Certainly the value of the model would be less if it were so generalized that it could not distinguish variety within its principles from a challenge to those principles. If nothing could be excluded we would be in Fish's position, claiming that all readers are in one community.

We therefore have to put the preference model to a test as a method of describing competing interpretations produced by it. The theoretical inadequacies of the purely conventionalist or intentionalist models motivate the preference model, but the test of the model must be whether it can in fact describe a reading by any reader. For this test, we will examine a series of reviews of Ernest Hemingway's *For Whom the Bell Tolls*, focusing on Lionel Trilling's essay in the *Partisan Review* and making comparisons with other contemporary reviews, all published within a few months of the appearance of the novel in 1940, and all written by members of a single (though, as will emerge, not totally unified) critical community, centered in New York City and made up of mainly academics and journalists. Although the community shared well-formedness conditions, the novel's political reference became the catalyst by means of which different conditions of significance and different weightings produced a variety of interpretations.

For Whom the Bell Tolls was immediately acclaimed a success. Most reviewers, according to Robert O. Stephens's "Introduction" to a collection of reviews (1977), felt that it was the fulfillment of Hemingway's long-delayed "promise." It was described as being one of the major American works of fiction of the century. It was certainly the most important American book about the Spanish civil war (p. xxiii). But, as Stephens says (p. xxiv), not all critics concurred in the judgments: "As reviews accumulated it became apparent that there were areas of disagreement . . . [some thought] the novel focussed too little on Robert Jordan in its attempt to encompass the wider war and, as a result, Jordan became a puppet who merely spoke Hemingway's undramatized ideas"; also (p. xxv), "a significant issue developed over the question of whether the love story was integral or extraneous to the whole action."

In general, critics who liked the novel attempted to describe a coherent pattern, and those who disliked it justified their views by saying that it was seriously flawed because it did not have a coherent pattern. Lionel Trilling (*Partisan Review*, Jan.–Feb. 1941), although generally praising what he called a new maturity in Hemingway's style, complained that the prose of the love scenes was strained: "obtrusively 'literary' and oddly 'feminine' . . . used for the emotions of love [it is] false and fancy." Howard Mumford Jones (*Saturday Review of Literature*, Oct. 26, 1940), thought the language particularly appropriate for a love story, but he found the characterization of the heroine flat: "She is tenderly presented . . . and the lovemaking is beautiful and frank. But . . . Maria is little more than pathetic." Jones pointed out that the weak characterization was

even more disappointing in contrast to the rich pattern of characterization that joins Pilar (the female protagonist) to the other characters. Trilling, along with Hemingway and many of his admirers,
liked Maria's "essential innocence and responsive passion."

Jones's remarks indicate that some readers were able to rational-
ize the change in diction by recognizing a partial match between the
language patterns in the love scenes and those in the other scenes:
the language between Jordan and Maria was appropriate to night
and love, and the language in other parts of the text was appropriate to day and politics. This partial match satisfies a typicality condition (GTC 1) describing a term in the Structural Description of a
transformation: A unit of a text counts as a term in a Structural Description when there is a partial match between that unit and another part of the text. On the basis of these partial matches, several
transformations are applied that produce a conventional literary
pattern in which changes in diction correspond to changes in thematic content and mood. By making inferences from this conventional pattern of opposition between day and night, rationality and
love, the reader understands diction as mirroring the emotional situation—as an imitation of the change from ordinary rationality and
the sensible, matter-of-fact relationships of daytime to the passionate and irrational relationships of night and love. So understood, the
language could then be satisfactorily patterned with other idio-
syncrasies of diction, such as Hemingway's invented language for
the Spanish guerrillas, and also with other symbolic fantasy such as
Pilar's palm reading and her awareness of the "smell of death." In
this way several different kinds of details in the text could be accounted for in one complex pattern. These transformations and inferences would not create a satisfying pattern for all readers, however. The objection was made that in spite of its controlled and
patterned use in the text, such fantasy is, as reference, naïve, and
that asking readers to believe in these various kinds of magic was
asking them to ignore some fundamental inconsistencies in the
whole novel. Was there not an inconsistency in an author who
could discuss the subtleties of Spanish civil war politics with sophis-
tication but at the same time fail to recognize the complexity of relationships between men and women?

A second group of critics exhibited their competence by attempting to name a genre that could provide a pattern for all the incidents

of the plot, and then, by inferring its mode and purpose, claiming the right to apply transformations to its incidentals to derive a highly abstract level in order to argue the merits of the novel. Not all were ready to allow the novel any great merit, on the grounds (in our terms) that according to their conditions of significance they could not get a strong interpretation. Still another group derived weak interpretations, but they are of little interest here because they were unconcerned about the inconsistencies in language or characterization or the uncertain balance of the political and romantic aspects of the novel.[3] We leave them out of consideration because they cannot be said to have used the model fully.

All the critics who derived stronger interpretations noticed at least one of these inconsistencies. Edmund Wilson (*New Republic*, Oct. 28, 1940) notes that Hemingway "poured in a certain amount of conventional romance. . . . A love story headed straight for Hollywood. . . . The whole thing has the too-perfect felicity of a youthful erotic dream." Wilson nevertheless considers the novel a success because others of his criteria for "best" are met:

There is in *For Whom the Bell Tolls* an imagination for social and political phenomena such as he has hardly given evidence of before. . . . There is here a conception of the Spanish character, very firm and based on close observation, underlying the various social types; and in approaching the role of the Communists in Spain, Hemingway's judgments are not made to fit into the categories of a political line . . . but seem to represent definite personal impressions.

Wilson was one of a number of critics who, in various ways, appreciated the balanced presentation of the political situation and also attempted to account for the inconsistencies. He is able to find value in the novel in spite of its overall lack of stylistic coherence because his conditions of significance weight the balanced presentation of a fictionalized social and political situation as highly, presumably, as they would weight what he would consider an honest journalistic account of the war. His interpretation is stronger than those that ignore the inconsistencies, although it is inevitably weakened by his failure to apply transformations and inferences that would allow more inclusive patterning.

[3] For example, J. Donald Adams in the *New York Times Book Review* and Dorothy Parker in *PM*.

John Chamberlain (*New York Herald Tribune Books*, Oct. 20, 1940) uses the familiar strategy of calling a text sui generis as a way of accounting for the presence of the unintegrated patterns of the love story and the gypsy magic. He finds a genre categorization that would include these features as well as the more realistic plot events:

The idyll remains the same [as in *A Farewell to Arms*], but there is more than just a love story here. On one level it is a thriller which yields nothing to Malraux's *Man's Fate*—for that matter, to Nick Carter or *The Perils of Pauline*. It moves along from high spot to high spot with tumultuous abandon. . . . On another level *For Whom the Bell Tolls* is a political novel. . . . And on still another level the novel is a paean to the landscape and spirit of Spain. . . . Finally, the novel has a faint touch of a very terrible satire: Hemingway seems to be hinting that all noble causes must end in the triumph of the bureaucrat.

It is a novel, in other words, "that has something for every one," and Chamberlain tries to save the text from accusations that it is flawed in any one place by declaring it too powerful to be confined by the bounds of unity. He calls it a "superb series of annotations on how a great variety of men go to meet their Maker." Seeking a pattern to fit the text, he reads according to the well-formedness condition for patterning that says that the units or patterns must form either a pattern of dominance and subordination or a pattern of symmetry. In order to form the pattern of symmetry, he must extract units of the text and apply transformations so that each seems in some way equivalent to the others (the "superb series of annotations"). Each of the symmetrical units satisfies a condition of a genre, and the combination of different genres makes up a pattern from which the genre name is taken—"political novel," "thriller," etc. These labels satisfy the Structural Description for a transformation that combines the new labels (the embedded subtexts) into a symmetrical pattern. A pattern of subordination is thus formed in which a head is created for a set of symmetrical units ("how to meet one's maker"). The interpretation therefore amounts to a hierarchical combination of patterns in which each retains its own generic conditions. By combining a dominance pattern and a symmetrical pattern Chamberlain produces a stronger interpretation than Wilson's, which recognizes the love story as a relevant unit but is unable to pattern it.

Mark Shorer (*Kenyon Review*, Winter 1941) tries to arrive at a strong interpretation by finding a genre for the novel that has a pattern of dominant realism with subordinated elements of myth and fantasy, exemplified but not exhausted by the love story. He decides that *For Whom the Bell Tolls* is a "partisan novel": "The defects of characterization are the conventional defects of partisan novels, in which personalities always threaten to vanish in abstractions." If, as Shorer claims, one or more other characters besides the two lovers can also be seen as abstractions, then the lack of realism in the novel can be interpreted as a sustained pattern of mythic characterization—a heavily weighted typicality condition that determines a genre rather than an unassimilable feature. Instead of the structural genre determination "novel," which was for many readers a sufficient genre categorization, Shorer supplies a functional genre categorization to account for seeming inconsistencies. This may answer Shorer's demand, and Shorer expresses respect for the novel, but it is nonetheless a weak interpretation. The genre itself weakens the interpretation because of its own typicality condition that the novel's significance is ephemeral. Though Shorer says that the flexibility of Hemingway's new style gives a "bigger writer" and a story with "moral greatness," his interpretation, even if coherent, is undercut by the limitations of the genre he chooses.

Another path followed by some of the novel's first readers in the search for a stronger interpretation was to deny that *For Whom the Bell Tolls* is primarily a realistic novel. In effect, they showed that the partial match between the nonmimetic, impressionistic parts of a novel and the realistic parts directs a series of transformations and inferences which can result in an interpretation of more generalized significance. Since the application of transformations is structurally unconstrained, the only limits to what may be claimed are the critic's conditions of significance. Clifton Fadiman (*New Yorker*, Oct. 26, 1940) claims that the book demands this kind of reading: "It touches a deeper level than any sounded in the author's other books. . . . It is [more than] a thrilling novel about love and death and battle. . . . There is in this book a certain process of etherealization . . . the small boy Spartanism and the parade of masculinity which weakened the earlier books are transformed into something . . . spiritual."

Malcolm Cowley (*New Republic*, Jan. 20, 1941) also applies

transformations to the details of Hemingway's story according to the conditions of significance that he presumes he shares with Hemingway:

In addition to being a fine novel, *For Whom the Bell Tolls* is also an interesting and very complicated political and moral document. . . . He is trying here not only to write the best novel, but also to state and justify an attitude toward the Spanish revolution, and toward the whole set of beliefs that dominated the 1930's besides implying an attitude toward what has happened since his story ended. It is an ambitious undertaking, but then Hemingway has written a very long book, and everything is there if you look for it.

Howard Mumford Jones, despite his disappointment with the flatness of Maria, was able to generalize about the higher implications of the novel. His claims were perhaps the grandest of any of the contemporary critics:

For Whom the Bell Tolls is one of the finest and richest novels of the last decade. . . . Hemingway disappears, and in his place is the sorrowful majesty of a cause in which he believed and which did not triumph, at least superficially. But it is only superficially that this lost cause is to be identified with the Spanish Republic. More deeply, the cause is *not* lost, because (and I am not trying to be magniloquent), it is the cause of Humanity itself— that vague and splendid cause in which the nineteenth century liberal believed with a faith that we have almost lost, and which inspired some of the best pages of Victor Hugo and Charles Dickens and Dostoievski and Tolstoy. [*Saturday Review of Literature*, Oct. 26, 1940]

Questions about the verisimilitude of the love scenes pale before such claims, as indeed is the intention of their makers. The mysticism of the love affair in conjunction with the mysticism implied by the reference to John Donne in the title is read not as a flaw in an otherwise successful realistic war novel but as the partial match that triggers transformations the reader applies in order to generate interpretation on a much wider scale. These lofty interpretations proceed from conditions of significance that weight the inferred generalizations more heavily than they weight detailed textual examination. If the more generalized patterns can subsume the details of language patterning the interpretation has a good chance of being considered a strong one, even if it does not explicitly address those issues. Whether it will be considered both coherent and satisfying depends on the prevailing conditions of significance. We will see, for example, that the highly generalized patterns proposed for *For Whom the Bell Tolls* did not satisfy all readers.

Lionel Trilling was one of those who refused to infer coherence. In a studiously academic essay (*Partisan Review*, Jan.–Feb. 1941), he claims that the inconsistencies are the source of a tension which itself is not sufficiently satisfying to balance the dissatisfaction generated by those inconsistencies. He cannot agree that the book is serious enough to attain the most general significance:

The power and charm [of *For Whom the Bell Tolls*] do not arise from the plan of the book as a whole; when the reading is behind us what we remember is a series of brilliant scenes and a sense of having been almost constantly excited, but we do not remember a general significance. Yet Hemingway, we may be sure, intended that the star-crossed love and heroic death of Robert Jordan should be a real tragedy, a moral and political tragedy which should suggest and embody the tragedy of the Spanish war. In this intention he quite fails; he gives us astonishing melodrama, which is something, but he does not give us tragedy.

Trilling attributes Hemingway's failure to his hero's inability to transcend his own individual experience: not only does Robert Jordan not understand the full political significance of his death, he actually rejects that understanding; and Hemingway, by implication, also rejects the understanding of the death he invents, even though, as Trilling admits, he seems to understand the political issues thoroughly. Because Hemingway insists on portraying "naked experience," Jordan's death is "devastatingly meaningless." Trilling makes the point that since the political and social insights that would form the basis of a tragedy are in the concluding pages of the book almost entirely outside the hero's consciousness, they cannot be interpreted as part of Jordan's experience. If they had been kept in focus, Trilling says, "we should have had a personal tragedy which would have truly represented the whole tragedy of the Spanish war—the tragedy, that is, which was not merely a defeat by superior force but also a moral and political failure; for tragedy is not a matter of fact, it is a matter of value."

The title, which for other readers was sufficient evidence that Hemingway had indeed made a statement about all of humanity, is to Trilling only evidence that he intended to do so. Trilling wants more than only expressed intention; he here displays a more heavily weighted literary rule that gives significance to particular kinds of narrative ordering. For Trilling, Hemingway's portrayal of Jordan's preoccupation with himself and the issue of personal bravery in his last moments is an "implied rejection of the rest of humanity," which in effect negates the meaning deliberately implied by the epigraph from Donne's XVIIth Meditation. Important moral lessons might have been inferred from Jordan's experience, Trilling says, but "by some failure of mind or of seriousness, [Hemingway] cannot permit these political facts to become integral with the book by entering importantly into the mind of the hero." Trilling is reacting, not to the absolute absence of the author's expressed intentions—which to him are not absent—but to their absence in a place where he expects them to be, namely in the concluding scenes of the narrative. In sum, Trilling cannot find a unified interpretation. He claims one must infer "the rejection of the rest of humanity" from Hemingway's failure to encourage all the necessary inferences: he fails to find partial matches that trigger the transformations, so the individual personal experience of Jordan remains for him particular rather than generalized as Hemingway intended it to be.

As for the implications of the style, Trilling believes that the stark realism characterized by Philip Rahv (1940) as "the cult of experience" is too sentimentally ego-centered to allow a reader to draw universal inferences from it. The issue here is the by now familiar question of the necessary relationships between language structures and their implications. Rahv apparently insists on a necessary connection between this particular kind of American realism and the implications he reads into it and Trilling assents to this necessity, but it has not yet been demonstrated that such necessary connections exist. While it certainly can be argued that it is difficult to find universal implications in a text of the "cult of experience" that has as a necessary condition a hero who is sentimentally ego-centered, one cannot absolutely exclude the possibility of such implications. If the context—in this case the rest of Hemingway's novels and Hemingway's publicly expressed sympathy with the Spanish republicans—provides enough evidence to suggest inferences toward universality, the inferences about egocentricity can be muted, although they will not disappear and will still exist along with the universal inferences.

The question therefore becomes whether or not the weight of the evidence in *For Whom the Bell Tolls* is sufficient to draw universal inferences. Trilling argues that the lack of focus on the Spanish civil war in the final pages of the book leaves the reader without any explicit encouragement to find patterns that allow for inferences of the universal implications the title invites. He believes that the only implications that can be drawn from it "glorify the isolation of the individual ego." Yet many experienced readers clearly make the inferences Trilling would deny, presumably weighting only lightly the literary rule that patterns narrative ordering and thematic significance. These inferences, furthermore, override for many readers the implications from the necessary conditions of a style centered on realistic experience in favor of the other evidence. The limits Trilling places on transformations and inference are not inherent in the process but are imposed by his conditions of significance and genre expectations.

Trilling's critique of Hemingway provides an example of the interactions of the conditions of significance and their weightings. The "academic's academic," Trilling seems to have been particularly anxious to demonstrate how lightly he valued the narcissistic element in Hemingway's public personality. He seems to have used his ability to manipulate formalist rules as a weapon against the claims of the "cult of experience": he weighted heavily the condition of significance describing the congruence between language structures and propositional content, thereby limiting the inferences he was prepared to draw from Hemingway's style. At the same time, despite his hostility to what he apparently considered a pose, he felt he had to respect the author's intention that the life and death of Robert Jordan symbolize the tragedy of Spain. The interpretation rejected by Trilling was required to satisfy this second heavily weighted condition of significance, which respects authorial intention, creating a conflict. Trilling judged the tension to be dissatisfying and thereby to weaken the novel.

Trilling may be right in his judgment that the conflict weakens the book; but in any case, his refusal to draw the intended inferences would seem to suggest that he weights congruence of language structures and propositional content more heavily than he weights authorial intention. It also could be the case that he weights *this* author's intention lightly, because, like Rahv, he does not consider the cult of experience to be of any positive social or literary value. Trilling clearly feels that the conflict between the style and his interpretation of it compromises the value of the book; if these same conditions of significance were weighted differently, the interpretation would be stronger. If the condition of significance that values the presence of such tension were still heavily weighted, but an author's intentions were very lightly weighted, the tension in *For Whom the Bell Tolls* between its ostensible claims and its failure to fulfill them would be a source of value.

The disagreements about the value or weight of partial matches between social upheaval and fiction are seen especially clearly in Alvah Bessie's review (*New Masses*, Nov. 1940). Bessie, like Trilling, denies that *For Whom the Bell Tolls* achieves high seriousness: "Depth of understanding there is none; breadth of conception is heartbreakingly lacking; there is no searching, no probing, no grappling with the truths of human life that is more than superficial . . . there is no tragedy here, merely pathos." Hemingway's subjects, Bessie says, fail to achieve "the stature of universality, perhaps because Hemingway cannot see them in perspective, cannot see them more than sentimentally." Bessie's perspective was, of course, that of the radical left. His own conditions of significance, a reflection of his politics, dictated that he take issue with Hemingway's treatment of the Soviet role in the Spanish war and with his balanced presentation of barbarity and corruption on both the left and the right. Whereas Wilson and Fadiman welcomed the balance, Bessie took it as a sign of muddleheadedness.

Bessie's political position also influenced his expectations of the genre in that his ideas about Hemingway, reinforced by the book's title and subject matter, led him to expect a proletarian novel. Such a political novel would be written from the point of view of the Spanish republicans, and so, in accordance with one of its necessary conditions of significance, would assert the value of the proletariat and its struggle, and portray or predict the ultimate victory of the Left. Unlike Trilling, Bessie had no doubt that realism could achieve this end if the author would "expand his personality as a novelist to embrace the truths of other people, everywhere." The book, however, did not meet the conditions of the genre he expected from Hemingway, and he judged it a bad book: "There are many references in the *Bell* to various political aspects of the struggle in Spain. And few of these references do more than *obscure* the nature of that struggle." Unlike Chamberlain and Shorer, Bessie could not readjust his political position to meet the book. Under the circumstances he makes as strong an interpretation as he can and finds the book disappointing. His heavy weighting of the condition of significance that describes the political position the text must espouse outweighs all the other conditions.

In the preference model, the well-formedness of literary interpretation and the value attributed to the text meet at this point. A strong interpretation is an indication of value because only when the particular set of conditions of significance in force can generate a strong interpretation can the text be valued. This is hardly surprising; it is a truism to say that unless the conditions of significance can provide a satisfying and coherent reading of a text, its value cannot be great. But formal specification reveals that this situation amounts to a refutation of the enforced separation of valuation and interpretation that literary formalism and structuralism in general have insisted upon. Since a book that cannot be satisfactorily read cannot be positively valued, and, conversely, a book that is positively valued has by definition been coherently interpreted, not only is there no reason why one model cannot account for both in some basic ways, but as we will see more clearly in Chapter Ten, a model of interpretation would seem to be required to do so.[4]

In view of the disagreements about the significance and value of the text, one must ask again whether the reviewers of *For Whom the Bell Tolls* can be said to belong to a single literary community. We define community as a pragmatic unit describable by necessary and typicality conditions that specify the structure of the unit (the community) and how it functions. A community functions, for example, to allow communication among its members, and to define status relationships between the members of the community and the larger critical community. The judgment about who is a member of a particular community and who is not is therefore a preference judgment and, like all preference judgments, the decision will be clearer in some cases than in others.

The necessary rules in the grammars of the members of a community include the general well-formedness and preference rules for categorization, inference, transformations, reference, and pattern-

---

[4]We are not the first to raise the issue of the place of evaluation in a theory of literature. See Smith (1979) and (1983); the latter was included in a special issue of *Critical Inquiry* dedicated to canon.

ing. An automatic consequence of necessary conditions is that members of the same community can communicate and argue. The typicality conditions of the description of a literary community include the conditions of significance. Typically, but not necessarily, members of a community share conditions of significance and their weightings. The apparent distance between Trilling and Bessie on the spectrum of competent interpretations is determined by their differently weighted conditions of significance: Bessie's political condition of significance heavily outweighs all other conditions, whereas Trilling is very interested in the structural issues Bessie seems uninterested in. It follows that the fewer the number of conditions that are shared, the more difficult communication and argument will be. Members of a community also typically share descriptions of categories, such as the conditions of genres. Descriptions, too, being made up of many conditions, can be partly shared, and agreement will be more likely between readers who share the weightings of the conditions.

Communities are usually labeled by shared typicality conditions. Any individual reader will be more or less clearly a member of a community depending on which and how many typicality conditions and their weightings are or are not shared. A reader will belong to a selection of partly overlapping communities (e.g., Trilling, an anti-Soviet liberal and an academic; Bessie, a communist and a journalist). Like genre categories, communities are fluid, easily changed by the addition, deletion, modification, and reweighting of typicality conditions, so that within one broad community a number of subcommunities are possible.

The Hemingway reviewers, although in many ways members of the same community, can be grouped into subcommunities according to their differing typicality conditions along any number of axes. In addition to the differences between the academics and the journalists, they can also be grouped according to preferred interpretive strategies. Chamberlain and Shorer attempt genre recategorization; Fadiman, Cowley, and Jones, thematic generalization; Trilling takes a primarily formalist approach. These approaches differ in their primary foci, which in turn reflect variations in weighted conditions of significance, depending on the nature of the problem. By and large, groupings are not permanent; different critical problems produce new groups.

In spite of their varying sets of differences, however, the interpretations of the community as a whole are similar in that they are all produced by the general preference rules and well-formedness rules for categorization and patterning. If more than one interpretation produced by the preference model is held at the same time, and if the conditions of significance and their weightings necessary for interpretation do not conflict, the interpretations would be called complementary interpretations. A somewhat more complex question is whether two interpretations based either on different conditions of significance or on different weightings of the same conditions can be said to be competing. Since typicality conditions are by definition non-necessary, a condition of significance, insofar as it seems to be a typicality condition, cannot stop transformations and therefore cannot exclude any other reading. Within a community, pluralism cannot, in principle, be denied: its existence is the inevitable result of the choices the system allows and is not dependent merely on high-minded toleration (see W. Booth, 1979). Competing interpretations are produced by members of the same community, by interpreters who share necessary conditions but differ in the weightings of typicality conditions. Incompatible weightings of conditions, as Chapter Nine will show, necessarily introduce conflict.

Challenging the System

Having shown how the preference model can handle competing interpretations essentially deriving from a single critical community that follows a similar pattern of evaluation, we must now put the model to a more serious challenge—one that questions the fundamental well-formedness rules for categorizations. To fulfill this second test, we will discuss Cynthia Chase's 1978 *PMLA* essay, "The Decomposition of the Elephants: Double-Reading *Daniel Deronda*." This essay is an example of an interpretation based on deconstructionist principles and therefore of the kind of interpretation that has, in recent years, presented itself as an attack on the fundamental principles described by the preference model. In our discussion of the challenge we will demonstrate why it is a strong interpretation, but not in fact an attack. We will differentiate deconstructionist theory from the practice of American deconstructionist critics and will assess separately the challenge posed by theoreticians from the challenge posed by their interpretations. The exercise demonstrates how, for deconstructionists as for the New Critics before them, practice is not totally consistent with theory, but is certainly consistent with the kind of interpretive perspectives that are described by the preference model.

Chase's elegant essay, published almost forty years after the appearance of *For Whom the Bell Tolls* and superficially so different from the reviews of the 1940's, makes an interesting comparison with the Hemingway criticism for several reasons. Unlike Hemingway's first critics, Chase is not concerned with historical parallels. Although *Daniel Deronda* would certainly lend itself to interpretation as a treatise on the feminist politics of the 1970's, Chase seems interested only in critical politics in this essay. Her particular critical politics, of the school of American deconstructionists, denies the assumption implicit in all the Hemingway essays: that narrative fiction can authoritatively refer to, that is, make truthful statements about, such things as wars and fascists. Referring to Paul de Man (1975), she argues that Eliot's text itself demonstrates the limitation of language:

Both the origin of Deronda's history (the fact of his birth) and its goal (the act of restoration [of Jewish nationhood]) are excluded from his history proper. . . . His birth is located in a past prior to the time of the novel [and] Deronda's activity in Palestine is . . . not an actuality but . . . an eventuality subsequent to the novel's time.
   To put it another way, the text brackets the decisive assertion in a story within a story and banishes the decisive performance to a fictive future beyond the story's end. This exclusion of knowledge and action from the realistic narrative proper signifies an acknowledgment of their constitutionally fictional status and with that an acknowledgment of the limited possibilities of language. It is implicitly acknowledged that "the possibility for language to perform is just as fictional as the possibility for language to assert." [p. 223]

Most important for the argument we are making here, Chase's article is a contrast to the Hemingway criticism in its claim to represent a truly new, a "radically" new, critical community on the scene of American academic criticism. The reviewers of Hemingway's book, although presumably liberal-leftist in their views on the politics of nations, did not, with some variations, consider themselves radicals in their critical methodology. Even the communist critic Bessie wanted "good" literature, by established criteria, to espouse his point of view. Despite their disagreements, they presumably all took the classical position that a new or current political situation (such as the one in which they all found themselves after the defeat of the Spanish republicans by Franco) would provide exactly the kind of situation in which great fiction had traditionally been produced and might again be. Their essays therefore assess Hemingway's success or failure in living up to inherited critical standards. The authority, in the 1940's, is clearly on the side of the critics: does Hemingway's novel make the grade by living up to its responsibility to fictionalize history and politics according to inherited standards?

In 1978 the situation of authority is somewhat different: the critic reads an old book, already approved by generations of readers, and applies a new system of interpretation. She finds, in the end, that the book satisfies: she produces a coherent reading that demonstrates what she wanted to demonstrate. Rather than vindicating the text under review, she vindicates the critical methodology. The authority, in any case, remains with the critic: the book and its author are at the mercy of the system by which she chooses to read. Since Chase's article was accepted by the journal of the American literary establishment, presumably it was not perceived as threatening. Yet it makes claims to philosophical foundations that are very threatening indeed to the interpretive principles of that literary community whose rules the preference model has described. A close examination of Chase's argument will reveal why it is acceptable while seeming to threaten, and will also shed light on the issue of challenges to the system.

Chase's argument can be evaluated in two ways. As an example of literary criticism, it can be evaluated in terms of the preference model already developed; as a representation of a theoretical position, it can be evaluated in terms of the conditions that theoretical position would require of a model that could generate it. Although at first glance Chase's interpretation seems markedly different from the earlier ones, it is in fact made in the traditional way, using the same strategy used by the Hemingway critics who, unsatisfied with the inconsistencies in other interpretations of a text, tried to find ways of repatterning to create an interpretation that would satisfy their ideas of coherence. Chase's notion of "best" interpretation requires her to define and weight the conditions of significance in accordance with a deconstructionist epistemology. Even so, she does not abandon her traditional literary competence; the well-formedness of her reading derives from her control of the well-formedness and preference rules of patterning that she uses to build her argument.

As traditionally competent critics do, Chase sets out some of the old problems of inconsistency with which earlier criticism of the novel is familiar. One of these difficulties is that by the time the story comes to the revelation of Deronda's Jewish birth, the plot has already made it inevitable; the critic's pragmatic sense of causality has been offended. But it is not offended, Chase notes, when the plot of *Oliver Twist* achieves a similar inverted revelation. This comparison of plot patterns and critical reactions suggests to her that more is involved than the implausibility or inevitability of the plot.

Chase's knowledge of the pragmatic context of the novel further allows her to notice (pp. 220–23) the social pattern that contributes to the creation of "the scandal of the referent": "For the men of Eliot's day, sexual identity and Jewish identity did have a kind of structural similarity. Each claimed, on the one hand, an irreducible physical element and, on the other, an enormous burden of cultural, spiritual, and historical significations." The "embarrassment" of Jewish identity is thus the impossibility, on the one hand, of Deronda's simply "becoming" Jewish gradually, under the spiritual tutelage of Mordecai, and the simultaneous impossibility of Deronda's having always been Jewish without knowing it—as if, as Stephen Marcus says (1976:212n.), he had "never looked down."

Chase's specific contribution is to note a problem of sequence and origin not previously noticed—in the letter from Hans Meyrick to Deronda. She quotes these sentences from the letter (p. 215):

In return for your sketch of Italian movements and your view of the world's affairs generally, I may say that here at home the most judicious opinion going as to the effects of present causes is that "time will show." As to the present causes of past effects, it is now seen that the late swindling telegrams account for the last year's cattle plague—which is a refutation of philosophy falsely so called, and justifies the compensation to the farmers.

In a footnote (p. 226) in which she describes the other notes and letters in the novel, Chase says, "In contrast with these decisive missives, the gratuitous, purposeless character of Meyrick's letter stands out sharply." Chase regards Meyrick's letter (p. 215) as "aberrant as interpretation and superfluous to the plot," and these literary and pragmatic difficulties lead her to a new interpretation: they beg for reconciliation, or, as Chase puts it, for deconstruction.

According to the typicality conditions on transformations, the process begins with any partial match; the partial matches that are most attractive to a given reader are described by that reader's conditions of significance. In her "recipe" for deconstruction, Gayatri Spivak (Derrida, 1976: lxxv) says that the starting point for a deconstructive reading is usually a small detail "that seems to harbor an unresolvable contradiction" or "to suppress its implications." Details of this kind are heavily weighted in deconstructionist readings; here it provides the partial match that serves as the basis for the application of transformations.

The partial matches significant to Chase are (1) the match between Meyrick's concern with both causality and origins and the importance of those subjects in Nietzschean epistemology; (2) the match between his ironic tone and the attack on irony which the book, when partially matched with Kierkegaard's *The Concept of Irony*, can be read as providing; and (3) the match between structurally similar parts of the text, that is, between Meyrick's letter and the other four letters in the text. (A formalist reading, prompted by different typicality conditions of significance, would consider the third of these partial matches significant, might possibly be interested in some version of the second, but less in the first.) Chase then works through a chain of references, transformations, and inferences until she has demonstrated that Meyrick's letter, generally considered the least significant of all the letters and notes (according to traditional interpretation considered by the narrator and Deronda to be nothing more than evidence of its author's superficiality), is considered the most important.

The interesting twists of argument cannot be traced in detail here; it will have to suffice to say that Chase reads the letter as the head of a pattern of deconstruction, both because of its own self-deconstructing irony and because of the seemingly unresolvable contradiction it embodies between causes that are conventionally understood to precede effects and the causes Meyrick mentions that seem to follow them. Chase thinks that the Meyrick letter stands out sharply because it is the head of a pattern of dominance, just as units that are syntactically subordinate may be semantically dominant. In other words, the letter, though semantically subordinate, becomes, through transformations, symbolically dominant, and thus (p. 215) the key to the interpretation: "It sets the reader on the traces of the rhetorical principles by which the text is constructed, principles at odds with the meanings indicated by *Deronda*'s narrator and dissimulated by the novel's narrative mode. In short, the letter functions as a deconstruction of the novel."

In a way, Chase's claim for the letter as a "deconstruction" of the novel is similar to the formalist use of the microcosmic episode as the head of a pattern of dominance. A small detail, both the deconstructionist and the New Critic claim, when examined closely, may be repatterned to have revelatory power disproportionate to its size. The well-formedness conditions for patterning describe both claims in the same way. The power of the letter after the application of transformations is not only to dominate the pattern of the letters but to dominate the pattern that is Chase's interpretation of the text as a whole.

The basis for Chase's interpretation is the symbolic significance of Meyrick's letter in combination with her version (p. 215) of "one of the main ostensible meanings of the novel," namely the triumph of (Deronda's) idealism over (Gwendolen's) irony. The letter's "parodic mode" or irony becomes the dominating symbol in the new double reading which sets the "triumph of idealism over irony" alongside the triumph of irony over idealism. By deconstructing the "ostensible meaning" of the novel, the letter achieves a "refutation" of causality: the letter (p. 217) "names what is vitally at issue: not a violation of genre conventions or of *vraisemblance* but a deconstruction of the concept of cause."

Chase's argument (p. 219) identifies the letter with its questioning of the received philosophical notions of causality as the device by which the text asks the reader to consider it as "the construction of a discourse and a history" rather than as "the reconstruction of the sequence of events in an imaginary human life." Chase then makes a further twist (p. 220): "At the moment that deconstruction claims to achieve a 'refutation' of causality or of the subject or whatever, the argument deconstructs itself in turn, ironized through the very process of making its pretension explicit."

As the letter deconstructs the pretenses of Eliot's plot to reflect a convincing sense of causality, the deconstruction itself is deconstructed by the "exemplary signifier," Deronda's circumsized penis. The "exemplary signifier" is "preposterous" by simultaneously being there and not being there: either its presence or its absence would make impossible difficulties in the text. Chase reads its presence/nonpresence as signifying the impossibility of authoritative interpretation, her own deconstruction included. In a compressed but not implausible argument, she refers to the conventional connection between the covenant of circumcision and the biblical story of the binding of Isaac in which the notions of origin and significance are linked:

> The unacknowledged mark is the circumcized phallus emblematizing the powers of constatation, performance, and reference. It is the exemplary signifier, and it commemorates a fiat allowing the possibility of signification. It is a sign that stands for a story, told to account for the origin of Jewish identity: the story, namely, of Abraham and Isaac and of Jehovah's intervention to prevent the completion of an act of autocastration. An account that would link the possibility of signification with the possibility of origin and of identity must invoke a divine power. Deus ex machina cuts short the cutting off of the race: so the mark of circumcision signifies. Divine dispensation grants genealogy, history, and signifying power. [p. 224]

Chase is now in a position to explore two more embedded partial matches, one between circumcision as signification and the "institution of signification" itself suggested by another partial match, that is, that between Eliot's epigraph to the chapter in which Meyrick's letter appears (a quotation from La Rochefoucauld), and another between references within Meyrick's letter and a distinction between art and forgery. The working out of these particular partial matches serves a double purpose. First, Chase leads her reader to this conclusion (p. 225): "*Daniel Deronda* presents as its point of departure a prior text, a rhetorical and syntactic structure, rather than the dilemmas of subjectivity. The starting point of the novel's discourse is, not the subject, but written language." Second, at the point at which the reader grows impatient with the seemingly interminable reference, and so infers the difficulty of ending the movement of deconstruction, Chase announces (p. 225) that she will "cut short the process."

The originality of Chase's interpretation lies in its neat patterning not only of all the units of the text that were previously patternable, but also of one particular one (the exemplary signifier) that could not previously be patterned and of many that had never before been valued as units at all. Chase pulls these new units into the interpretation as partial matches, more or less in two cycles. First she makes Meyrick's letter the dominant unit of a pattern that reflects ironically off the idealistic reading, and then she creates a larger pattern dominated by the "exemplary signifier," itself part of a pattern that includes the reference to the binding of Isaac. This second deconstructionist cycle, which undermines the authority of Chase's first-stage interpretation, demonstrates the deconstructionist position on the perpetual self-deconstruction of authority in general. After two cycles, the first deconstructing earlier critical readings of *Daniel Deronda* and the second deconstructing her own reading, Chase suggests the beginnings of a third cycle, but does not fully work its deconstruction through. Its presence in embryo is sufficient to make her point that there is no natural or logical end to deconstruction.

ASSESSING THE CHALLENGE

The test we set for our preference model was the challenge of Chase's nontraditional deconstructionist reading of a traditional literary text. Our comparison of Chase's essay with the model showed that, in terms of the preference model, Chase's reading is well-formed. The aspects of the reading that seem so radically different from, for example, formalist readings are accounted for by changes in typicality conditions and by reweightings of conditions of significance. Deconstructive epistemology narrows the range of interpretations considered interesting or nontrivial no more severely than any other set of conditions of significance. As has often been noted, deconstructionist interpretations tend repeatedly to arrive at the conclusion that "the starting point of the novel's discourse is, not the subject, but written language"; but this does not make deconstructionism any less satisfactory as a critical methodology than others that the preference model describes. New critical readings of literary texts, as Cleanth Brooks pointed out (1947:3), tend to demonstrate in a wide variety of texts that "the truth which the poet utters can be approached only in terms of paradox"; yet that both kinds of readings were reductive in similar ways does not mean that American deconstruction is in all ways similar to the critical methodology that preceded it and has nothing new to teach. Rather, it shows that both approaches as practiced by academic critics are self-conscious enough to watch a critical performance as it proceeds and to appreciate its process as well as its conclusion. Gilbert's obeisance to the critical cliché, his claim to have "saved"

Tennyson's *Idylls* from undervaluation, does not blind readers to the more interesting aspects of his reading. The balance between thematic and methodological interest in critical essays would seem to depend on their relative weightings in the interpretive community. This makes them clearly matters of typicality conditions, particularly the typicality conditions describing the reviewers themselves as academics—the absence of such self-consciousness was obvious in many of the Hemingway reviews, for example. What is crucial here is that these attitudes are not represented by necessary rules.

Although any one way of weighting typicality conditions of significance necessarily conflicts with other ways of weighting, and therefore cannot exist simultaneously within the same interpretive system, in principle no set of weightings is excluded. The model as an idealization of competence encompasses all possible sets. Chase has retooled some conditions of significance and introduced some new ones. Since typicality conditions are always subject to addition, deletion, and reweighting, her interpretation can certainly be said to fall within the scope of the preference model.

Even at the point where Chase's essay might have violated a necessary condition, it does not do so. That is, while an interpretation on deconstructionist principle is *necessarily* deconstructed by its supplement in an endless sequence, a supplement of meaning always remaining, Chase allows the supplement to have relevance only when and where she wants it—which is as the preference rule would have it. Throughout the two major cycles of the essay, Chase is careful to select for our attention specifically those fragments of supplemental meaning that contribute to the pattern she is building. She is never swamped by all the possibilities, although in the concluding paragraphs she allows them in, just to indicate that she knew all along that they were there. Chase's deconstruction of *Daniel Deronda* therefore seems to put some distance between itself and deconstructionist theory.[1] Certainly it appears that a serious gap exists between the problems deconstructionist theory presents

---

[1] Gasché (1979) and Spanos (1980), e.g., also present, from a different perspective, the view that deconstructionist criticism is not the challenge to the preference model that it might be. Lentricchia (1980, ch. 5) argues the continuity of New Criticism and American deconstructionism.

for making categorization judgments and deconstructionist literary critical methodology itself: deconstructionist theory would seem to be committed to a set of necessary conditions for categorization different from the one that Chase depends on.

Derrida's supplementarity of meaning presents a problem for him in that it confounds the boundaries of categories: no unit, no semantic unit, for example, can be "purely" that unit—it always implies, among other things, its opposite. Impurity always threatens. Derrida maintains in his article "The Law of Genre" (1980) that no unit can be absolutely categorized because any mark of a unit will itself be outside that unit:

> I submit for your consideration the following hypothesis: a text cannot belong to no genre, it cannot be without or less a genre. Every text participates in one or several genres, there is no genreless text; there is always a genre and genres, yet such participation never amounts to belonging. And not because of an abundant overflowing or a free, anarchic, and unclassifiable productivity, but because of the *trait* of participation itself, because of the effect of the code and of the generic mark. Making genre its mark, a text demarcates itself. If remarks of belonging belong without belonging, participate without belonging, then genre-designations cannot be simply part of the corpus. [p. 65]

The logic of this argument prevents Derrida from explaining the situation that he acknowledges obtains: people do make categorization decisions, even though the units they categorize are impure or fuzzy. They do seem to be able to avail themselves of contextual clues that permit them to distinguish fuzzy units from their supplements. Presumably it is Derrida's desire to refrain from exclusionary categorization that makes his own literary essays so flooded with supplement as to be almost unreadable.

Derrida thus regards the gradient typicality condition concerning the existence and significance of traces as a discrete necessary condition. His concept of unit determination would therefore have to be described by the modification and promotion of a gradient typicality condition in the preference model to a discrete necessary (well-formedness) condition. Thus what in the preference model would be

> GTC: A category (e.g., a unit of a text) includes a supplement of meaning that in a given context is more or less equal in importance to the unit itself and to all other traces of the unit.

becomes

WFC: *A category includes a supplement of meaning that is absolutely equal in importance to the unit itself and to all other traces of the unit.*

In the preference model, the gradient typicality condition recognizes that a trace is weaker or stronger depending on its context both in relation to the unit of the text of which it is a condition, and in relation to other traces.[2] The noncancelability of the stages of metaphoric transformations in many (but not all) genres is an example of the continued strong presence of traces or supplements even when they have been, as it were, replaced, and their presence would, on a binary model, be "illogical." Phonological absences, or echoes, which would have no place in the interpretation of nonliterary texts, have a place in the preference model, their strength or weakness being determined by the conditions of the genres. The differential weighting of implicatures and assertions (the former can, in the pragmatic system, even be canceled) is another example of one of the ways the preference model handles supplementarity on a gradient.

In principle, the preference model can accept a change from gradience to discreteness. In the example above, however, the change insists on a simultaneous change from typical to necessary. It is necessary rather than typical *as a consequence* of being discrete, since discreteness leaves no way of differentiating the relevance of the details and patterns that are discussed from those that are not.[3] The nature of this particular condition on unit determination is such that the result of a change from gradience to discreteness is that all supplements are now required in the system, and therefore the rule has become a necessary rule in the system. This happens because in the case of this particular condition gradience is the only feature that allows the exclusion of some traces from categorization and therefore from patterning and meaning. Without a principle of gradience there is no way of explaining how it is that readers who do admit all kinds of traces when and where they want them, also manage to exclude traces brought in on the coattails, as it were, of a unit which itself has been brought in on a typicality condition. Derrida's

[2] Prince (1980) demonstrates some of the dimensions of the gradient.
[3] Abrams (1979) calls this Derrida's absolutism. See also Altieri (1977).

version of this particular condition, while necessary to deconstructionist philosophy, creates an impossible interpretive system: it is impossible to satisfy because the condition itself precludes the possibility of categorization. But categorization continues to be necessary.

Since relevant units must be determined somehow for any pattern including a deconstruction to emerge, and since deconstructionist philosophy cannot give a rationale for the discovery of any units even while recognizing their necessity, the blanket permission for bricolage may be invoked (Derrida, 1972). Chase thus falls back on the principles of categorization and patterning described by the preference model. Preference rules, of course, describe the categorization of impure units, and as Wittgenstein and Jackendoff recognized, most categorization is of impure units. The preference model provides an account of how it is that people in fact categorize, in spite of the difficulties to which Derrida alludes. In addition, the preference model has the capacity to account both for a derivation such as Trilling's, which is restricted and determinate, and for Chase's derivations, which are, in potential, infinitely cyclical, open-ended.

Chase can develop an interpretation that satisfies deconstructionist conditions for best pattern, if not best categorization, this latter being a theoretical impossibility. Like Trilling, Chase depends on the gradient typicality condition on traces, which allows her to decide which traces to admit as relevant and which to ignore. But as a consequence of her sympathy with the absolutist philosophical position, she grants heavy weighting to a new typicality condition of significance, a condition that gives equal value to presence and to absence, that is, to the units and the meanings that are included by exclusion; this means that she devalues the conditions of significance that involve the notion of closure. These consequences make her essay look very different from Trilling's. Examples of conditions whose satisfaction, in principle, invites closure are the typicality conditions of significance that Trilling weights so heavily: "partial matches between language structures and propositional content is significant," and "partial matches between patterning and the author's expressed or implied intentions is significant." Having valued these conditions of significance so heavily, Trilling is left with no alternative but to conclude that Hemingway's performance is flawed, and so the interpretive process comes to an end. In Bessie's review, the interpretive process ends essentially at the point when references, transformations, and inferences have created a pattern that represents his political position. Bessie's preferred closure results from weighting one typicality condition of significance so heavily: "partial matches between patterning and a favored political position is significant."

Chase, on the other hand, implicitly claims to weight more heavily the conditions of significance that pursue references without the limitation that would be the consequence of discounting some of them—for example, references the author probably did not intend or references that produce patterns contradictory to other patterns in the text. Such a weighting does not limit inferences in the way Trilling's does. While there seems to be one kind of pattern favored by deconstructionist reading, the pattern of symmetrical opposition—the reversal and its supplement—the inferences that can be drawn from that pattern are unlimited. Chase (p. 216) makes extraordinarily large claims for the implications of her patterns: "[The letter] offers a deconstruction of the narrator's story and, by implication, of story in general—both of history, with its system of assumptions about teleological and representational structures, and of discourse, with its intrinsic need to constitute meaning through sequence and reference." (Howard Mumford Jones, while "not trying to be magniloquent," made similarly grand claims for *For Whom the Bell Tolls*.)

Chase here uses inference in a familiar way. She categorizes and patterns according to the rules of the preference model, and she weights supplements of meaning according to the gradient typicality condition on unit determination that assigns relative significance to traces, even though they are allowed, in the end, to imply the arbitrariness of closure. In deconstructionist literary criticism, the reweighting of some familiar conditions of significance conspires with a new condition (a typicality condition that gives equal significance to the presence and absence of traces) to delay, though not prevent, closure. Thus, while Chase's deconstructionist vocabulary and the implications she draws from her interpretive patterns suggest her sympathy with a radical revision in the preference model, her interpretation of *Daniel Deronda* does not actually require such fundamental revision for its own description. It requires only the additions and reweightings that the system permits, namely, additions and reweighting of typicality conditions.[4]

We conclude, then, that while the (impossible) interpretation entailed by deconstructionist philosophy would be excluded from the preference model, Chase's readings, and Derrida's as well, can be accommodated. Derrida certainly makes choices—that is, prefers to attend to one rather than another partial match—and it is unlikely that his choices are entirely unmotivated.

The hypothesis that there can never be a true deconstructionist interpretation is hardly surprising since deconstructionist philosophy is self-consciously a critique and not a methodology (see Rorty, 1978; Johnson, 1980). The critique of interpretation that deconstruction offers does, however, prevent those who accept its premises from proceeding with the old critical methods. In that respect it has led to a critical practice that, if not consistent with the deconstructive critique, at least demonstrates its sympathy with it by adding, as we have shown, new typicality conditions and by reweighting conditions of significance. We can therefore say that while deconstructionist philosophy has significant consequences for literary critical interpretations, producing readings that are very different from the kinds of readings the literary establishment had been accustomed to, the readings themselves are accounted for by the preference model, that is, they do not represent an entirely new kind of interpretation. Deconstructionist literary interpretations that approach the revised preference model implied in Chase's essay (as Derrida's reading of Blanchot, 1980, for example, does) are readable within the preference model.

The challenge of deconstructionist philosophy has already had a noticeable influence on the model's use within the academic literary community. If nothing else, it has made critics in many subcommunities conscious of some of their assumptions and of the power of their interpretive model. Since the definition of the model allows for its own revision, the model is patchable: necessary conditions in a

---

[4]The reanalysis of a condition from typical to necessary because of a change in the typicality condition has analogies in linguistic change. An example from word-formation rules would be the reanalysis of the suffix "nik" from "foreign (and therefore nonproductive)" to "English (and therefore productive)." Words such as "nudnik" and "sputnik" lost their feature "foreign" in a younger generation of speakers, that is, a different community of speakers, allowing the formation of new English words by suffixing "nik," e.g., "beatnik" and "refusenik."

challenging paradigm can be reinterpreted as typicality conditions. It is precisely because of this power of the preference model to absorb change through typicality conditions that we assume deconstructionist theory cannot have much more impact on the model than it already has had, though that impact will continue to be disseminated throughout the literary community.

THE SPECTRA OF INTERPRETATION

Turning once again to our earlier questions about the power of the model and about communities, we see that rather than having clarified the issue we have introduced an interesting new complication. If American poststructuralist criticism turns out not to be a radically different kind of criticism from earlier pre–poststructuralist criticism, then perhaps the model *is* too powerful: that is, right, but so overgeneralized as to fail to distinguish between clearly distinguishable types of interpretation. Earlier, we accused Fish of evading this very issue. If we find Trilling and Chase to be interpreting under the same rules, as Fish found himself and Abrams to be, can we say that we have made an advance? What claims can we make for the preference model as a tool for distinguishing either major interpretive paradigms or, more simply, schools of interpretation?

We will defend our model by making two claims. The first claim is that since the preference model allows description and discussion of differences between interpreters in terms of weighted typicality conditions, it allows us to be specific about the differences and similarities between Chase and Trilling. Since every text is in some way different from other texts, at one level of abstraction at least, every text is sui generis; by the same logic, every interpreter is his or her own community. At another level, however, because all interpreters share a set of necessary conditions that are universal, it is also correct to say, with Fish, that academic readers are all one community. We distinguish interpretive communities along a spectrum. The decisions about boundaries, being preference decisions, will be made to suit the context of the moment, and they will be distinctions that are not absolute but are only relatively stronger or weaker. The differentiation of systems of interpretation according to their typicality conditions is a rhetorical exercise: its goal is the recovery of the presuppositions of discourse. As long as differences in interpretive method can be accounted for as differences of typicality conditions, the preference model would not exclude any system of interpretation.

Our second claim is the claim that, indeed, the model can be attacked, cannot co-opt any challenge to its description by the claim that any variation can be accommodated. A change in a necessary condition (as opposed to a typicality condition) is a challenge to the preference model. The model cannot accommodate conflicting necessary conditions. To suggest a change in a necessary condition is, by definition, to challenge the model, because necessary conditions are meant to be just that—necessary. This is a truth *by definition*, but it is not an arbitrary definition. Necessary conditions correctly described, like Kantian categories or Chomskyan universals, have a psychological reality. They are subject to what Jackendoff (1983*a*) calls the cognitive constraint: the necessary conditions of the model must be described so that they are in harmony with what is known about the biological equipment that is the human genetic inheritance. The necessary conditions and their limits are coextensive with the possibilities of human minds. The necessary conditions of an interpretive system play a role comparable to the role of language universals in syntax. They are one of the points of interface between biology and culture and individual experience.[5] At the level of the necessary conditions, then, there is no other paradigm that can be distinguished from the one all people work with. The question is simply whether it has or has not been correctly described.

We have emphasized the point that, although these necessary conditions will not account for vast amounts of what happens when readers read, they do account for a crucial part of it. What they do not account for is described by typicality conditions—conditions that vary according to context. It is not highly controversial to argue that universals of interpretation must exist (see, e.g., Chomsky, 1965; Jackendoff, 1983*a*) but identifying and describing them is another matter.[6] Describing the biological, or more exactly, the neuro-

[5] See Jackendoff (1983*a*: ch. 1 and p. 56) for the argument that the total set of ontological categories (e.g., thing, place, action, direction, event) is necessarily universal.

[6] Like the search for universals, the search for the necessary conditions of interpretation can proceed in two ways. One way would be to collect and study many seemingly different systems of interpretation and look for similarities. Such a "theory of substantive universals claims that items of a particular kind in any language must

physiological parameters of understanding is an empirical enterprise of enormous difficulty and ultimately a study for psycholinguistics and neurology.

The distinction in the preference model between necessary and typicality conditions, however, allows us to specify how Derrida's epistemology challenges the interpretive model that has been assumed for the last few centuries and that the preference model attempts to describe. Derrida's idea of reading, as we have seen, is in principle described by a *necessary* condition about meaning different from the one the preference model has described. His position thus represents a claim that the fundamental processes of human cognition, the necessary conditions of categorization, have been misunderstood and that the border between nature and culture must be redrawn. Although Derrida makes no such explicit empirical claim, his speculation would seem to have been influenced by, among other things, Freud's demonstration of the availability of meaning that had been considered unavailable, and indeed the evidence from psychoanalysis would have to be taken into account, as would the evidence that people process meanings differently, and that the same people process differently at different times. The physiology of storage and retrieval would seem to be highly relevant. These topics are mentioned simply to suggest some of the dimensions of the empirical problem that would have to be investi-

---

be drawn from a fixed class of items" (Chomsky, 1965 : 28). Although this approach has had some success, especially in phonology with its theory of distinctive features, it has two interconnected major weaknesses. (1) The choice of methodology would ensure that one could never have any confidence in current hypotheses. They are in principle not verifiable, as the very basis of the method is the search for counter-evidence, since one can never know whether it will eventually show up. There is no system that might be indirectly substantiated. (2) Even if the counter-evidence did show up, without some system from which it would have to follow, it probably would not be recognized as such but simply reinterpreted to fit the extant framework.

The second approach would be to seek more abstract universals—Chomsky's formal rather than substantive universals (Chomsky, 1955 : 129)—to understand the concept of universals as the set of constraints on the form of a possible human interpretive system. As the parameters of a general language theory, universal grammar would thus focus "on principles that hold of rules and representations of various sorts" (Chomsky, 1982 : 6). This approach still requires attention to rules and is also not directly verifiable, but, as Keenan notes (1978 : 89), it provides a logical basis "for extrapolating from known languages to the full class of possible human languages" and so can be indirectly substantiated. Chomsky (n.d.) now supports this approach over the procedure described here first. It has allowed a refocusing and advancement in his own work.

gated before it could be decided how the necessary conditions of understanding should be written. If it could be demonstrated that units of meaning are not genetically distinguished or weighted, that traces or supplements are freely recategorizable and absolutely available until they are contextually valorized, then the necessary conditions of the model would have to be revised. Current work suggests that Derrida's work is seriously oversimplified (see Fodor, 1983; Jackendoff, 1983*b*; Chomsky, n.d.), but the challenge Derrida presents to include the unconscious and the absent as present is a powerful and important one. Because it crucially involves the physiology of memory, an area that remains mysterious in spite of advances in other areas of brain science, the arguments that might support its validity have barely begun to be investigated.

Chapter Ten

Literature and Value

Our claim for the preference model has been that the model would have to be the test of its own categories and rules, that there was no set of primitives that could be justified prior to the operation of the model, not even the category "literature." Earlier chapters have implied, and here we make it explicit, that in the model, what counts as literature is described by a preference rule in the competence of an experienced reader. A set of well-formedness conditions and weighted preference conditions describes the category of literary texts. The category is, in addition, described by the description of the literary system, itself consisting of the descriptions of the individual literary genres. A judgment about whether a particular text is considered literary demonstrates, as does any judgment, the theoretically infinite contextual embedding to which judgments are subject: it is possible for an experienced reader to recognize that a given text was once considered literary, or that a text might, in another context, be considered literary. In this concluding chapter we will suggest some of the conditions of the rule of literature that our model implies and then will examine some of the conditions suggested by various contemporary critics as a way of summarizing the power of preference rules in the description of interpretive competence.

As a competence model, the preference model describes the competence to interpret literary texts. In the same way that a grammar is both the competence to manage the language system and the formal description of that system, the preference model is a description simultaneously of an internalized literary competence and of a public (shared) system of literary interpretation. Literature is identical with its interpretation: what is interpreted as literature is literature. Thus we may postulate two rules for the description of a category of literary texts. The first rule recognizes that the job is a categorization task:

GNC: *Make the best categorization possible under the circumstances.*

The second rule specifies the necessary condition:

WFC: *Literature is described by the literary system.*

Stanley Fish (1973) thought the circularity implicit in this rule was self-defeating, but Roland Barthes, writing in 1963 (Lodge, 1972:650), recognized circularity as being inherent in all interpretation: "Critical writing, like logical writing, can never be other than tautology; in the last resort, it consists in the delayed statement (but the delay, through being fully accepted, is itself significant) that 'Racine is Racine,' 'Proust is Proust.'" But if circularity is not the problem, then the level of abstraction of the claim is. A statement that whatever one has decided is literature is therefore literature leaves unexplained, for example, the diachronic question of how texts come into or leave the canon, or, in a broader sense, why the canon of literary texts changes. It is by means of detailed description of the literary genres that the preference model can go further than this first definition. Because the preference model describes a process of interpretation in which the presence of some conditions triggers further transformations, inferences, and references, it does not require that texts come to it already labeled as canonical literary works, nor does it make every language text literary.

Even though the description of the literary system remains incomplete, the preference model posits certain characteristics of the conditions of literary genres that should be specified before proceeding with our description of the literary system per se. We may begin by noting that the conditions of the various literary genres come from all three systems, that is, the autonomous, the pragmatic, and the literary. The same conditions circulate freely among genres, though any one of the conditions may be heavily weighted in one genre and lightly weighted in another. Rhyme, for example, an autonomous structural pattern, is a heavily weighted typicality condition of the structural literary genre "poem"; "story" is a pragmatic structural category that is a typicality condition of, among other things, the novel; and family structures, including, say, the patterns of socially acceptable marriages, are themselves categorized as pragmatic patterns, but act as typicality conditions of the novel. "Telephone conversation," on the other hand, is a structural pragmatic genre. Although a literary text may describe a telephone conversation, telephone conversations are not part of any typicality condition of any literary genre, and therefore they are not a typicality condition in the literary system.

Conditions that have been typical of a genre in a particular historical period remain typicality conditions of the genre as long as the works in which they are evident are familiar to readers. Even though writers in other periods have not incorporated them, may even have explicitly rejected them, their presence in the literary experience of readers makes them a part of their expectations of the genre; an author can count on readers' genre expectations in the same way that speakers always count on shared assumptions, so that either their presence or their absence can be meaningful. Furthermore, like all other typicality conditions, these dated ones can be contradicted by other expectations. The same condition may occur in the same genre in different historical periods, though it may be weighted differently. A reader of the canon of Western literature is entitled to expect Shakespearean romance to end with marriage, but expects much less certainty of marital happiness and fruition from twentieth-century romances such as *Children of a Lesser God*, even when they have many of the other typicality conditions of romance. Marriage as an ending would therefore be a heavily weighted typicality condition in the earlier periods, but a weakly weighted condition of otherwise similar twentieth-century works. It is the specification of the conditions of the genre rules that makes it possible to see how judgments can change over time, which conditions remain constant and which disappear or are reweighted.

The preference model thus accounts for the diachronic dimension of an experienced reader's competence by including historically contingent lists of typicality conditions for literary genres and also of conditions of significance. All this is no more than to say that an experienced reader can hold several conceptions of "romance," or indeed of "literature," simultaneously, each marked socio-politically or historically.

Even when typicality conditions from earlier historical periods are lightly weighted in a reader's experience, they can still be useful referents when they are revived, suggested, or parodied in works of later periods. The ambiguous ending of a book like John Fowles's *The French Lieutenant's Woman*, for example, counts on the reader's familiarity with the endings of nineteenth-century novels about marriages and fortunes. The experienced reader will recognize (among the three alternative endings Fowles provides for his story) three alternatives to the conventional happy ending. Typicality conditions, even if they no longer seem to be productive categories for writers, cease to be conditions in the experienced reader's literary system only when the works in which they were originally present drop out of the literary canon entirely. When, for example, the listener has no recognition of the classical Greek verse forms on which some of Gilbert and Sullivan's songs are based, one aspect of the parody vanishes.

It hardly needs to be said that the weighting for each condition comes from the conditions of significance in force for a reader at any particular time, simply because the literary system is inextricably intertwined with a socio-political system that defines significance and value within the pragmatic and literary systems. Still, a glance at the history of terms that have been important in conditions of significance suggests that there are in practice a remarkably small number of significant factors whose weights change in relationship to each other. These have endured in pronouncements that have, in the times of their ascendancy, claimed to assert some permanent truth. Aristotle's word "mimesis," Horace's "ut pictura poesis," Sidney's claim, following Horace, that the aim of poetry is to teach and delight, or that the poet can create a golden world, Keats's conclusion that truth is beauty, all express relative values or weights among conditions that seem in one way or another permanently a part of the social institution of Western literature. Texts have been valued because they provide aesthetic pleasure or moral or pragmatic instruction, because they make people happy, or discontented, because they help them to live in their world, or help them to escape from it. The emergence of new scales of value cannot, of course, be denied. The theories of both Freud and Marx eventually produced new criteria of value. The work of Derrida and of feminist criticism seems to be doing the same. The history of critical theory may be viewed as the history of the ways in which a relatively few moral, epistemological, and aesthetic possibilities have been weighted by readers and writers in their judgments of whether or not a text is to be valued as literature.

The presence of one or another statement about the value of literature is by definition a necessary condition of the literary genres. As gradient conditions these statements of value serve at least two purposes. They describe, for one, the distinction between a text like Shakespeare's *The Tempest* and the stories in the comic book *Career Girl Romances*, which in fact satisfy many of the same conditions. When Northrop Frye banished evaluation (1957) in an effort to make the study of literature more "scientific," he also banished the distinction between popular literature and the literature of high culture. Having a condition of value to attach where warranted allows the system to describe communities for whom oral myths or comic books teach and delight.[1]

The conditions that describe value also serve competent readers when the text they want to categorize does not fit an already labeled literary genre, or when they want to argue that a text that has been conventionally labeled nonliterary should be relabeled. The rule needed here is a rule in the pragmatic system. It is a rule that makes a decision, one might say, to call the literary system into action. Within the context of recent theoretical debate about the ontological status of literary texts, various attempts have been made to state these gradient conditions. As a group they may be seen as the conditions of a generalized rule of literature.[2] Most do not claim to present a complete description of literature, but only to make a start on listing conditions.

---

[1] We would not deny that this banishment had a salutory effect on the understanding of the universals of literature, but it necessarily concentrated on the continuities at the expense of the discontinuities.

[2] Many, but not all, of these statements are culled from a collection edited by Paul Hernadi, *What Is Literature?* (1978).

Culler, for example (1975 : 264), proposes a gradient condition: "Literature offers the best of occasions for exploring the complexities of order and meaning." Gerald Graff (1979 : 2) is committed to a different gradient typicality condition: "Literature ought to play an adversary role in society." Charles Altieri (Hernadi, ed., p. 72) suggests two gradient conditions that he calls "basic expectations": "that we should be able to sympathize with the conditions, actions, feelings, and thoughts of the principal characters and that we should be able to reflect upon the potential general significance of their actions, feelings, etc., by considering the rhetorical and structural patterns informing the text." Monroe Beardsley (Hernadi, ed., p. 165) claims that, among other things, "a literary work is something produced intentionally." Murray Krieger (Hernadi, ed., p. 179) claims "the literary work to be an illusion"—an illusion that is conscious of itself as illusion, as vision.

In an attempt to describe a condition of literary texts, Pratt (1977 : 144−45) makes a claim that resembles the distinction made earlier by the anthropological linguist Carl Voegelin (1960) between casual and noncasual utterances. She suggests the notion of a "display text" that is "detachable" from its immediate context in that it does not "relate to the concrete momentary concerns of the addressee" and is highly "tellable"—"unusual," widely appealing, "adaptable" to a variety of audiences, and subject to elaboration and exaggeration. According to Pratt, the display text that occurs in daily life when someone bursts in with "The funniest thing happened today . . ." is not functionally different from literary texts that are equally detachable, tellable, and subject to elaboration; the various conventions of public refereeing and formal presentation are what turn a particularly tellable display text into literature. A reader infers from the circumstances of its presentation that it is to be treated as such: it is more carefully presented than an oral and spontaneous display text, and it is understood to possess aesthetic qualities that make it worthy of sustained attention as a literary text.

It is not surprising that some of the conditions overlap. Beardsley and Pratt both assume that a literary text must be something that its author intended to be a literary text, and Barbara Herrnstein Smith's conditions, too, begin with this requirement. Smith (1978 : 111) says that the reader recognizes an author's intention to free the reader from the "economics of the linguistic marketplace" and to present a text that meets two specific conditions (the first overlapping with one of Pratt's conditions): (1) the text is "historically indeterminate" (p. 140), and (2) the text is in some ways "nonnatural" (p. 131), a "fictive utterance" (p. 138). (This latter perhaps overlaps with Krieger's "illusion.") Once the primary authorial intention is recognized (and honored), Smith continues, the reader's responsibility to the author can end, and is indeed licensed to do so by the author's own categorization of the text as fiction. Readers are then free to make of the material what they will, according to the needs and desires that guide their reading. Having said this, Smith shifts her thesis from social to psychological grounds that recall Aristotle's theory of catharsis: the literary work allows the reader to experience emotions that are otherwise, as Smith says, "unspeakable" and come away undamaged or even improved by the experience. Norman Holland makes a somewhat similar point. Describing literary texts (1968, 1975a, 1975b) he says that they can "gratify our wishes and defeat our fears" (Hernadi, ed., p. 213).

This overlapping and the references to Aristotle and Voegelin together suggest that these resemblances, which appear despite the different goals of their work, far from denying originality, show how critics like Pratt and Smith, for example, are right about literary texts in some fundamental ways. In other words, we suggest that all the various conditions discussed are involved in the categorization of a text as literary. When taken together as a set of conditions— with no stipulation that the set is closed to additional conditions— the insufficiency of any one of these conditions by itself does not spoil the categorization. That Graff's condition would not distinguish *The Scarlet Letter* from an editorial in the *New Republic*, that Altieri's would describe biography and Krieger's some of the prophetic books of the Bible, that Pratt's would describe a sophisticated advertisement in the *New Yorker*, and that Smith's freedom from the marketplace is the freedom granted in psychoanalytic dialogue does not disqualify any of these conditions from being conditions of literature. The preference model does not require necessary and sufficient conditions. Fighting against aphorism, that is, the single-term description, the model opens the set of conditions to all these statements, making them conditions of the individual literary genres and of the rule of literature. A strong judgment, then, about whether or not a text is literary is reached when more rather than fewer of the conditions are met. Furthermore, all the complex terms within these conditions ("illusion," "nonnatural"), are described in turn by preference rules, that is, by further sets of conditions that are embedded in the rule of literature. Each attempt at specification will in turn produce new difficult terms, and the embedding of conditions continues, in principle, indefinitely. The limit to the embedding is ultimately a pragmatic limit: as far as interest and memory will take an interpreter, the model can follow.

These conditions, variously proposed and described, and including their various ambiguities and complexities, represent claims for the value of literary texts. Literature, when one is speaking about the general category in the pragmatic system, is always Literature in the honorific sense. When Culler says that literature offers the best occasions for exploring the complexities of order and meaning, we understand him to mean that he values the complexities and the exploration of the complexities. That literature, for Holland, can defeat fears, is a measure of its value. We therefore suggest that in the pragmatic system the general rule that distinguishes literary texts from nonliterary has the following gradient necessary condition:

GNC: A literary text is a valuable text, with value being assigned by the prevailing conditions of significance.

Value, of course, can never be a condition of a structure qua structure but is a function that must be inferred from it. Inferences, as we have discussed, are dependent on the contexts in which they are made and the conventions in force in those contexts. Therefore value, like other inferences, is determined in large part by the conventions of a particular socio-political system. Insofar as a function is a meaning, there is no meaning, no interpretation without evaluation: conditions of significance cannot be suspended, and interpretation cannot proceed without them.

The same weightings of conditions do not have to apply in both the pragmatic and the literary systems. Nor does what counts as satisfying a condition have to be the same in those two systems. Closure, for example, has conventionally been valued in a literary text, as two important books of the sixties argued (Kermode, 1966; Smith, 1968), but closure is also valued in pragmatic texts. The notion of what counts as closure, however, differs in different systems. The aesthetic aspects of design and pleasure are also valued in both the pragmatic and the literary systems, although the weighting may be different. If Aristotle and Peckham (1978) are correct, the right kinds of discomfort may be highly valued in the artistic and literary experience while not normally valued pragmatically. Smith exemplifies the different weightings in her argument that a crucial value of literary texts is their "very endlessness" (1978: 144), by which she means their permanently being open to new readings. Contrast the frustration that would presumably accompany the endlessness of a communication with the telephone company about a billing error.

Personal inclinations and experiences, as opposed to communal values, also have an effect on the interpretive system insofar as they influence the conditions of significance and their weighting. The system accommodates idiosyncracies in the same way as it accommodates social conventions: by allowing addition, deletion, modification, and relative reweighting of typicality conditions of significance. All these possibilities allow readers with different experiences to make different decisions about what is literary and what is not. But because these are differences in typicality conditions, not changes in well-formedness conditions, they do not imply different literary systems. A community is made up of people who agree about what is *not* arguable: they agree on the necessary conditions (e.g., of literature) but will argue about typicality conditions. Readers who do not share necessary assumptions have no foundation for arguments about typicality conditions, among which are the conditions of significance. That is, so long as these are conditions held in common but weighted differently, the differently weighted conditions of significance can be debated.

The preference model is by definition not concerned with all the arguments that can be made about typicality conditions: people will always argue about political positions, for example, but these arguments need hardly be accounted for by a theory of literary interpretation. On the other hand, what may reasonably be argued about within the parameters of a literary discussion is the weighting of a shared condition of significance. One specifically literary argument would concern how heavily to weight the condition of significance respecting the congruence between an interpretation and a favored political position.

In spite of the theoretical arguability of typicality conditions, it seems to be the case that only certain sets of conditions of significance are in fact acceptable within a literary community at any one time (see Fish, 1980, and recent arguments about canon formation in *CrI*, vol. 10, no. 1, especially Ohmann and Smith). Again, this is not a literary matter but a matter of the power relationships within the social system. Socially sanctioned value is no less important in the evaluation of what counts as a literary text than it is in the sanctioning and evaluation of new genres. The theoretical possibilities for variation are much greater than the experienced reading public ever actually deals with at one time. As in the autonomous linguistic system, overgeneration in part of the system is balanced by rules in another part.

In describing the system of literary interpretation we have pointed out places where so much variation is allowed that interpretation has to be indeterminate. We are now in a position to summarize our claim to locate both the points of determinacy and of indeterminacy in the literary system. In the literary system, as in the two other systems, the well-formedness conditions represent points of determinacy. We have not discussed these rules in syntax or phonology, but we have claimed that the necessary conditions in the literary system ultimately derive from human capacities for making categorization judgments, applying transformations, determining references, and figuring inferences. The difficulty of deciding just which capacities are universal, however, is not to be underestimated. About all we can say is that the well-formedness conditions represent such determinacy as there is in an interpretive system, and only a small part of a satisfying and coherent interpretation can ultimately be accounted for as determinate.[3]

The preference model describes several different kinds of indeterminacy. We begin with the issue of the infinite regression of rules and conditions as it accounts for variation in the interpretive sys-

---

[3] We are not making the claim that Todorov makes (1969), and that Lentricchia (1980:116) reads as a kind of platonism, namely that grammar "coincides with the structure of the universe itself." Rather, we are suggesting that there must be some connection between how human animals act and how they are built. (This idea underlies Todorov's claim but Lentricchia seems unaware of the notion.) Lentricchia chooses to read Saussure's evidence of the arbitrariness of language as "apparently incontrovertible" but it is hardly that. Saussure (1959) points to the different ways languages divide up a conceptual field as evidence of the arbitrariness of language, but if this were the whole truth then the Whorfian hypothesis (Whorf, 1950) would be watertight and it has been shown not to be. (See Fishman, 1960, 1980, 1982, and for its relevance to interpretive theory, Spolsky, forthcoming in *NLH*.) The other evi-

tem. This kind of variation differs from Chomsky's notion of creativity, though both have a place in the preference model. Chomsky (Parret, 1974:28) assumed that "a language is infinite," by which he meant that there is, in principle, no limit (though there are practical limits) to the number of new sentences that a speaker of the language can produce and understand. This unlimited creativity derives from a necessarily finite grammar, and a finite grammar can produce an indefinite number of sentences only if it has at least one component with recursive rules.[4] Chomsky finds recursion in the syntactic component. His grammar interests us because of its potential to account for creativity. But in order to overcome the exclusionary logic inherent in the well-formedness rules of his system that necessarily restricts interpretive freedom, we have argued that preference rules must also be part of the grammar. Preference rules, themselves describable by conditions, provide infinite embedding, which not only can handle gradience but also can provide additional avenues for variation and change.

Reviewing the points in the preference model at which variation of different kinds is accounted for, we would begin with the creativity that comes from the autonomous linguistic system, that is, the generative component that Chomsky describes, with recursive rules and options in lexical insertion, in well-formed underlying trees and in application of transformations. We would note, next, that in the pragmatic and the literary systems there is no end to the possible applications of transformations. They are iterative and unordered, and the output of one can always be the input for another one. Furthermore, the inclusion in the preference model of pragmatic and literary references and inferences floods the interpretive system with new units which are then available to more rules which are themselves limited only by personal or conventional conditions of

---

dence is that My Man Friday *does* learn Robinson Crusoe's language. He learns it badly, but well enough so that Robinson Crusoe correctly understands he can trust his Man. Languages are arbitrary but they are also, with fuzzy edges, translatable one to another. The assumption that there are language universals need not be an assumption of fully grown platonic ideas such as truth and beauty, but may be, as it is in our model, the more modest assumption of shared processing machinery producing shared limitations on the possibilities for interpretation.

[4]See Radford (1981:49–53) for a standard discussion of the significance within generative grammar of recursion, the ability of a category to self-embed and thereby create infinite structures from a finite set of rules.

significance; they are not in theory subject to limitation. We have seen that deconstructionist criticism lays bare the full potential of the creative power of recursive devices in a grammar by refusing in principle to limit (for example) the number of ironic reflections an interpretation can engender.

The possibilities for recombination are made even greater, not only in the autonomous system but also in the pragmatic and literary systems, by the existence in each system of an open-ended component to which new categories can always be added. There is the open lexicon in the autonomous system and the open list of genres in the pragmatic and literary systems. Just as language depends on the existence of a lexicon that is in principle open to additions, so a system that values creativity, as does the literary system, takes advantage of the addition of new possibilities, of new genres, as the list of genres is the framework for text interpretation. In addition, transformations, inferences, and references bring new units into the interpretive purview to be patterned with already existing rules. All this richness is of course characteristic of a pragmatic competence as well as of a literary one. In the area of literary interpretation it allows the competent reader to produce and understand an unlimited number of interpretations, and to judge them as well- or ill-formed, weaker or stronger.

That new sentences can be understood by speakers of the language, or new interpretations understood by experienced readers, was attributed by Chomsky simply to knowledge of the structural system. Our recognition of the ease with which new genres can be named and our analysis of the reasons for this allow us to hypothesize that it is, rather, the double axis of the system—the functional in addition to the structural dimension—that allows this freedom. Inference works in either direction: knowing the function allows an inference about the new meaning of the structure, and familiarity with the meaning conventionally associated with a structure allows the inference of a nonconventional function for that structure. New conventions can be established almost as easily as a new word can be added to the vocabulary. Since the constraints on interpretation are pragmatic, it can only be through a formally more complex semantics than that originally described by Chomsky, a semantics with both well-formedness conditions and preference conditions, that the interactions between the infinite structures produced by the autonomous sytem and the pragmatic constraints on those structures can be specified.

The preference model is a language theory much of whose strength comes from contemporary theoretical linguistics and philosophy of language. We have learned several crucial notions from them. Speech act theory and Gricean implicature, for example, have provided us with a way of talking about function in language and about the ways indirection is institutionalized in language. The division into systems of language competence in generative grammars has taught us the value of dividing literary competence into subsystems, allowing separate examination of interacting parts. We have described the three systems by two kinds of rules, well-formedness and preference rules (the rules themselves described by four kinds of conditions), which we have adapted from the semantics of Jackendoff. Our further division of the semantic operations of categorization and patterning into their structural and functional aspects allows additional insight into the interpretive activity. For the same reason, we have insisted on the distinction between a text and the rules describing how the text can be read.

The division into systems is done at least in part for the sake of methodological convenience. Specifically, the division into these systems is an artificial one, three being the smallest number of systems that allows us to reach the level of specificity that we have.[5] Clearly, other choices could have been made. For a study of how specific literary genres are interpreted in specific social subsystems, further breakdown would be necessary. For a study of the comparative capabilities or styles of individual critics, we could explore in greater depth the embedded structures of specific textual interpretations. Presumably the varying sensitivity of interpreters is to some extent at least a variation in their ability to keep multiple levels of embedded preference judgments available to the ongoing interpretive process.

While others have argued for the inseparability of systems, this theoretical issue is still open to argument, as is, also, the practical

[5] Traugott (1973) and Iser (1979) have also suggested that tripartite models with parts similar to ours will be maximally efficient.

one of how best to study various aspects in detail. One advantage to our approach, which includes the separation of a text from the grammar of its interpretation, is that the ways in which variation between interpreters is produced can be explored.

The theoretical transparency of levels should be stressed here. In principle, the model allows not only the specification of well-formedness conditions and the preference conditions on which preference judgments are based but also the specification of the well-formedness and preference conditions of the components of the conditions on which a judgment is based, ad infinitum. Jackendoff (1983*a*) points out that the presence of a complex interpretive challenge is a condition of art. What he has to say about music is worth quoting at length:

> Much of the interest in "art" music comes from its exploitation of conflict among preference rules to increase tension and ambiguity. Characteristically, multiple interpretations at a local level are resolved by global considerations [i.e. conditions of significance], themselves often kept ambiguous by conflict among preference rules. It is these complexities that make such music in all its richness inaccessible to unsophisticated listeners. By contrast, most folk music and "popular" music is characterized by strong reinforcement of preference rules at all levels, so that the most salient structure is computable largely on the basis of local considerations and is never open to doubt. This means that increased musical sophistication may be partially attributed to increased capacity for entertaining multiple large-scale structures simultaneously, hence to a more effective ability to resolve conflicts between local and global factors. Thus music that is considered more "difficult" does in fact put greater demands on the listener's computational capacity. [pp. 138–39]

The kinds of conditions we have proposed for the preference model, in their ability to describe judgments ranging from the superficial and conventional to the complex and original, not only are methodologically serviceable but also make some claim to match the cognitive capacities of readers. They are at least a beginning step in the description of a human cognitive capacity that manifests itself as nonbinary and makes weighted judgments along gradient scales. The preference model is, not incidentally, itself a demonstration that the kind of linguistics needed for an interpretive theory must be one that can handle such gradience.

The preference model turns out to be extremely powerful in understanding a variety of troublesome issues that have seemed unrelated. It can, for example, account for metaphor without the problematic notion of deviance, as we discussed in Chapter Six. Arguments against a closed set of universal genre types also fall out from the description of the model. Clarification of the notion of an interpretive community is another consequence of the project, and the relationships among deconstructionist philosophy, current deconstructionist literary criticism, and other sections of the literary community are thereby illuminated. The preference model also provides a way of accounting for the processes of change as they operate within the literary genres, in the evaluation of texts, and in their interpretation, although issues of literary change such as the development of the canon, communal acceptance of changes in literary conventions, and the structure of literary history remain to be explored. The common denominator for the discussion of these and other issues turns out to be the preference rule with its necessary and typical, discrete and gradient conditions. Furthermore, the preference model has allowed us to specify points of freedom and creativity in the model as well as to locate the constraints on that freedom. It has allowed us to chart the interrelationships of the two, and thus, we suggest, to make a start on answering some of the questions that literary theorists have been struggling with. The work has hardly begun.

Reference Matter

References

The following list of references makes no attempt to be a comprehensive bibliography of the topic. Rather, it includes references cited in the text plus a selection of other books we have used and found particularly relevant. The following abbreviations are used in the References:

CrI	*Critical Inquiry*
MLN	*Modern Language Notes*
NLH	*New Literary History*
PhilRev	*Philosophical Review*
SCE Reports	*Society for Critical Exchange Reports*

Abrams, M. H. 1979. "How to Do Things with Texts," *Partisan Review*, 46:566–88.

Akmajian, Adrian, and Frank Heny. 1975. *An Introduction to the Principles of Transformational Syntax.* Cambridge, Mass.

Akmajian, Adrian, Susan Steele, and Thomas Wasow. 1979. "The Category AUX in Universal Grammar," *Linguistic Inquiry*, 10:1–64.

Allott, Miriam, ed. 1970. *Emily Brontë: Wuthering Heights, A Casebook.* London.

——, ed. 1974. *The Brontës: The Critical Heritage.* London.

Altieri, Charles. 1975. "The Poem as Act: A Way to Reconcile Presentational and Mimetic Theories," *Iowa Review*, 6:103–24.

——. 1976. "Wittgenstein on Consciousness and Language: A Challenge to Derridean Theory," *MLN*, 91:1397–1423.

———. 1977. "The Qualities of Action: A Theory of Middles in Literature," *Boundary 2*, 5:323–50.

———. 1978. "The Hermeneutics of Literary Indeterminacy: A Dissent from the New Orthodoxy," *NLH*, 10:71–99.

———. 1979. "Presence and Reference in a Literary Text: The Example of Williams' 'This is Just to Say,'" *CrI*, 5:489–510.

Armstrong, Nancy. 1982. "Emily Brontë In and Out of Her Time," *Genre*, 15:243–64.

Austin, J. L. 1962. *How to Do Things with Words*. Cambridge, Mass.

Bach, Emmon, and Robert T. Harms, eds. 1968. *Universals in Linguistic Theory*. New York.

Bach, Kent, and Robert M. Harnish. 1979. *Linguistic Communication and Speech Acts*. Cambridge, Mass.

Baird, James. 1968. *The Dome and the Rock*. Baltimore, Md.

Banfield, Ann. 1979. "The Nature of Evidence in a Falsifiable Literary Theory." In *The Concept of Style*, edited by Berel Lang. Philadelphia.

———. 1982. *Unspeakable Sentences*. Boston.

Bates, Elizabeth, et al. 1979. *The Emergence of Symbols: Cognition and Communication in Infancy*. New York.

Bateson, F. W. 1950. *English Poetry: A Critical Introduction*. London.

Beardsley, Monroe. 1958. *Aesthetics: Problems in the Philosophy of Criticism*. New York.

Beckett, Lucy. 1974. *Wallace Stevens*. Cambridge, Eng.

Black, Max. 1962. "Models and Archetypes." In Max Black, *Models and Metaphors*. Ithaca, N.Y.

———. 1972. "Meaning and Intention," *NLH*, 4:257–79.

Blackmur, R. P. 1932. "Examples of Wallace Stevens," *Hound and Horn*, no. 5. Reprinted in *The Achievement of Wallace Stevens*, edited by Ashley Brown and Robert S. Haller. Philadelphia, 1962.

Bleich, David. 1978. *Subjective Criticism*. Baltimore, Md.

Bloom, Harold. 1971. *The Ringers in the Tower: Studies in Romantic Tradition*. Chicago.

———. 1972. *The Anxiety of Influence: A Theory of Poetry*. New York.

———. 1975. *A Map of Misreading*. New York.

Bloomfield, Morton. 1972. "Allegory as Interpretation," *NLH*, 3:301–17.

Booth, Stephen. 1969. "On the Value of *Hamlet*." In *Reinterpretations of Elizabethan Drama*, edited by Norman Rabkin. New York.

Booth, Wayne C. 1961. *The Rhetoric of Fiction*. Chicago.

———. 1979. *Critical Understanding: The Powers and Limits of Pluralism*. Chicago.

Bové, Paul. 1976. "The Poetics of Coercion: An Interpretation of Literary Competence," *Boundary 2*, 5:263–84.

Bresnan, Joan. 1971. "Sentence Stress and Syntactic Transformations," *Language*, 47:257–81.

———. 1972. "Stress and Syntax: A Reply," *Language*, 48:326–42.

———. 1978. "A Realistic Transformational Grammar." In *Linguistic*

Theory and Psychological Reality, edited by Morris Halle et al. Cambridge, Mass.

———. 1982. *The Mental Representation of Grammatical Relations.* Cambridge, Mass.

Brodkey, Linda. n.d. "Brutal Words: Speech Acts in *A Modern Instance.*" Photocopy.

Brooke-Rose, Christine. 1976. "Historical Genres / Theoretical Genre: A Discussion of Todorov on the Fantastic," *NLH*, 8 : 145 – 58.

Brooks, Cleanth. 1947. "The Language of Paradox." In Cleanth Brooks, *The Well-Wrought Urn: Studies in the Structure of Poetry.* New York.

———. 1951. "Irony as a Principle of Structure." In *Literary Opinion in America*, edited by M. D. Zabel. 2nd ed. New York.

Brown, Robert L., Jr., and Martin Steinmann, Jr. 1978. "Native Readers of Fiction: A Speech-Act and Genre-Rule Approach to Defining Literature." In Hernadi, ed.

Brown, Roger. 1976. "Reference: In Memorial Tribute to Eric Lenneberg," *Cognition*, 4 : 125 – 53.

Butcher, S. H., trans. and ed. 1951. *Aristotle's Theory of Poetry and Fine Art.* With a critical text and translation of the *Poetics.* 4th ed. New York.

Buttel, Robert. 1967. *Wallace Stevens: The Making of the Harmonium.* Princeton, N.J.

Chase, Cynthia. 1978. "The Decomposition of the Elephants: Double-Reading *Daniel Deronda*," *PMLA*, 93 : 215 – 27.

Chomsky, Noam. 1957. *Syntactic Structures.* The Hague.

———. 1965. *Aspects of the Theory of Syntax.* Cambridge, Mass.

———. 1972a. *Studies on Semantics in Generative Grammar.* The Hague.

———. 1972b. *Language and Mind.* Enlarged ed. New York.

———. 1973. "Conditions on Transformations." In *A Festschrift for Morris Halle*, edited by S. Anderson and P. Kiparsky. New York.

———. 1975a. "Introduction." In Noam Chomsky, *The Logical Structure of Linguistic Theory.* New York.

———. 1975b. *Reflections on Language.* New York.

———. 1977a. "Conditions on Rules of Grammar." In Noam Chomsky, *Essays on Form and Interpretation.* New York.

———. 1977b. "On Wh-Movement." In Culicover, Wasow, and Akmajian, eds.

———. 1980. "On Binding," *Linguistic Inquiry*, 11 : 1 – 46.

———. 1981. *Lectures on Government and Binding.* Dordrecht, Neth.

———. 1982. *Some Concepts and Consequences of the Theory of Government and Binding.* Cambridge, Mass.

———. N.d. [1984]. "Changing Perspectives on Knowledge and Use of Language." Photocopy.

Chomsky, Noam, and Morris Halle. 1968. *The Sound Pattern of English.* New York.

Clark, Eve V., and Herbert H. Clark. 1978. "Universals, Relativity, and Language Processing." In Greenberg, ed.

Clark, H. H. and S. E. Haviland. 1977. "Comprehension and the Given-New Contract." In *Discourse, Production, and Comprehension*, edited by R. O. Freedle. Norwood, N.J.

Cole, Peter. 1981. *Radical Pragmatics*. New York.

———, ed. 1978. *Syntax and Semantics, 9: Pragmatics*. New York.

Cole, Peter, and Jerry Morgan, eds. 1975. *Syntax and Semantics, 3: Speech Acts*. New York.

Cole, Peter, and Jerrold Sadock, eds. 1977. *Syntax and Semantics, 8: Grammatical Relations*. New York.

Colman, Linda, and Paul Kay. 1981. "Prototype Semantics," *Language*, 57:26–44.

Conrad, Carol. 1974. "Context Effects in Sentence Comprehension: A Study of the Subjective Lexicon," *Memory and Cognition*, 2:130–38.

Craig, Hardin and David Bevington, eds. 1973. *The Complete Works of Shakespeare*. Rev. ed. Glenview, Ill.

Crane, Ronald. 1953. *The Languages of Criticism and the Structure of Poetry*. Toronto.

Culicover, Peter, Tom Wasow, and Adrian Akmajian, eds. 1977. *Formal Syntax*. New York.

Culler, Jonathan. 1973. "Phenomenology and Structuralism," *The Human Context*, 5:35–42.

———. 1975. *Structuralist Poetics: Structuralism, Linguistics, and the Study of Literature*. Ithaca, N.Y.

———. 1976. "Beyond Interpretation: The Prospects of Contemporary Criticism," *Comparative Literature*, 28:244–56.

———. 1981. "Convention and Meaning: Derrida and Austin," *NLH*, 9:15–30.

———. 1983. *On Deconstruction*. London.

Daiches, David. 1963. *George Eliot: "Middlemarch."* London.

Derrida, Jacques. 1972. "Structure, Sign, and Play in the Discourse of the Human Sciences." In *The Structuralist Controversy*, edited by Richard Macksey and Eugenio Donato. Baltimore, Md.

———. 1976. *Of Grammatology*. Translated by G. C. Spivak. Baltimore, Md.

———. 1977. "Signature Event Context," *Glyph*, 1:172–97.

———. 1980. "The Law of Genre," *CrI*, 7:55–81.

Dijk, Teun Van. 1972. *Some Aspects of Text-Grammars: A Study in Theoretical Linguistics and Poetics*. The Hague.

Dillon, George L. 1978. *Language Processing and the Reading of Literature: Toward a Model of Comprehension*. Bloomington, Ind.

Donaldson, E. Talbot. 1954. "Chaucer the Pilgrim," *PMLA*, 49:928–36.

Eagleton, Terry. 1975. *Myths of Power: A Marxist Study of the Brontës*. London.

Easthope, Antony. 1981. "Problematizing the Pentameter," *NLH*, 12:475–92.

Eco, Umberto. 1976. *A Theory of Semiotics*. Bloomington, Ind.

————. 1979. *The Role of the Reader*. Bloomington, Ind.

Ellmann, Richard. 1957. "Wallace Stevens' 'Ice Cream,'" *Kenyon Review*, 19:89–105.

Enck, John J. 1964. *Wallace Stevens: Images and Judgments*. Carbondale, Ill.

Erteschik, Nomi. 1973. "On the Nature of Island Constraints." Ph.D. dissertation, MIT.

Evans, Martha, Bonnie Litowitz, Judith Markowitz, Raoul Smith, and Oswald Werner. 1980. *Lexical-Semantic Relations: A Comparative Study*. Carbondale, Ill.

Ferguson, Charles A. 1978. "Historical Background of Universals Research." In Greenberg, ed.

Fillmore, Charles. 1968. "The Case for Case." In Bach and Harms, eds.

————. 1975. *Santa Cruz Lectures on Deixis*. Bloomington, Ind.

————. 1976. "Pragmatics and the Description of Discourse." In *Pragmatik/Pragmatics II*, edited by Siegfried J. Schmidt. Munich.

————. 1977. "The Case for Case Reopened." In Cole and Sadock, eds.

Fischer, Michael. 1979. "Why Realism Seems So Naive," *College English*, 40:740–50.

Fish, Stanley. 1970. "Literature in the Reader: Affective Stylistics," *NLH*, 2:123–62.

————. 1971. *Surprised by Sin*. Berkeley, Calif.

————. 1973. "What Is Stylistics and Why Are They Saying Such Terrible Things About It?" In *Approaches to Poetics*, edited by Seymour Chatman. New York.

————. 1976. "How to Do Things with Austin and Searle: Speech Act Theory and Literary Criticism," *MLN*, 91:983–1025.

————. 1978. "Normal Circumstances, Literal Language, Direct Speech Acts, the Ordinary, the Everyday, the Obvious, What Goes Without Saying, and Other Special Cases," *CrI*, 4:625–44.

————. 1979. "What Is Stylistics and Why Are They Saying Such Terrible Things About It? Part II," *Boundary 2*, 8:129–45.

————. 1980. *Is There a Text in This Class? The Authority of Interpretive Communities*. Cambridge, Mass.

————. 1982. "With the Compliments of the Author: Reflections on Austin and Derrida," *CrI*, 8:693–721.

Fishman, Joshua. 1960. "A Systemization of the Whorfian Hypothesis," *Behavioral Science*, 5:323–39.

————. 1980. "The Whorfian Hypothesis: Varieties of Valuation, Confirmation, and Disconfirmation, I," *International Journal of the Sociology of Language*, 26:25–40.

————. 1982. "Whorfianism of the Third Kind: Ethnolinguistic Diversity as a Worldwide Societal Asset; The Whorfian Hypothesis: Varieties of Valuation, Confirmation, and Disconfirmation, II," *Language in Society*, 11:1–14.

Fleishman, Avrom. 1978. *Fiction and the Ways of Knowing: Essays on British Novels*. Austin, Tex.

Fodor, Jerry A. 1979. *The Language of Thought*. Cambridge, Mass.
———. 1983. *The Modularity of Mind*. Cambridge, Mass.
Forster, E. M. 1927. *Aspects of the Novel*. London.
Fowler, Alistair. 1982. *Kinds of Literature: An Introduction to the Theory of Genres and Modes*. Cambridge, Mass.
Frame, Donald M., trans. and ed. 1963. *Montaigne's Essays and Selected Writings: A Bilingual Edition*. New York.
Fraser, Bruce. 1974. "An Analysis of Vernacular Performative Verbs." In *Towards Tomorrow's Linguistics*, edited by R. W. Shuy and C. J. N. Bailey. Washington, D.C.
Frye, Northrop. 1957. *Anatomy of Criticism: Four Essays*. Princeton, N.J.
Garvin, Paul, trans. and ed. 1964. *A Prague School Reader on Esthetics, Literary Structure, and Style*. Washington, D.C.
Gasché, Rodolphe. 1979. "Deconstruction as Criticism," *Glyph* 6: 177–215.
Gazdar, Gerald. 1979. *Pragmatics: Implicature, Presupposition, and Logical Form*. New York.
———. 1981. "Speech Act Assignment." In *Elements of Discourse Understanding*, edited by A. Joshi, B. Webber, and I. Sag. Cambridge, Eng.
Gibson, W. M., ed. 1957. *A Modern Instance*, by William Dean Howells. Boston.
Giglioli, Pier Paolo, ed. 1972. *Language and Social Context*. Harmondsworth, Eng.
Gilbert, Elliot L. 1983. "The Female King: Tennyson's Arthurian Apocalypse," *PMLA*, 98: 863–78.
Goffman, Erving. 1974. *Frame Analysis: An Essay on the Organization of Experience*. New York.
Goodman, Nelson. 1968. *Languages of Art: An Approach to a Theory of Symbols*. Indianapolis, Ind.
Gordon, David, and George Lakoff. 1971. "Conversational Postulates." In *Papers from the Seventh Regional Meeting, Chicago Linguistic Society*. Chicago.
Graff, Gerald. 1979. *Literature Against Itself: Literary Ideas in Modern Society*. Chicago.
———. 1981. "Culler and Deconstruction," *London Review of Books*, Sept. 3–16, 1981. Review of Jonathan Culler, *The Pursuit of Signs* (London, 1981).
Green, Georgia. 1982. "Linguistics and the Pragmatics of Language Use," *Poetics*, 11: 45–75.
———. 1983. Review of Bach and Harnish (1979), *Language*, 59: 627–35.
Greenberg, Joseph H., ed. 1978. *Universals of Human Language, Vol. I: Method and Theory*. Stanford, Calif.
Grice, H. P. 1957. "Meaning," *PhilRev*, 66: 377–88. Reprinted in *Readings in the Philosophy of Language*, edited by Jay F. Rosenberg and Charles Travis. Englewood Cliffs, N.J., 1971.

———. 1969. "Utterer's Meaning and Intentions," *PhilRev*, 78:147–77.

———. 1975. "Logic and Conversation." In Cole and Morgan, eds.

Guillen, Claudio. 1971. "On the Uses of Literary Genre." In Claudio Guillen, *Literature as System*. Princeton, N.J.

Hale, Kenneth, LaVerne Masayesva, Jeanne and Paul Platero. 1977. "Three Cases of Overgeneration." In Culicover et al., eds.

Halliday, M. A. K. 1973. *Explorations in the Functions of Language*. Guildford, Eng.

———. 1979. *Language as a Social Semiotic: The Social Interpretation of Language and Meaning*. London.

Hancher, Michael. 1977. "Beyond A Speech-Act Theory of Literary Discourse," *MLN*, 92:1081–98.

———. 1978. "The Classification of Cooperative Illocutionary Acts." Photocopy.

———. 1981. "Humpty Dumpty and Verbal Meaning," *Journal of Aesthetics and Art Criticism*, 40:49–58.

Hans, James S. 1979. "Derrida and Freeplay," *MLN*, 94:809–26.

Hardin, Richard F. 1983. "'Ritual' in Recent Criticism: The Elusive Sense of Community," *PMLA*, 98:846–62.

Harman, Gilbert, ed. 1974. *On Noam Chomsky: Critical Essays*. New York.

Hartman, Geoffrey. 1980. *Criticism in the Wilderness*. New Haven, Conn.

Harvey, W. J. 1965. *Character and the Novel*, Ithaca, N.Y.

Hawkes, Terence. 1972. *Metaphor*. London.

Hemingway, Ernest. 1940. *For Whom the Bell Tolls*. New York.

Hernadi, Paul. 1978. "Order Without Borders: Recent Genre Theory in the English-Speaking Countries." In *Theories of Literary Genre*, edited by Joseph P. Strelka. *Yearbook of Comparative Criticism*, vol. 8. University Park, Pa.

———, ed. 1978. *What Is Literature?* Bloomington, Ind.

Hirsch, E. D., Jr. 1967. *Validity in Interpretation*. New Haven, Conn.

———. 1976. "Stylistics and Synonymity." In E. D. Hirsch, Jr., *The Aims of Interpretation*. Chicago.

Holland, Norman. 1968. *The Dynamics of Literary Response*. New York.

———. 1975a. *5 Readers Reading*. New Haven, Conn.

———. 1975b. "Unity Identity Text Self," *PMLA*, 90:813–22.

Holland, Peter. 1979. *The Ornament of Action*. Cambridge, Eng.

Horn, Laurence. 1984. "Toward a New Taxonomy for Pragmatic Inference: Q-Based and R-Based Implicature." In Schiffrin, ed.

Hornback, Bert G., ed. 1977. *Middlemarch* by George Eliot. New York.

Hyman, Larry. 1975. *Phonology: Theory and Analysis*. New York.

Hymes, Dell. 1972. "Models of the Interaction of Language and Social Life." In *The Ethnography of Communication*, edited by Dell Hymes and John Gumperz.

———. 1973. "Toward Linguistic Competence." In *Working Papers in Sociolinguistics*. Austin, Tex.

———. 1974. *Foundations in Sociolinguistics: An Ethnographic Approach*. Philadelphia.

Iser, Wolfgang. 1971. "Indeterminacy and the Reader's Response in Prose Fiction." In *Aspects of Narrative*, edited by J. Hillis Miller. New York.

———. 1972. "The Reading Process: A Phenomenological Approach," *NLH*, 3:279–99.

———. 1974. *The Implied Reader: Patterns of Communication in Prose Fiction from Bunyan to Beckett*. Baltimore, Md.

———. 1978. *The Act of Reading: A Theory of Aesthetic Response*. Baltimore, Md.

———. 1979. "The Current Situation of Literary Theory: Key Concepts and the Imaginary," *NLH*, 11:1–20.

Jackendoff, Ray. 1972. *Semantic Interpretation in Generative Grammar*. Cambridge, Mass.

———. 1978. "An Argument About the Composition of Conceptual Structure." In *Theoretical Issues in Natural Language Processing*, edited by David Waltz. New York.

———. 1983a. *Semantics and Cognition*. Cambridge, Mass.

———. 1983b. "Music and the Modularity of Mind." Photocopy.

———. N.d. "Generative Music Theory and Its Relevance to Psychology." Photocopy.

Jackendoff, Ray, and Fred Lerdahl. 1980. "A Deep Parallel Between Music and Language." Photocopy.

Jakobson, Roman. 1956. "The Metaphoric and Metonymic Poles." In Roman Jakobson and Morris Halle, *Fundamentals of Language*. The Hague.

———. 1960. "Linguistics and Poetics." In Sebeok, ed.

Jameson, Frederick. 1971. "Meta-Commentary," *PMLA*, 86:9–18.

Johnson, Barbara. 1980. "Nothing Fails Like Success," *SCE Reports*, 8:7–16.

Josipovici, Gabriel. 1971. *The World and the Book: A Study of Modern Fiction*. London.

Karttunen, Lauri, and Stanley Peters. 1977. "Requiem for Presupposition," *Proceedings of the Annual Meeting of the Berkeley Linguistics Society*, 3. Berkeley, Calif.

———. 1979. "Conventional Implicature." In Oh and Dinneen, eds.

Katz, Jerrold J. 1980. *Propositional Structure and Illocutionary Force: A Study of the Contribution of Sentence Meaning to Speech Acts*. Cambridge, Mass.

Keenan, Edward L. 1971. "Two Types of Presupposition in Natural Language." In *Studies in Linguistic Semantics*, edited by Charles Fillmore and D. Terence Langendoen. New York.

———. 1978. "Language Variation and the Logical Structure of Universal Grammar." In *Language Universals*, edited by Hansjakob Seiler. Tübingen, W. Ger.

Kempson, Ruth. 1984a. "Pragmatics, Anaphora, and Logical Form." In Schiffrin, ed.

———. 1984*b*. "Weak Crossover, Logical Form, and Pragmatics." Paper delivered to GLOW (Generative Linguists in the Old World).

Kermode, Frank. 1966. *The Sense of an Ending: Studies in the Theory of Fiction*. Oxford.

Knoepflmacher, U. C. 1971. "Wuthering Heights—A Tragic Comic Romance." In U. C. Knoepflmacher, *Laughter and Despair*. Berkeley, Calif.

Koelb, Clayton. 1980. "'Tragedy' and 'The Tragic': The Shakespearean Connection," *Genre*, 13:275–86.

Koffka, Kurt. 1935. *Principles of Gestalt Psychology*. New York.

Köhler, Wolfgang. 1947. *Gestalt Psychology*. New York.

Kravec, Maureen. 1979. "Let Arcade Be Finale of Arcadia: Stevens' 'Emperor of Ice-Cream'," *The Wallace Stevens Journal*, 3:8–11.

Krieger, Murray, ed. 1966. *Northrop Frye in Modern Criticism*. New York.

Kuhn, Thomas. S. 1970. *The Structure of Scientific Revolutions*. 2nd ed. Chicago.

Labov, William. 1966. *The Social Stratification of English in New York City*. Washington, D.C.

———. 1972*a*. "On the Mechanism of Linguistic Change." In *Directions in Sociolinguistics: The Ethnography of Communication*, edited by John J. Gumperz and Dell Hymes. New York.

———. 1972*b*. *Sociolinguistic Patterns*. Philadelphia.

Lakatos, Imre. 1970. "Falsification and the Methodology of Scientific Research Programmes." In *Criticism and the Growth of Knowledge: Proceedings of the International Colloquium in the Philosophy of Science* (London, 1965), vol. 4, edited by Imre Lakatos and Alan Musgrave. Cambridge, Eng.

Lakoff, George. 1972. "Hedges: A Study in Meaning Criteria and the Logic of Fuzzy Concepts." In *Papers from the Eighth Regional Meeting, Chicago Linguistic Society*. Chicago.

Lakoff, George, and Mark Johnson. 1980. *Metaphors We Live By*. Chicago.

Langacker, Ronald W. 1972. *Fundamentals of Linguistic Analysis*. New York.

Lentricchia, Frank. 1980. *After the New Criticism*. Chicago.

Lerdahl, Fred, and Ray Jackendoff. 1983. *A Generative Theory of Tonal Music*. Cambridge, Mass.

Levin, Samuel R. 1977. *The Semantics of Metaphor*. Baltimore, Md.

Levinson, Stephen C. 1983. *Pragmatics*. Cambridge, Eng.

Lévi-Strauss, Claude. 1967. "Structural Analysis in Linguistics and Anthropology." In Claude Lévi-Strauss, *Structural Anthropology*, translated by Claire Jacobson and Brooke Grunfest Schoepf. New York.

Li, Charles, ed. 1976. *Subject and Topic*. New York.

Lodge, David, ed. 1972. *20th Century Literary Criticism*. London.

Lyons, John. 1977. *Semantics 1 and 2*. Cambridge, Eng.

McCawley, James D. 1976. *Grammar and Meaning: Papers on Syntactic and Semantic Topics*. New York.

———. 1979. "Presupposition and Discourse Structure." In Oh and Dinneen, eds.

———. 1981. *Everything That Linguists Have Always Wanted to Know About Logic (But Were Ashamed to Ask)*. Chicago.

McNeill, David. 1970. *The Acquisition of Language*. New York.

Mailloux, Steven. 1977. "Reader-Response Criticism," *Genre*, 10:413–31.

———. 1979. "Learning to Read: Interpretation and Reader-Response Criticism," *Studies in the Literary Imagination*, 12:93–108.

Man, Paul de. 1971. *Blindness and Insight*. New York.

———. 1975. "Action and Identity in Nietzsche," *Yale French Studies*, 52:16–30.

———. 1979. *Allegories of Reading: Figural Language in Rousseau, Nietzsche, Rilke, and Proust*. New Haven, Conn.

Marcus, Stephen. 1976. *Representations: Essays on Literature and Society*. New York.

Meyer, Leonard B. 1983. "Innovation, Choice, and the History of Music," *CrI*, 9:517–44.

Miller, J. Hillis. 1963. *The Disappearance of God: Five Nineteenth-Century Writers*. Cambridge, Mass.

———. 1982. *Fiction and Repetition: Seven English Novels*. Cambridge, Mass.

Mukarovsky, Jan. 1932. "Standard Language and Poetic Language." In Garvin, ed.

———. 1940. "The Esthetics of Language." In Garvin, ed.

Nagel, E. 1961. *The Structure of Science*. New York.

Newmeyer, Frederick. 1980. *Linguistic Theory in America: The First Quarter-Century of Transformational Generative Grammar*. New York.

———. 1983. *Grammatical Theory: Its Limits and Its Possibilities*. Chicago.

Oates, Joyce Carol. 1982. "The Magnanimity of *Wuthering Heights*," *CrI*, 9:435–49.

Oh, Choon-kyu, and David Dinneen, eds. 1979. *Syntax and Semantics, 11: Presupposition*. New York.

Ohmann, Richard. 1970. "Speech Acts and the Definition of Literature," *Philosophy and Rhetoric*, 4:1–19.

———. 1972. "Instrumental Style: Notes on the Theory of Speech as Action." In *Current Trends in Stylistics*, edited by B. B. Kachru and H. F. W. Stahlke. Edmonton, Ill.

———. 1973. "Literature as Act." In *Approaches to Poetics*, edited by Seymour Chatman. New York.

Olson, Elder. 1952. "William Empson, Contemporary Criticism, and Poetic Diction." In *Critics and Criticism, Ancient and Modern*, edited by R. S. Crane. Chicago.

Ortony, Andrew, ed. 1979. *Metaphor and Thought*. Cambridge, Eng.

Page, Norman. 1973. *Speech in the English Novel*. London.

Parret, Herman. 1974. *Discussing Language: Dialogues*. The Hague.

Partee, Barbara. 1975. "Montague Grammar and Transformational Grammar," *Linguistic Inquiry*, 6:202–300.

Peckham, Morse. 1965. *Man's Rage for Chaos: Biology, Behavior, and the Arts.* New York.
———. 1978. "Perceptual and Semiotic Discontinuity in Art," *Poetics,* 7:217–30.
Perelman, Ch., and L. Olbrechts-Tyteca. 1969. *The New Rhetoric: A Treatise on Argumentation.* Translated by John Wilkinson and Purcell Weaver. Notre Dame, Ind.
Perlmutter, David. 1980. "Relational Grammar." In *Syntax and Semantics, 13: Current Approaches to Syntax,* edited by E. A. Moravcsik and J. R. Wirth. New York.
Peters, P. S., and R. W. Ritchie. 1973. "Context-Sensitive Immediate Constituent Analysis: Context-Free Languages Revisited," *Mathematical Systems Theory,* 6:324–33.
Pratt, Mary Louise. 1977. *Toward A Speech-Act Theory of Literary Discourse.* Bloomington, Ind.
———. 1981. "The Ideology of Speech-Act Theory," *Centrum,* n.s. 1, no. 1: 5–18.
Prince, Gerald. 1976. Review of Culler (1975), *PTL,* 1:197–202.
———. 1980. "Notes on the Text as Reader." In *The Reader in the Text,* edited by Susan R. Suleiman and Inge Crosman. Princeton, N.J.
Pullum, Geoffrey. 1981. "Evidence Against the 'AUX' Node in Luiseno and English," *Linguistic Inquiry,* 12:235–64.
Rabinowitz, Peter J. 1981. "Assertion and Assumption: Fictional Patterns and the External World," *PMLA,* 96:408–19.
Radford, Andrew. 1981. *Transformational Syntax; A Student's Guide to Chomsky's Extended Standard Theory.* Cambridge, Eng.
Rahv, Philip. 1940. "The Cult of Experience in American Writing," *Partisan Review,* November–December: 412–24.
Reichert, John. 1977. *Making Sense of Literature.* Chicago.
Riddel, Joseph N. 1965. *The Clairvoyant Eye: The Poetry and Poetics of Wallace Stevens.* Baton Rouge, La.
Robinson, F. N., ed. 1957. *The Works of Geoffrey Chaucer.* 2nd ed. Cambridge, Mass.
Robinson, Richard. 1950. *Definition.* Oxford.
Rogers, Andy, Bob Wall, and John J. Murphy, eds. 1977. *Proceedings of the Texas Conference on Performatives, Presuppositions, and Implicatures.* Arlington, Va.
Rommetveit, R. 1979. "Language Games, Syntactic Structures, and Hermeneutics." In *Studies of Language, Thought, and Verbal Communication,* edited by R. Rommetveit and R. M. Blakar. New York.
Rorty, Richard. 1978. "Philosophy as a Kind of Writing: An Essay on Derrida," *NLH,* 10:141–59.
Rosch, Eleanor. 1977. "Human Categorization." In *Advances in Cross-Cultural Psychology,* vol. 1, edited by N. Warren. London.
Ross, John Robert. 1967. *Constraints on Variables in Syntax.* Bloomington, Ind. Excerpts reprinted in Harman, ed.

———. 1970. "On Declarative Sentences." In *Readings in Transformational Grammar*, edited by R. A. Jacobs and P. S. Rosenbaum. Waltham, Mass.

Ryan, Marie-Laure. 1979. "Toward a Competence Theory of Genre," *Poetics*, 8:307–37.

Sacks, Sheldon, ed. 1979. *On Metaphor*. Chicago.

Sadock, Jerrold M. 1974. *Toward a Linguistic Theory of Speech Acts*. New York.

Sale, William M., Jr., ed. 1963. *Wuthering Heights* by Emily Brontë. New York.

Sampson, Geoffrey. 1979. *Liberty and Language*. Oxford.

Sapir, Edward. 1921. *Language: An Introduction to the Study of Speech*. New York.

Saussure, Ferdinand de. 1959. *Course in General Linguistics*. Translated by Wade Baskin, edited by Charles Bally and Albert Sechehaye in collaboration with Albert Reidlingers. New York.

Schaefer, William D. 1978. "Editor's Column," *PMLA*, 93:179–80.

Schane, Sanford. 1973. *Generative Phonology*. Englewood Cliffs, N.J.

Schauber, Ellen. 1979. *The Syntax and Semantics of Questions in Navajo*. New York.

Schauber, Ellen, and Ellen Spolsky. 1981. "Stalking a Generative Poetics," *NLH*, 12:397–413.

———. 1983. "Conversational Noncooperation: The Case of Chaucer's Pardoner," *Language and Style*, 16:249–61.

Schiffrin, Deborah. Forthcoming. *Georgetown University Roundtable on Language and Linguistics, 1984. Meaning, Form, and Use in Context: Linguistic Applications*. Washington, D.C.

Scholes, Robert. 1974. *Structuralism in Literature: An Introduction*. New Haven, Conn.

Searle, John R. 1958. "Proper Names," *Mind*, 67:166–73.

———. 1969. *Speech Acts: An Essay in the Philosophy of Language*. Cambridge, Eng.

———. 1971. "Introduction." In John R. Searle, ed., *The Philosophy of Language*. Oxford.

———. 1974. "Chomsky's Revolution in Linguistics." In Harman, ed.

———. 1975a. "The Logical Status of Fictional Discourse," *NLH*, 6:319–32.

———. 1975b. "Speech Acts and Recent Linguistics." In *Developmental Psycholinguistics and Communicative Disorders*, edited by Doris Aaronson and Robert W. Rieber. *Annals of the New York Academy of Sciences*, vol. 263. New York.

———. 1975c. "Indirect Speech Acts." In Cole and Morgan, eds.

———. 1976. "A Classification of Illocutionary Acts," *Language in Society*, 5:1–23.

———. 1979a. "What Is an Intentional State?" *Mind*, 88:74–92.

———. 1979b. "Metaphor." In Ortony, ed.

————. 1979c. "Literal Meaning." In John R. Searle, *Expression and Meaning: Studies in the Theory of Speech Acts.* Cambridge, Eng.

Searle, John R., Ferenc Kiefer, and Manfred Bierwisch, eds. 1980. *Speech Act Theory and Pragmatics.* Dordrecht, Neth.

Sebeok, Thomas A., ed. 1960. *Style in Language.* Cambridge, Mass.

Segré, Cesare. 1973. *Semiotics and Literary Criticism.* The Hague.

Slobin, Dan Isaac. 1979. *Psycholinguistics.* 2nd ed. Glenview, Ill.

Smith, Barbara Herrnstein. 1968. *Poetic Closure: A Study of How Poems End.* Chicago.

————. 1978. *On the Margins of Discourse: The Relation of Literature to Language.* Chicago.

————. 1979. "Fixed Marks and Variable Constancies: A Parable of Literary Value," *Poetics Today,* 1:7–22.

————. 1981. "The Exile of Evaluation." Photocopy.

————. 1983. "Contingencies of Value," *CrI,* 10:1–35.

Spanos, William. 1980. "Retrieving Heidegger's De-Struction: A Response to Barbara Johnson," *SCE Reports,* 8:30–53.

Sperber, Dan, and Deirdre Wilson. Forthcoming. *Relevance: Foundations of Pragmatic Theory.*

Spolsky, Ellen. Forthcoming. "The Conditions of Meaning," *NLH.*

Stankiewicz, Edward. 1977. "Poetics and Verbal Art." In *A Profusion of Signs,* edited by Thomas A. Sebeok. Bloomington, Ind.

Stephens, Robert O., ed. 1977. *Ernest Hemingway: The Critical Reception.* N.p.

Stevens, Holly, ed. 1966. *Letters of Wallace Stevens.* New York.

Stevens, John. 1973. *Medieval Romance: Themes and Approaches.* New York.

Stevens, Wallace. 1976. *The Collected Poems of Wallace Stevens.* New York.

Strawson, P. F. 1964. "Intention and Convention in Speech Acts," *PhilRev,* 73:439–60. Reprinted in Searle, ed., 1971.

————. 1971. "Meaning and Truth." In P. F. Strawson, *Logico-linguistic Papers.* London.

Sukenick, Ronald. 1967. *Wallace Stevens: Musing the Obscure.* New York.

Thomas, Owen. 1969. *Metaphor and Related Subjects.* New York.

Todorov, Tzvetan. 1969. *Grammaire du Décameron.* The Hague.

————. 1976. "The Origin of Genres," *NLH,* 8:159–70.

Tolkien, J. R. R. 1936. "Beowulf: The Monsters and the Critics." In *An Anthology of Beowulf Criticism,* edited by Lewis E. Nicholson. Notre Dame, Ind. 1963. Reprinted from *Proceedings of the British Academy,* 22:245–95.

Traugott, Elizabeth. 1973. "Generative Semantics and the Concept of Literary Discourse," *Journal of Literary Semantics,* 2:5–22.

Vendler, Zeno. 1972. *Res Cogitans: An Essay in Rational Psychology.* Ithaca, N.Y.

Voegelin, Carl F. 1960. "Casual and Noncasual Utterances Within Unified Structure." In Sebeok, ed.

von Wright, Georg Henrik. 1971. *Explanation and Understanding*. Ithaca, N.Y.

Walcutt, Charles Child. 1966. *Man's Changing Mask: Modes and Methods of Characterization in Fiction*. Minneapolis, Minn.

Wall, Robert. 1972. *Introduction to Mathematical Linguistics*. Englewood Cliffs, N.J.

Weber, Samuel. 1980. "Closure and Exclusion," *Diacritics*, 10:35–46.

Wertheimer, Max. 1923. "Laws of Organization in Perceptual Forms." In *A Source Book of Gestalt Psychology*, edited by W. D. Ellis. London, 1938.

Whorf, Benjamin Lee. 1950. "An American Indian Model of the Universe," *International Journal of Anthropological Linguistics*, no. 16. Reprinted in *Language, Thought, and Reality: Selected Writings of Benjamin Lee Whorf*, edited by J. B. Carroll. Cambridge, Mass., 1956.

Wittgenstein, Ludwig. 1953. *Philosophical Investigations*. Translated by G. E. M. Anscombe. 2 vols. Oxford.

Index

Library of Congress Cataloging-in-Publication Data

Schauber, Ellen.
  The bounds of interpretation.

  Bibliography: p.
  Includes index.
   1. Criticism. 2. Literary form. 3. Semantics.
I. Spolsky, Ellen, 1943–   II. Title.
PN81.S2286 1986   801'.95   85-26218
ISBN 0-8047-1300-6 (alk. paper)